**Postwar Economic
Reconstruction
and Lessons for the
East Today**

**Postwar Economic
Reconstruction
and Lessons for the
East Today**

edited by Rudiger Dornbusch,
Wilhelm Nölling, and
Richard Layard

The MIT Press
Cambridge, Massachusetts
London, England

This book was set in Palatino by Asco Trade Typesetting Ltd., Hong Kong, and was printed and bound in the United States of America.

Library of Congress Cataloging-in-Publication Data

Postwar economic reconstruction and lessons for the East today /
  edited by Rudiger Dornbusch, Wilhelm Nölling, and Richard Layard.
     p.   cm.
  Includes bibliographical references and index.
  ISBN 0-262-04136-7
    1. Europe—Economic conditions—1945– 2. Reconstruction (1939–1951)—Europe.
  3. Europe, Eastern—Economic conditions—1989– I. Dornbusch, Rudiger.
  II. Nölling, Wilhelm. III. Layard, P. R. G. (P. Richard G.)
  HC240.P634 1993
  338.94′009′045—dc20   92-34804
                                                                            CIP

Contents

Introduction   vii
Participants   xiii

1 **Openness, Wage Restraint, and Macroeconomic Stability: West Germany's Road to Prosperity 1948–1959**   1
Herbert Giersch, Karl-Heinz Paqué, and Holger Schmieding

2 **The Lucky Miracle: Germany 1945–1951**   29
Holger C. Wolf

3 **Inflation and Stabilization in Italy: 1946–1951**   57
Marcello De Cecco and Francesco Giavazzi

4 **Economic Reconstruction in France: 1945–1958**   83
Gilles Saint-Paul

5 **Reconstruction and the U.K. Postwar Welfare State: False Start and New Beginning**   115
Patrick Minford

6 **A Perspective on Postwar Reconstruction in Finland**   139
Jouko Paunio

7 **The Reconstruction and Stabilization of the Postwar Japanese Economy: Possible Lessons for Eastern Europe?**   155
Koichi Hamada and Munehisa Kasuya

8 The Marshall Plan: History's Most Successful Structural Adjustment Program   189

J. Bradford De Long and Barry Eichengreen

9 Panel Discussion: Lessons for Eastern Europe Today   231

Olivier Blanchard, Richard Portes, and Wilhelm Nolling

Index   243

Introduction

The extraordinary problems faced by Eastern Europe and by the former Soviet Union make us search for parallels. When did countries in modern history face similar problems of rebuilding their economies; how did they cope with the challenge; what lessons follow for Eastern Europe today? At a conference organized by the Center for Economic Policy Performance of the London School of Economics, with the warm hospitality of the Landeszentralbank Hamburg and the support of the Anglo-German Foundation, these questions were explored.

Much of the debate focused on a reassessment of the reconstruction experience in Europe and Japan and on the role played by the Marshall Plan. But the parallel to the current challenge was never out of sight.

The Issues

Characteristics of the postwar reconstruction in most countries do not fully overlap; the chief problems differed and so did the approach. But it is interesting nevertheless to highlight some dimensions in which comparisons will be useful.

• What was the relative role of government and the market? During the Great Depression (and more so in the fascist or militaristic countries) intervention became the rule. Was reconstruction built around a central role for the market?

• What was the role of economic openness—convertibility, free trade, access to imports?

• What was the relative role of industrial conversion from war to peacetime production, of actual rebuilding after wartime destruction and of building up new productive structures?

Table I.1
Industrial production: 1946–60

	Index 1937 = 100			Growth (%)
	1946	1949	1960	1948–1960
Austria		118	293	9.9
Belgium	72	94	140	3.5
Denmark	101	137	229	4.8
Finland	107	143	282	6.0
France	73	112	208	5.9
Germany (W)	34	90	283	12.9
Italy	71	109	292	9.0
Netherlands	75	127	266	7.1
U.K.	90	117	177	4.0

• What was the role of institutions and of behavior and attitudes of the work force and business community?

• What was the composition of enterprises, that is, of their size (small or medium-sized, monopolies) and their working staff?

• What was the role of external control of policy measures, of resources made available by the outside world, and of the general external environment?

• All things considered, was reconstruction easy?

An Overview

We will not try to answer each question in detail; that is what the entire collection seeks to accomplish. But we offer nevertheless some assessment here. We start immediately with the bottom line: reconstruction was a very, very tough job everywhere. There was hunger and cold; unemployment and hardship were the rule. Reconstruction did not happen from one day to the next (table I.1).

It is important to bear this in mind as we look at the former Soviet Union today. Sure, we would like to alleviate pain and suffering and certainly prevent famine, but is there not an assumption that we can do miracles? Even with very generous U.S. support and massive efforts of adjustment, life in the forties was very tough. That is bound to be the case in the East, perhaps far more than it was the case after World War II.

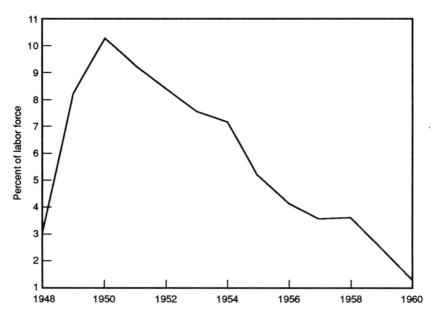

Figure I.1
German unemployment rate, 1948–60

An indication of just how difficult and gradual adjustment was in fact is suggested by German unemployment. Wartime displacement and flight from communism led to an inflow of almost 10 million refugees. How were they absorbed into jobs? Figure I.1 shows that unemployment was high and persistent for many years. True, employment grew very rapidly, but unemployment took a full decade to decline to modest levels.

Consider now the economic ideology prevalent at the time. In Germany Erhard set the tone: a stark monetary reform that eliminated the overhang and rapidly liberalized prices. An entire school of thought on economic policy soon flourished and became the ruling ideology—"social market economy." The social market economy philosophy emphasizes free markets, competition, stability of rules, and an emphasis on competition where the latter need by no means be the byproduct of free markets. In Italy, Luigi Einaudi played much the same role as Erhard had in Germany, and his philosophy ran in the same direction. In sharp contrast, Britain stayed in an interventionist mode. The welfare state, rather than free markets, seemed to offer the better promise for social stability. On the surface, Germany had the better model, at least as judged by growth (table I.2).

Table I.2
Comparative economic performance: 1950–59

	Growth	Unemployment rate
Germany	7.9	6.7
U.K.	1.9	1.5

An interesting point to make on the perspective of current policy prescriptions is this: advisors are almost unanimous that an immediate move to convertibility is the best prescription for Eastern Europe or the Soviet republics. That is not a lesson from the postwar reconstruction. Convertibility took a long time coming and was formally achieved only by 1958. It remains an open question whether Europe would have been served better by an earlier move to convertibility.

Economic openness and access to imports is identified invariably as a key element of reconstruction. Trade brought the essential raw materials that Europe was lacking and the capital goods as well. Import liberalization created intra-European growth opportunities, but openness of the dollar area was just as essential in that it made hard currency earnings possible.

But the role of the external environment went far beyond market access and an increasingly free trade environment. The United States directly and very early on provided the resources for European nations to import beyond their export earnings. The Marshall Plan—worth 2 percent of U.S. GNP for several years in a row, provided balance of payments support and avoided restrictive trade strategies. Once the Korean War boom started, rising world demand for Europe's goods provided an extra dose of foreign exchange earnings. Both the Marshall Plan and the subsequent boom gave the extra support that helped countries in severe trouble to avoid budget deficits, inflation, and recession. And for countries without severe trouble, the resources were the foundation for more stellar investment and growth performance. It is difficult to believe that reconstruction could have been as successful without these ingredients.

The United States played a key role in one further dimension, and that is in promoting cooperation in Europe. Out of a concern to check the spread of communism, the United States insisted on a cooperation strategy in Europe. Intra-European trade liberalization and the European Payments Union were the concrete measures, and the United States cheerfully accepted the implied trade discrimination against the dollar area. Europe might have gotten there by itself, but it is hard to believe that we would have today the prospect of Europe 92 and a common currency were it not for the U.S. insistence on cooperation.

Friedman's law asserts that physical destruction of capital is the fastest way to growth. Countries with newer capital can take advantage of state of the arts technology; the shock of destruction forces rebuilding. Where destruction is absent, there may be no incentive to make a Schumpeterian jump. In judging the growth performance of the postwar period, we must ask a few questions. First, what was actual wartime destruction? One argument is that destruction concentrated substantially on housing and much less on industrial structures and even less on equipment. If so, the high rates of investment meant extra investment, coming on top of a high capital stock. The second question is whether the wartime accumulation of capital was very specific to the war effort or else quite malleable. If the latter is the case, high growth in the postwar period is largely a reflection of significant accumulation over as much as a decade. Finally, how much did shortages, wartime constraints, discipline, and need teach people to use resources more carefully and to stretch their use much further? How much did they learn to just cope and get a job done? Clearly, that too is a source of growth.

These issues are relevant as one faces the question of rebuilding Eastern Europe. Will it take five, ten, or twenty years to raise the level of output and productivity to British standards? It must be clear that there cannot be the same answer for all the countries of that region. Whereas some smaller Eastern countries are well on their way to market economics, the situation in the Soviet Union is absolutely disastrous.

The European postwar experience may not apply; rebuilding a plant is easier than building one that was never there. It should be borne in mind that the rapid and successful reconstruction process in postwar Germany was largely due to psychological factors in terms of work ethic, initiative, and market behavior, with market relevant institutions still intact. The German population wanted to work and was prepared to make great efforts in order to overcome poverty and destitution. Turning to the Soviet Union, working hard may be a difficult discipline in a country where it never was the rule.

The Approach

The book does not try to offer new findings or a radically new interpretation of the postwar reconstruction in the way that an economic historian would like to see. In other words, there is no testing of rival hypotheses and no attempt at major primary research. Rather, we offer here a collection of essays or opinions that review what is known about the postwar reconstruction from particular points of view.

The essays try to fit the facts into a way of thinking. The reader will find that the authors of this volume do not view the world from a common vantage point: for some authors, pervasive economic freedom would have offered an express lane to prosperity, *especially* in the conditions of postwar Europe; for others, the special conditions of the time made controls a constructive solution because a free market would not function. The issue arises, for example, with respect to convertibility: was inconvertibility in the early fifties an inevitable precaution that helped make the return to normalcy more smooth and perhaps more rapid than in a situation of unrestricted payments, or was it a counterproductive interference with the market that stalled progress without offsetting benefits? That is very much the question in the post-Communist world, just as it was then.

Abstract arguments will not convince, but a review of the historical experience may. Implicit in either judgment is, of course, a political economy opinion about what markets do or don't do, how important equity is, and how best to achieve it. Interestingly, in the fifties, even after such a long period of control (or perhaps because controls had become the modus vivendi?), there was a lot of tolerance for continued control and the free market approach was the untested, bold if not reckless revolution.

From the diversity of the studies, from the overlap in their coverage by issue and by periods, we hope to discern an impression of what reconstruction was about and what lessons might be derived from Western Europe's experience for the post-Communist economies today.

Participants

Olivier Blanchard
Department of Economics
Massachusetts Institute of
Technology
Cambridge, MA 02139

Marcello De Cecco
University of Rome
Via Nomentana 41
Rome 00161 Italy

J. Bradford De Long
Department of Economics
Harvard University
Cambridge, MA 02138

Barry Eichengreen
University of California
Department of Economics
Berkeley, CA 94720

Francesco Giavazzi
Bocconi University
I. Gasparini Institute for Economic
Research
Abbazia de Mirasole
Opera (Milano) 1-20090 Italy

Herbert Giersch
Institut für Weltwirtschaft
Dusternbrooker Weg 120.122
D-2300 Kiel 1 Germany

Koichi Hamada
Department of Economics
Yale University
New Haven, CT 06520

Munehisa Kasuya
Bank of Japan
2-1-1 Nihombashi Hongoku Cho
Chuo-ku
Tokyo 103 Japan

Patrick Minford
University of Liverpool
P.O. Box 147
Liverpool L69 3BX
United Kingdom

Wilhelm Nölling
Präsident der Landeszentral Bank
Ost-West-Straße 73
2000 Hamburg 11 Germany

Karl-Heinz Paqué
Institut für Weltwirtschaft
Dusternbrooker Weg 120.122
D-2300 Kiel 1 Germany

Jouko Paunio
University of Helsinki
Department of Economics
Aleksanterinkatu 7
SF 00100 Helsinki, Finland

Richard Portes
CEPR
Duke of York Street
London SW1Y 6LA
United Kingdom

Gilles Saint-Paul
Delta
Ecole Normale Superieure
48 Boulevard Jourdan
75014 Paris, France

Holger C. Wolf
Stern Business School
New York University
New York, NY 10006

1

Openness, Wage Restraint, and Macroeconomic Stability: West Germany's Road to Prosperity 1948–1959

Herbert Giersch, Karl-Heinz Paqué, and Holger Schmieding

1 1945–48: The Starting Conditions

From 1936 onward, the Nazis transformed the German economy into a centrally administered system. The main measures they imposed were the fixing of prices and wages at the levels of autumn 1936, the rationing of consumer goods and foodstuffs, the central allocation of labor and raw materials, a system of compulsory delivery quotas for farmers, and a tight rent control. During the war this system worked reasonably well for the purposes of the war economy. After the end of the war, however, it became impractible due to the breakdown of the public administration, the collapse of communications and transportation, the fragmentation of the German reich, and the general postwar disruptions of the pattern of production.

The frozen price level was much too low relative to the stock of money, which had been inflated by a factor of ten as a result of financing the war through the printing press. Germany found itself in a state of "repressed inflation."[1] The official currency lost its value because economic agents were reluctant to accept it as a medium of exchange. Instead, people and firms used cigarettes as the standard means of payment or resorted to barter and to complicated compensation deals, often involving chains of bilateral trade, to obtain scarce inputs. The need of firms to have commodities at hand for eventual bartering and a flight into physical assets as durable stores of value (*Flucht in die Sachwerte*) led to a large-scale hoarding of raw materials and semifinished products.

The old structure of relative prices did not reflect the relative scarcities of the postwar period. There were no adequate economic incentives to raise the production of bottleneck commodities such as fertilizers and coal mine equipment, in contrast to the profit opportunities offered by the free pricing for new goods that had played no role before the war. Thus, despite postwar misery, West Germany turned into something like a "hair-oil ash-tray herb-tea economy."[2]

Industrial production between 1945 and early 1948 was about one third of its pre-war level and food output not more than 70 percent (1946–47) and as low as 58 percent (1947–48). Although the United States and, to a lesser extent, the United Kingdom financed food imports, the rations actually supplied frequently fell below the target of 1550 calories, that is, about half the level of prewar consumption. The postwar misery also showed up in a run-down of the capital stock: three years after the war, it was 21 percent below its 1944 peak and 7.4 percent below its 1945 level, with machines being on average older than before.[3]

Exports and imports lagged far behind the sluggish recovery of domestic economic activity. In addition to the Allied restrictions and the bureaucratic red tape, there were monetary arrangements that provided little incentive to exporting: apart from a minor foreign exchange retention quota (introduced in the U.S.-British Bizone in September 1947), German firms received almost useless reichsmarks for their exports whereas home markets at least offered opportunities for profitable barter transactions.

The turnaround was initiated by a political reassessment of the situation by the Western Allies. When Communists pushed their way into power in the countries occupied by the Soviet Union, the Western Allies decided to go ahead with rebuilding the German economy in their three zones of occupation and—if necessary—to establish a separate West German state. By mid-1948, the time had come for radical change, notably for a currency reform on the macro level and the decontrol of markets on the micro level.

2   West Germany's Transition to a Market Economy: The Internal Reforms of 1948

The transition toward a market economy consisted of three major reform steps: the currency reform, a "little" tax reform, and the reinstitution of markets in the U.S.-British Bizone in late June 1948.

The *currency reform* was enacted by the military governments in all three Western zones of occupation on June 20, 1948 and comprised a drastic contraction of the money supply and the substitution of the deutsche mark (DM) for the reichsmark (RM); moreover, it provided for restructuring and consolidation of existing private and public debt and the establishment of institutional safeguards against inflationary policies.[4]

As an initial endowment, individuals received DM 40 (plus DM 20 two months later), firms received DM 60 per employee, and public authorities were given the equivalent of one month's revenue. Private bank deposits, including savings accounts and time deposits, were to be scaled down by a factor of ten.[5] Half of this amount became available after the income tax office had checked the registered sums for prior tax evasion; the other half was blocked. In late September, 10 percent of the original total was released, 5 percent was credited to a special account for investment purposes, and 35 percent was cancelled. Thus, the effective conversion rate turned out to be 10:0.65 for reichsmark balances exceeding RM 600.

While official prices and recurrent payments (wages, rents, and pensions) remained unchanged (1 RM = 1 DM), almost all debts were scaled down by a factor of ten. For their reichsmark balances and government bonds, commercial banks received low-interest "equalization claims" amounting to roughly 4 percent of the reich debt. Banks obtained deposits with the central banking system (15 percent of their demand deposits plus 7.5 percent of their time and savings deposits). This was 50 percent more than the new minimum reserves required; thus, considerable leeway for credit expansion was created.

The Western Allies established several safeguards against a future financing of public debt by money creation. The new central bank (*Bank deutscher Länder*), which had been established in March 1948, became the sole provider of legal tender; it was to be independent of the government and all other political bodies.[6] Moreover, the conversion law explicitly forbade excessive budget deficits: public authorities had to cover their expenditures by current income; the financing by credit was to be permitted only in anticipation of future revenues.

Together with the currency reform, the military governments changed the *tax system* with a view to promoting the formation of capital. The top marginal income tax rate, which had been as high as 95 percent (Boss 1987, 4), was cut by roughly one third; the corporate income tax rate was reduced from 65 to 50 percent. For income saved and invested, important tax exemptions were granted. On the other hand, many local taxes were substantially raised and a high excise tax on coffee was introduced (Mendershausen 1949, 660).

Immediately after the currency reform, Ludwig Erhard, the head of the Bizonal economic administration, abolished *central planning* in the Bizone. Guidelines on the decontrol of the economy (*Leitsätze*) that had passed the Bizonal parliament on June 18, 1948, gave him the right to remove price controls for almost all manufactured goods and some foodstuffs. By fully using this authorization, Erhard made the Bizonal economy begin the second half of 1948 with free markets in most goods.

Contrary to the suggestions of many German and foreign experts, the currency reform was not immediately complemented by a one-time *redistribution of wealth* to achieve an equalization of war and postwar burdens (*Lastenausgleich*). But it was made clear by mid-1948 that, at some time in the not too distant future, some such scheme would be implemented.[7]

3   The Impact of the Reforms

3.1   The Immediate Aftermath: Rising Production

The currency reform quickly became a great success. On the morning after the introduction of the deutsche mark, people readily accepted money in exchange for goods and labor services. The shop windows were full of products that had not been available before, at least not over the counter. Parallel markets practically disappeared. At the same time production soared: in the second half of 1948, the 1936-based index of industrial production leaped from 50 in June to 77 in December. The incentive to work in factories was restored since no longer did people need to spend their scarce time searching and bartering for food and other basic necessities. In December 1948, workers stayed on the job for 42.4 hours per week, 4.2 hours longer than they had in June.[8]

As soon as the utilization of existing capacity began to rise, the depletion of the physical capital stock was stopped: in the second half of 1948 the capital stock started to grow at an annualized rate of 5.6 percent. The investment surge could be financed although private households turned into net dissavers.[9] It was funded largely out of business profits and to a lesser extent out of foreign aid and the fiscal surplus of the public sector, which amounted to about 1.5 percent of GNP from July 1948 to March 1949.[10]

The positive account of the 1948 reforms is largely based on the official index of Bizonal industrial production in 1948. These numbers and the general assessment of the reforms have been brought to doubt by Abelshauser (1975). As the immediate prereform figures may have significantly understated true activity (because firms did not report part of the output they hoarded in anticipation of the reform), Abelshauser used statistics on the electricity consumption of industrial firms to reestimate actual output. According to his calculation, industrial production in the last quarter of 1948 was just 33 percent instead of 51 percent above the level of six months earlier. Moreover, he concluded that what happened after the currency reform was mainly a continuation of the general recovery that followed the deep crisis of early 1947.

Prima facie, Abelshauser's arguments look plausible as the official production indices for May and June 1948 do in fact show incredibly low figures for some specific consumption goods. Nonetheless, his case is still unconvincing for a variety of reasons: (i) the incentive to underreport actual output was in general rather small before the reforms as firms ugently needed the official allocations of inputs.[11] (ii) Abelshauser's reestimate assumes a constant ratio of the input of electricity to output. This assumption is unrealistic: the productivity of electricity rose in line with the volume of industrial production. The official figures that imply that firms made a better use of electricity after the reforms thus become more plausible.[12] (iii) Even if the official figures for May and June 1948 were biased downward (because firms secretly hoarded part of their output in anticipation of the reforms), this would not speak against the significance of the regime switch. Given the general shortage of inputs, firms might not have produced these extra goods at all had they not expected to sell them for real money in the near future. (iv) Whereas the period until mid-1948 had been characterized by a decline in the capital stock, investment surged in the second half of 1948. (v) The crucial months of late 1948 and early 1949 in West Germany come close to being a controlled experiment. While the new currency was introduced in both the Bizone and the French zone, decontrol measures in the French zone were not enacted before 1949. Industrial production, which had been roughly on a par in both parts of Western Germany before the reforms, showed a sizable gap thereafter; recovery in the French zone was much slower. The gap began to narrow once markets were liberalized in the French zone as well (figure 1.1). (vi) In a broader perspective, the importance of the regime switch can be gathered from a comparison between East and West Germany. Until 1948, the economic situation was roughly similar on both sides of the Elbe. After the regime switch in the West, East Germany—which was gradually transformed into a Soviet-type economy—began to lag behind dramatically.

3.2   Inflation, Stabilization, and Export-led Growth

As to the macroeconomic performance, the decade after the currency reform can be divided into three distinct phases, namely (i) the period of adjustment inflation (July to December 1948), (ii) the period of consolidation (January 1949 to mid-1950), and (iii) the period of export-led growth (from mid-1950 on).

Despite the spectacular advance of aggregate supply, the transition to a market economy was endangered in fall 1948. The reason was an unexpected surge of monetary demand. It resulted from a considerable credit

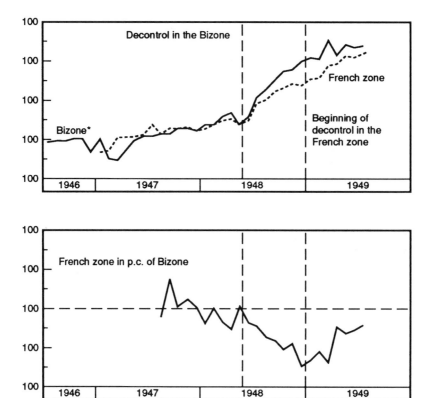

Figure 1.1
Industrial production before and after the liberal reforms of June 1948[a]
Source: Ritschl (1985), p. 164; own calculations

expansion due to the generous endowment of commercial banks with central bank deposits. While the quantity of money (M3) grew faster than anticipated, the velocity of money also rose when firms learned to live with rather small cash balances and when private households, presented with full shops after more than five years, revealed their high propensity to consume.

Until the end of October 1948, consumer prices (as measured by the cost of living index) increased at an annualized rate of 33 percent, producer prices at a rate of 45 percent.[13] In fall 1948, a reemergence of bartering arrangements and a renewed hoarding of inventories was observed; it seemed to indicate the danger of a repudiation of the new money. On November 12, 1948, the trade unions called for a one-day general strike to protest against the inflationary consequences of Erhard's economic policies.

The major concern of the unions was inflation itself rather than a deterioration of the standard of living in real terms. As prices and nominal wages had moved up in parallel, the real purchasing power had not been diminished.[14] Fortunately, the strike had no major consequences. In late 1948, the economy began to cool off, after the price level had approached the limit set by the monetary frame and the fiscal surplus.

What followed was a period of price stability and most of the time even price deflation until mid-1950. There can hardly be any doubt that a prolonged period of price stability was absolutely crucial in macroeconomic terms to establish confidence in the new currency. What is really remarkable—if not miraculous—about this period of consolidation is that it was a time of both stability and fast economic growth: despite a noticeable slowdown of economic expansion relative to the spectacular upsurge right after the currency reform, the growth of industrial production was still about 25 percent per annum in 1949. At the same time, the unemployment rate moved up continuously from about 4.5 percent in the second half of 1948 to a peak of about 12 percent in March 1950. As employment contracted slightly, aggregate output growth in this period was exclusively due to gains in labor productivity. These gains came about through essentially two distinct supply-side forces that had been freed by the liberal reform: first, a rapid reconstruction of the capital stock, and second, a powerful structural adjustment.

Concerning reconstruction, it soon became obvious that a good part of the capital stock that had been damaged in the war could quickly be repaired and put to use again. These repair investments raised output per worker for two reasons. In a quantitative sense, they allowed working hours to return to normal levels, from about 42 hours per week in 1948 to 48 hours per week in 1950. In a qualitative sense, they increased output per working hour since they provided industrial workers with a post-war endowment of properly functioning capital equipment. Thus, literally speaking, the economy's machinery was switched on again so that, probably not before mid-1950, anything like a normal utilization of productive capacities could be reached, independent of cyclical forces. With full analytical justification, this process may be called *reconstruction*.

Structural change usually receives less attention than reconstruction, but was probably of no less importance. Behind the veil of more or less stagnating employment, a massive reshuffling of labor was taking place. It had started in the second half of 1948, when substantial job losses in contracting sectors (370,000) were well overcompensated by job gains (600,000) in the expanding parts of the economy, and it forcefully continued in the consolidation period. In the year 1949 alone, employment grew by 260,000 in the expanding sectors and shrank by slightly above 400,000 in the contracting sectors, thus bringing about a net loss of employment of about 140,000 jobs. Apparently, the liberal reform had led to a thorough reorganization of the economy's production structure that was mostly independent of short-term cyclical forces. In low-productivity agriculture and forestry alone, 350,000 jobs were lost in the eighteen months after the reform, with half of this loss occurring in 1949. In turn, employment in construction and in high-productivity manufacturing—above all in investment goods industries—grew sharply. This rapid structural adjustment was bound to leave deep traces in any productivity statistics but it also, quite naturally, led to some unemployment, at least in the rural parts of the North and South-East that were crowded by refugees. In fact, by the time of the year 1949–50, the unemployment rate in the two northern states Schleswig-Holstein and Lower Saxony stood at 26.3 and 17.3 percent respectively, compared to the rate of 4.5 percent in urban and industrialized North Rhine-Westphalia and 4.6 percent in the area of the later state of Baden-Württemberg.

Note that real wages in industry grew by almost 16 percent in the year 1949, which was not bad by any historical standards, but still much lower than the 26 percent labor productivity growth in industry so that firms could cash in huge profits and thus stock up retained earnings for further investment. All this happened with no demand push of monetary and fiscal policy; in fact, the central bank loosened the monetary ties only very cautiously in the course of 1949 so as not to rekindle inflation and endanger the still shaky external balance.

Despite the stability-oriented fiscal and monetary stance, Ludwig Erhard received a full blessing for his economic policy in the political realm in the federal elections of September 1949, which were held when the unemployment rate already stood at 8.8 percent, seasonally adjusted not far from the peak of winter 1950. Although, with unemployment rising, there was some grumbling in the union ranks and among opposition social democrats, the general political atmosphere was far from explosive, at least with respect to economic matters. In fact, not before the Allies stepped in with a sharp call for expansionary measures in February 1950 did the debate dramatically heat up. Taking a detached view, it is very hard to see why the consolidation period should not be called a wholesale success, with unemployment being in effect a natural consequence of restructuring and the increase of the labor supply, with no need for any emergency policy activism.

In the second quarter of 1950, a long phase of sustained export-led growth began. The boom created by the Korean Conflict imparted an additional boost to the West German economy in late 1950 and early 1951. It put an end to the discussion about whether an expansionary demand policy might be called for to reduce unemployment. On the one hand, the surge in demand that was triggered by the hostilities in Korea may in itself be interpreted as a massive Keynesian-type stimulus. Unlike a domestically engineered macroexpansion, however, most of the extra demand came from abroad and therefore West Germany's reorientation toward a structure of production in line with the country's comparative advantages was hastened and not delayed or even distorted, as would have happened in the case of an unsustainable internal stimulus. After the Korea boom, the stability-oriented macroeconomic policy of both the central bank and the federal government was no longer seriously disputed for quite some time. In fact, sustained growth brought the unemployment rate down to 1.3 percent by 1960.

It has sometimes been argued that it was the fair dose of Keynesian medicine provided by the Korea boom that really pushed the West German economy onto the growth track.[15] In fact, the timing of the Korea boom was certainly good fortune as it helped to diminish the calls for more expansionary domestic policy measures. This is the kernel of Keynesian truth in the story. Nevertheless, there are good reasons not to overestimate the element of luck. After all, is it really luck when a country deliberately restrains absorption at a noninflationary level to be ready to service world markets if the opportunity arises? To be sure, this is precisely the right strategy to grow into an international division of labor and to avoid balance of payments disruptions in the long run. Under the constraints of the time, with no easy access to international capital markets, a homemade boom would probably have had undesirable side effects: a monetary expansion would have ended in a loss of confidence in the currency; a sizable fiscal expansion would have undermined the credibility of fiscal conservatism and thus mounted the threat of monetizing the emerging public deficits in the future.

The fundamental question—which separates a Keynesian from a neoclassical interpretation of the events—is whether the subsequent sustained growth of the West German economy would have been possible without the impetus of the Korea boom. Of course, nobody can answer this counterfactual question with any degree of precision. Nevertheless, it appears quite likely that, in the course of normal business cycle movements, some sort of export surge would have occurred and thus carried the economy over to grow into its supply-side potential. Given the traditional strength of the German capital goods industries and the excellent starting position these industries had established precisely through the strong profits they earned even during the period of consolidation, any other outcome would have been surprising. Hence, the real luck is to be located on the supply side, namely in the very high elasticity of goods supply that gave the whole expansion its noninflationary growth momentum.

3.3   The Puzzle: Labor's Acquiescence

The period after the currency reform up to the mid-1950s was a time of persistently high profit margins and a declining wage share in value added, which greatly facilitated the economic resurgence of West Germany. Why did labor—represented by unions—allow this to happen? After all, the principle of *Tarifautonomie* (autonomous collective bargaining) was reestablished by law in April 1949, and it gave unions and employers' associations the right to negotiate over working conditions and wages basically without any government interference, even without compulsory arbitration by the government, which had still been a last resort in the legal framework of the Weimar Republic from 1919 to 1933. Hence, in principle, the unions had a free hand to pursue an aggressive wage policy.

There are at least four plausible explanations for the unions' apparent restraint, which may be briefly described as (i) organizational weakness, (ii) political distraction, (iii) expectational errors, and (iv) social responsibility.

Organizational Weakness
It has been argued, by Mancur Olson among others that the caesura of a lost war and foreign occupation destroyed the traditional network of distributional coalitions in West Germany; as a consequence, unions lost part of their power and political strength.[16] Thus, for a decade or so, there was plenty of scope for the economy to grow unburdened by the corporatist sclerosis that is typical for stable democratic societies.

This theory contains an important element of truth for the explanation of union behavior in, say, the first two years after the currency reform of June 1948. Before that date, unions had been particularly favored by the Allied authorities in receiving permission and support for the rebuilding of their organizations since union leaders had been quite consistent in opposition to the National Socialist regime. Yet, the currency reform destroyed much of their funds so that, for a while, they were simply not able to carry out any major strikes. With the economy recovering quickly, however, this changed in a rather short time, and strikes again became financially feasible, probably as early as 1950. In this respect, West Germany in the fifties was a paradise of peaceful labor relations compared to other industrialized countries such as the United Kingdom, France, or Italy and compared to its own troubled past of the Weimar Republic. Yet, by West Germany's standards of later times, the 1950s were not quite so calm: out of ten years in the period 1950 to 1989 in which more than 1 million working days per year were lost through strikes, five—1951, 1953, 1954, 1956, and 1957— were in the first postwar decade.

Other indicators also point in the direction of organizational strength rather than weakness. Through the first half of the fifties, the unionization rate was high, both by international standards and by the historical standards of later periods: in 1951–52, more than 45 percent of all employees were union members, more than at any other later time of West German economic history up to the present. Until about 1965, this share declined to about 36 percent, due mostly to the sharp increase of employment of still nonunionized workers. In the fifties, however, the absolute number of union members grew quickly, by an average of about 1.6 percent per annum. Hence, it would be somewhat misleading to speak of a dramatic weakening of the unions' (numerical) power base. The same holds for the unions' voice in politics and economic policy counseling.

As to politics, it is clear that the center-right federal government as a whole and the Ministry of Economics in particular had, if anything, an antiunion bias. Nevertheless, it would be wrong to regard the unions' umbrella organization, the 1949-founded *Deutscher Gewerkschaftsbund* (DGB), as politically powerless: its first president, the prestigious Hans Böckler, was on good terms with Chancellor Adenauer (whom he had known well from the twenties when Adenauer was the mayor of Cologne). Most notably, the fierce political debate on the codetermination law in 1950–51 was settled by the deliberate use of the personal ties between the chancellor and the union leadership. In addition, the Labor Ministry was traditionally open-minded toward union concerns and remained a citadel of labor interests, as it had already been in the Weimar Republic.

Political Distraction

Henry Wallich argued that West German unions were distracted from pursuing an aggressive wage policy by their own syndicalist demands for codetermination that provoked a heavy political controversy over the passing of two laws, the *Mitbestimmungsgesetz* (codetermination law) in 1951 and the *Betriebsverfassungsgesetz* (company statute law) in 1952.[17] As both laws were bound to set the framework for industrial relations in the decades to come, it is not surprising that the unions, just like the employers' associations and the confederation of industry, took them very seriously and invested much effort and political argument in lobbying for their cause. Clearly, the protracted controversy over these laws makes Wallich's point look plausible: given the strong syndicalist aspirations of German unions, which go back to the twenties, it would have been a rational strategy for them to temporarily stand still at the wage front so as not to endanger the far more daring prospect of a thoroughly syndicalist "industrial democracy." Nevertheless, it is only a partial explanation of union restraint in the fifties since the codetermination issue virtually disappeared from the political agenda after 1952. The final outcome of the two laws, especially the later one, was widely regarded as a bad defeat for the union's cause; hence, a backlash would be expected, with wage policy picking up in aggressiveness. However, it took another two years until, in 1954, hefty wage increases were demanded and granted. Fortunately, they did not lead to a sharp rise of real unit labor costs since the onsetting boom pushed up labor productivity growth to a quite unexpected degree.

Expectational Errors
This leads to a kind of theory of expectational errors that states that union wage demands were not particularly cautious and restrained but were persistently outpaced by the actual supply-side expansion and the resulting labor productivity gains; thus, what ex-ante may have looked like an aggressive wage policy turned out ex-post to be quite moderate in terms of real unit labor cost.

In fact, the rhetoric of the unions was by no means moderate. In particular, the Marxist Victor Agartz, who was chairman of the unions' Economic Research Institute until the mid-1950s, repeatedly called for sharp wage increases either by criticizing productivity guidelines for wage policy or by arguing for a sort of purchasing power theory of wages that stated, in a quite unqualified fashion, that wage increases spur a noninflationary economic expansion by fueling demand and by forcing firms to raise labor productivity through rationalization investments. It was widely acclaimed that these calls were a prelude to the first major wave of strikes for higher wages in autumn 1954. On the other hand, the repeated warnings by the press that the wage claims were likely to lead into an inflationary spiral had quite often a tone of deep concern and urgency, especially in the boom periods 1950–51, 1954–55, and again in 1959–60. In the same vein, Minister of Economics Ludwig Erhard repeatedly issued passionate *Maßhalteappelle* (calls for moderation) to the public which were intended to ease inflationary pressures through moral suasion. Apparently, most professional observers underestimated quite consistently the potential for productivity growth. By any scientific standards, all these verbal statements are of course no more than soft evidence of repeated expectational errors; nevertheless, they indicate that neither the unions nor their critics had a realistic vision of the high supply elasticity inherent in the West German economy.

Social Responsibility
Whether some element of genuine social responsibility played a part in the unions' wage policy is difficult to say since the true motivation of union activities is usually well hidden in a cloud of moral and pseudo-moral arguments. Nevertheless, three particular circumstances of the fifties do in fact speak for the working of an element of group rationality that may deserve the name social responsibility.

First, in the public, the unemployment problem of the 1950s was visibly linked to the task of integrating immigrants and expellees. This task was widely regarded as something like a prime political aim of West German society since, if it were not reached, a resurgence of extreme right-wing ideas among the refugees could reasonably be expected. A temporary rise in 1950–1952 of a nationalist political party that represented the interests of expellees (the so-called BHE, *Bund der Heimatlosen und Entrechteten*) gave a warning signal that a right-wing potential of this kind might in fact become a threat to political stability. As the unions as a whole had left-wing and antinationalist leanings, some wage restraint to ease the integration of refugees would certainly have been a rational answer.

Second, the trauma of inflation remained virulent, particularly among low- and middle-income workers who had lost most of their savings in the currency reform. Clearly, an aggressive stance in wage policy, which would have run the risk of spurring a wage-price spiral, was not very popular among the rank and file, and union leaders could not simply disregard this mood. Thus, the repeated warnings by the press not to rekindle inflation might have frightened the average union member more than was officially admitted.

Third, the positive developments of the early fifties may have contributed to a calming down of the workers: even with some restraint, real wage growth by itself looked more than satisfactory for workers and gave them the confidence that, even without any turn to militancy, many of their material aspirations might be fulfilled within a fairly short time. Thus, the repeated attempts of union economists to bring the declining wage share to the attention of union members and the public at large did not initiate a persistent mass movement for higher wages.

To sum up, all four explanations of union restraint have their part to play: organizational weakness in the years 1948–50, but not later; political distraction in the period 1951–52; expectational errors and rational elements of social responsibility were present all the time, but maybe to a slowly decreasing extent since people gradually became accustomed to the fact that growth was fast and that the most urgent social problems were being solved. Hence, it is not surprising to see the first significant "wage revolution" happening in 1960 at the beginning of a new decade.

4 Setting the Stage for Export-led Growth: External Liberalization

In early 1948, the Western occupation zones were strongly dependent upon foreign aid to pay for two thirds of their desperately needed imports. By the mid-fifties, exports were ahead of imports to such an extent that West Germany came under frequent attacks from international organizations for its trade surpluses. And by 1960, West Germany's shares of world imports and exports—exceeded those that the much larger German reich had attained before the war. To some extent, the favorable development of West Germany's trade balance was a reflection of favorable price changes in world markets: from 1950 to 1960, the commodity terms of trade (average value of exports divided by average value of imports) improved by 40 percent. This was only partly due to the decline of raw material prices; more importantly, it reflected a rise of export relative to import prices for tradable manufactures.

4.1 The Dismal Starting Point

Europe's trading system in the late forties was very similar to the state of West Germany's internal economy before June 1948: the lack of sound money had its counterpart in the dollar gap that was due to an overvaluation of European currencies; and the administrative control over prices and production and the internal barter trade were paralleled by the network of bilateral trade agreements between currency areas. Although the internal reforms of the previous year proved very successful, the West German authorities did not dare to link the attainment of statehood and autonomy in late 1949 with a liberal reform of the foreign trade regime, that is, with a sharp devaluation (analogous to the currency reform) and a sweeping removal of import quotas and tariffs (analogous to the decontrol of the internal economy).

Four standard arguments were put forward by the center-right government against a radical liberalization of external transactions and a more realistic exchange rate: (i) the apprehension that a sufficiently large devaluation would make sensitive food imports from the United States more expensive; (ii) the fear that this would induce an inflationary wage-price spiral so shortly after the postreform inflation had run out; (iii) the desire to increase productivity by exposing firms, via an overvalued exchange rate, to fierce competition from abroad; and (iv) the bargaining argument that one's own import barriers would be used as a means to pry foreign markets open.[18]

While the 1948 reforms had put West Germany in the European vanguard with respect to internal deregulation, the external liberalization proceeded for the time being along the much slower path that most other West European countries followed after the war in the face of a severe shortage of foreign exchange.

4.2 European Liberalization and the Marshall Plan

Immediately after the war, the Americans dealt with the "dollar gap" by providing aid to "prevent unrest and diseases" in Europe. The European balance-of-payments crisis of 1947 and the fear that parts of Western Europe might turn communist induced the United States to become more involved in economic decision-making in Europe. In announcing the European Recovery Program (ERP)—the so-called Marshall Plan—on June 3, 1947, the United States decided:

• to replace the previous short-run relief efforts by medium-term aid for reconstruction,

• to provide Europe with some liquidity necessary for the conduct of intra-European trade on a multilateral basis, that is, without the need to balance trade accounts bilaterally, and

• to push for the removal of quantitative import restrictions within Europe.

Marshall Plan expenditures started in April 1948. In mid-1952, when expenditures had fallen to less than half of what they had been three years earlier, the Marshall Plan was replaced by the much less generous scheme of Mutual Security Assistance. All in all, European countries received roughly $12 billion of Marshall Plan assistance from the United States, a sum tantamount to roughly 2.1 percent of the recipients' GNP (1.4 percent in the case of West Germany). The funds were allocated according to the recipients' balance of payments situation vis-à-vis the dollar area, not according to investment needs or any productivity criterion.[19]

Nonetheless, the European Recovery Program had two important political effects: (1) As they received rather generous payments, France and the United Kingdom could more easily accept the reintroduction of West Germany into the politics and the trade circuits of Western Europe. (2) With its emphasis on medium-term aid for reconstruction, the Marshall Plan was interpreted as a lasting U.S. commitment to stay in Western Europe and thus enhanced investors' political confidence in that part of the continent.

Economically, Marshall Plan aid at least served to promote the gradual liberalization of trade and payments among the recipients who had formed the Organization for European Economic Cooperation (OEEC). In November 1949, the OEEC Council of Ministers agreed to abolish quantitative restrictions on 50 percent of intra-OEEC trade within six weeks. Shortly afterward, this liberalization target was raised to 60 percent as of autumn 1950 and to 75 percent as of February 1951. In early 1955, the target was finally fixed at 90 percent. In mid-1950, a few months after the first steps toward the removal of quantitative import restrictions had been taken, the European Payments Union (EPU) was established to replace the original arrangement for settling intra-OEEC payments imbalances.[20]

4.3   The "German Crisis"

From a contemporaneous West German standpoint, the European Payments Union had a good starting position: the West German trade deficit had narrowed to $45 million in June 1950, with exports rising rapidly while imports stagnated. However, the outbreak of war on the Korean peninsula changed the picture dramatically. The ensuing demand boom propelled West Germany into an unexpected balance-of-payments crisis. On November 14, when West Germany's cumulative deficit with the EPU had already surpassed its EPU quota, the OEEC council decided to grant a special credit of $120 million. In late January 1951, the West German central bank tightened the credit restrictions it had introduced in October 1950; one month later, West Germany suspended the previous relaxation of quantitative controls and temporarily ceased to issue any new import licenses.

This "Korea crisis" provided the last serious political challenge to West Germany's fledgling liberal economic order. Just as the post-currency-reform inflation in the fall of 1948, it put in jeopardy not only the details but also the essence of the social market economy. By early 1951, the conservative chancellor, Konrad Adenauer, the minister of finance, Fritz Schäffer, and even the Allies urged Erhard to return to a system of central administration and distribution, at least for major raw materials. Even a general price freeze was under discussion. However, as a notorious optimist, Erhard stuck to his predictions that the adjustment flexibility of the market economy was great enough to cope with the problem in due course.

He turned out to be right. From March 1951 onward, the West German overall balance of trade and its EPU position improved dramatically, enabling West Germany to repay the special assistance credit in May—five months ahead of schedule. West Germany even became a net creditor to the EPU by November 1951, a position the country continued to hold until the EPU was abolished in late 1958. The reimposed quantitative restrictions were progressively lifted from January 1952 onward.

The West German payments position improved so rapidly that one wonders how severe the crisis had actually been in the first place. Two considerations help to find an answer. (i) After January 1950 throughout 1951, exports rose faster than imports in terms of value and volume.[21] As exports increased from a much lower level, this difference in trend rates could go along with a balance-of-trade deterioration in late 1950. That was temporary. Given the difference in trend rates, the imbalance would soon have corrected itself. (ii) Prior to the Korea boom, capacity utilization in West Germany had been lower than in other industrial countries. This gave West Germany more scope for the expansion of output in the face of a boost in demand. A surge in raw material imports in advance of a surge in production and a parallel building up of stocks was inevitable and not disquieting.

The West German balance-of-payments crisis of late 1950 and early 1951, initially interpreted as a disaster, proved to be the counterpart of a resource inflow for widening production bottlenecks and for building up raw material stocks parallel to a quick expansion of production. To the extent that the current account deficit reflected a resource inflow for additional investment, it might well be interpreted as a sign of strength rather than a symptom of weakness.

All in all, the development of the West German balance of payments in late 1950 and early 1951 hardly deserves to be called the "German crisis." While the restrictions on the expansion of internal credit may have been justified to check the rise of prices during the Korea boom, the suspension of import liberalization was certainly not warranted by the actual development of trade. However, this criticism can hardly be directed at the West

German authorities, whose foreign exchange reserves were running out. Rather, it points to a deficiency of the international payments system—namely, to the lack of an adequate source of credit on commercial terms for a rapidly growing economy.

The handling of this crisis, together with the rapid improvement in the West German payments position in the same year, greatly enhanced the reputation of the EPU and the OEEC. The measures adopted set a precedent. By granting temporary balance of payments credits, the EPU and the OEEC council induced those debtor countries that were about to exceed their EPU quotas to pursue more restrictive monetary and fiscal policies and to quickly relax any reimposed import controls. As negotiations over the terms of renewal of the EPU were held every year after 1952, creditor countries had some leverage to push debtors toward less expansionary demand policies and a more liberal regime for trade and payments.

4.4   Becoming a Pacemaker for Liberalization

In the first years after the Federal Republic had come into being in late 1949, it pursued a trade policy almost exactly like that of every other country. The tariff policy was to put the new state in a good bargaining position, and the attitude toward nontariff barriers to trade was designed to fit into the framework of the OEEC and the EPU.

After 1952, concerns about imported inflation came to the fore in West Germany. The central bank—and the general public—gave high priority to price level stability. This manifested itself in a relatively restrictive monetary policy. As a consequence, the inflation rate in West Germany turned out to be lower than elsewhere: between 1950 and 1958, the GNP deflator increased at an annual average of 3.4 percent in West Germany as opposed to 5.5 percent in the other OEEC areas. At fixed nominal exchange rates, West German suppliers became ever more competitive. When the initial disturbance of the "Korea crisis" had been overcome, West Germany's current account quickly swung into surplus for a long time to come. In order to limit the inflow of exchange reserves—and hence the threat to internal monetary stability—the overriding imperative of trade policy was to relax import restrictions. West Germany thus became a pioneer of European liberalization. From 1953 onward, it took unilateral steps ahead during cyclical upswings when some debtor countries felt compelled to temporarily reintroduce trade restrictions.

West Germany's stepwise external liberalization in the fifties can hardly be explained—as Olson (1982) seems to imply—by a general weakness of organized interest groups in the wake of disruptions by war, occupation, and the division of the country. From the very beginning, the major interest groups participated actively in the process of trade policy formation. However, protectionist pressures arising from sectoral lobbies were effectively dampened by the umbrella organizations of capital and labor.

As a broad organization of labor, the *Deutscher Gewerkschaftsbund*, or DGB (German Federation of Trade Unions) often acted as an advocate of consumer interests. In the preparatory committee for the new West German tariff schedule (1949–1950), the delegate of the trade unions explicitly participated as the consumers' representative. In mid-1950, the DGB demanded sweeping reductions of many proposed tariffs. Throughout the period of rapid growth in the 1950s, the expected benefits of liberalization—namely, lower prices and higher productivity—were frequently regarded as outweighing the inconveniences of import-induced structural change.

The Bundesverband der Deutschen Industrie, or BDI, (Federation of Industries) tried to reconcile the interests of its branches by pleading for a general opening of markets, albeit with numerous exceptions and on the basis of strict reciprocity. Although the BDI resisted Erhard's unilateral steps, its influence was partly neutralized by pressures from abroad. From 1953 onward when the current account surplus became ever larger, the OEEC and the GATT repeatedly asked West Germany for a unilateral liberalization, sometimes coupled with unveiled threats of retaliation.

After 1951, the country's progress toward freer trade was paralleled by moves toward *currency convertibility on current account*—first within the EPU area, then with all countries except the dollar area, and finally with the dollar area as well. In 1952, Germany liberalized payments for trade in services with the EPU area; one year later this applied also for income transfers.[22] From April 1954 onward, the deutsche mark (DM) became freely convertible for residents of an increasing number of nondollar countries.[23] Simultaneously, the terms of bilateral trade and payments arrangements with non-EPU countries were hardened together with the EPU agreement itself. This made the discrimination between the hard-currency dollar area and the soft-currency rest of the world increasingly obsolete. Following a cyclical downswing and a drastic change in French policies, France finally agreed to dissolve the EPU as of December 27, 1958. On the same day, all OEEC members, except Greece (which followed in May 1959), Iceland, and Turkey, restored external convertibility of their currency into dollars for current transactions.

West Germany removed most of the remaining restrictions on *capital flows* in late 1958 and early 1959. The issue had not been under consideration before 1953 when the country's external indebtedness was still an unresolved problem. Most capital transactions were simply prohibited. First, two important steps had to be taken: a settlement with Israel (1952), which obliged West Germany to pay $3.5 billion as restitution over the course of the next twelve to fourteen years, and the London Debt Agreement (early 1953), which reduced the external indebtedness—prewar and postwar debt including obligations incurred under the Marshall Plan—by more than 50 percent from DM 29.3 to 14.5 billion.[24] After the London Debt Agreement had come into force as of mid-September 1953, West Germany swiftly began to lift the restrictions on capital flows. As the central bank feared a net inflow of capital that would boost the money supply at the fixed exchange rate, the liberalization of capital outflows usually preceded that of inflows.

5   Explaining the Postwar Growth Spurt: A Synopsis

1. The economic reforms of June 1948 are the demarcation line between postwar misery and the subsequent period of unprecedented growth. West Germany's experience demonstrates the importance of the *appropriate economic order*. Three empirical observations corroborate this hypothesis, namely, (i) the development of output in the Bizone before and after the reforms of June 1948, (ii) the comparison between the instant growth spurt in the Bizone and the belated recovery in the French zone where markets were deregulated with a delay of roughly six months, and (iii) the marked contrast between West Germany and East Germany where a command economy was maintained until mid-1990.

2. *Monetary and fiscal policy* provided individuals and firms with a relatively stable and reliable macroeconomic framework. Although West Germany was repeatedly criticized for its refusal to adopt expansionary demand policies on a grand scale, this restraint helped rather than hurt.

3. Initially, fast growth was comparatively easy: a *speedy return to normality* after a near collapse. This holds both for output and for (West) Germany's position in the world market. In 1948, favorable internal conditions for fast output growth were already in place. In terms of skills, experience, and motivation, West Germany's labor force was probably second to none; the capital stock was still among the most modern in the world. Apart from the damage done by bombing, the capital stock of firms was only slightly worse than during the war. Nonetheless, in early 1948 industrial production was less than one third of what it had been in early 1944. As soon as the reforms of June 1948 made production profitable again, output soared.

4. As the *capital stock* had been unevenly impaired by bombing, investments for repairing equipment and widening bottlenecks were highly productive. Part of the seemingly miraculous output growth in the period before 1950 must be ascribed to this repair effect. It was as if spare capacity had been waiting to be made accessible.

5. A similar argument applies to West Germany's exports and imports. The most obvious explanation for the spectacular expansion of its *foreign trade* in the late forties and the early fifties is that it had to start from an abysmally low basis. Given the chance, West German suppliers regained market positions they had held before the war.

6. West Germany's real miracle was that rapid economic growth went far *beyond a mere "reconstruction"*; it continued after previous levels of output and exports had been surpassed. This development was a miracle in the sense that it came as a surprise to almost everybody. The surprise may be part of the explanation. West Germany's economic performance would have been less spectacular had labor unions and employers' associations, when they agreed on wage increases, been fully aware of the future rise in distributable productivity. Without a wage lag, profits and business investment would have been lower, and unemployment would have persisted longer. To be sure, unexpected positive productivity shocks were not the only reason for wage moderation, although over the length of time they may well have been the most important single factor. Other reasons played their part as well: the destruction of unions' strike funds through the currency reform, which made long-drawn battles for higher wages impossible for a while; the strong syndicalist aspirations of the unions, which made them invest much effort in political lobbying for codetermination rather than in tough wage bargaining; and a sense of social responsibility especially in the unions' umbrella organization, the DGB, which made it hesitate to risk a most unpopular surge of inflation or a revival of right-wing radicalism among jobless refugees.

7. A major part of the explanation for the fast rise of distributable productivity was an *improvement in the external terms of trade*, which fed into a remarkable divergence between the producer price index (which includes exports) and the consumer price index (which includes imports of consumer goods). In line with the terms-of-trade improvement, the consumer prices in the 1950–1960 period lagged behind producer prices by an annual average of 1.1 percentage points. Producer wages thus rose considerably slower than consumption wages, and wage increases that appeared to be substantial from the point of view of workers were still easily bearable for firms.

8. The fortunate improvement in the external terms of trade was due to an *export mix* strongly biased in favor of machinery and equipment and of sophisticated durable consumer goods, which tend to face a demand with a high income elasticity. The export mix was related to the structure of production that West Germany had inherited from the past. West Germany's traditional strength in the production of investment goods brought high returns in the 1950s. The advantages of the export mix were important because the world economy enjoyed prosperous growth and hence had a particularly strong demand for such goods most of the time. German exporters deserve praise for having exploited these market opportunities.

9. A combination of *luck and monetary restraint* transformed West Germany into a country enjoying the benefits of export-led growth. Having less domestic inflationary pressure than other countries and benefiting from its traditional strength in sophisticated goods with a high income elasticity of demand, West Germany earned huge external surpluses—and had to cope with the corresponding influx of foreign exchange reserves. West Germany attempted to fend off an imported inflation via unilateral liberalization at fixed exchange rates. The liberalization process even tended to feed on itself as the removal of barriers to imports raised the degree of internal competition and hence the elasticity of domestic supply. West Germany's increasingly liberal trade policy contributed significantly not only to the growth in exports but also to the economic miracle itself. With a relatively far-reaching and rapid liberalization of imports and a faster growth of productivity than in most other EPU countries, West Germany outpaced its OEEC partners in terms of export and import growth and gained market shares overseas.

10. Apart from the factors mentioned so far, West Germany's rapid postwar recovery was due to *hard work*, conditioned by a traditional work ethic, desperate living conditions, and a widespread belief that self-help would be essential for regaining prewar living standards. The goal of catching up with past achievements (reconstruction) gave a strong motivation to the active population, including refugees, expellees from the former Eastern Germany, and exsoldiers returning from prisoner of war camps who were all highly motivated to work hard to regain prewar living standards.

11. *Human capital* turned out to be more important than physical capital, which can be restored and augmented in almost no time if external conditions permit. West Germany had an ample supply of human capital. There was immigration and hardly any outmigration at the beginning. Many former military officers became successful entrepreneurs. The formation of new human capital was facilitated by the postwar students' eagerness

to recoup whatever time they had lost since the outbreak of war. The dual system of professional schooling and apprentice work proved to be efficient for acquiring nonacademic qualifications.

12. The process of fast growth was accompanied by *internal migration* from the agricultural regions to the centers of industrial activity close to the Rhine. Mobility was particularly high among the refugees and ex-pellees from the East who were initially allocated to rural areas.

13. The 1948 reforms in West Germany had several *shortcomings*: there were exceptions from the decontrol of prices (basic foodstuffs and raw materials, housing rents, and public services) to prevent the real incomes of the poor from falling below the subsistence level; a better solution would have been direct income subsidies. Moreover, foreign trade and payments were kept under tight control until 1950, although a unified exchange rate was established already in 1948. Finally, the capital market remained subject to control so that retained profits were the major source for financing business investments.

14. Receipts under the *Marshall Plan* were not essential for West Germany's growth spurt after the reforms of mid-1948. In fact, the first major shipments did not arrive until early 1949, that is, at a time when the economy had already started to cool off somewhat. With less Allied red tape for exporters, a realistic valuation of the deutsche mark and access to short-term commercial credits to cushion the immediate J-curve effect of a deutsche mark devaluation, West Germany would not have needed any aid to pay for its food imports. While Britain and France, the major aid recipients, went through recurrent balance of payments crises in the fifties, West Germany experienced an unprecedented export boom although it had suffered a net outflow of resources in the postwar period if war reparations and the costs of military occupation are balanced against foreign assistance.

15. Although Marshall Plan aid helped to cope with the consequences of the *overvaluation* of West European currencies vis à vis the dollar, it reduced the need for a devaluation. A devaluation would have raised the competitiveness of the export sector and the import substitution sector and would even have accelerated the integration of the West German economy into the world economy.

16. Instead of *realigning the exchange rates*, West Germany—and Europe —waited for the special postwar import needs to abate before steps were taken to liberalize imports from the technologically most advanced part of the world. The United States provided Western Europe with the international liquidity necessary for intra-regional trade liberalization. Apart from

its political dimension, American aid and pressure to promote Europe's economic integration can be viewed as a strategy to redirect Europe's import demand away from the United States by removing intra-European barriers to trade and payments and by integrating West Germany into the European economy.

17. Import liberalization, later followed by the formation of the EEC customs union, must also be considered as a method of opening domestic markets to *competition* from abroad. In this sense, import liberalization served as a substitute for the competition law that did not pass the legislature before 1957.

18. The goal of *full currency convertibility* on the capital account could have been reached much earlier than 1958, though not before the London Debt Agreement had been concluded. Thanks to the high domestic savings rate, West Germany did not need capital imports. Otherwise, the postponement of full convertibility would have been more problematic.

19. West Germany, having been defeated in war, had no reservations against full *economic integration* into the international economy. Support for European economic integration became a substitute for patriotism, traveling abroad and gaining business experience in foreign countries was considered to be conducive to advancing professional careers. After a mere dozen years of control (1936–1948), the capitalist spirit quickly revived. There was need for industrial deconcentration and initially for the conversion of armaments production to civilian products but not for large-scale privatization (as in present-day Central and Eastern Europe). Similarly, the country after 1945 had an almost unimpaired system of private property rights. The clause in the constitution ("Basic Law") according to which private property rights can be constrained in the interest of the general welfare had no significant negative implication.

20. Finally, to Central and Eastern Europe, West Germany offers the political lesson that a liberal reform as tough and sweeping as that of late June 1948 can be *feasible in a democracy*: the two German parliamentary bodies, the Economic Council (the representatives of the freely elected state parliaments of the Bizone) and the *Länderrat* (the representatives of the Bizonal state governments) had endorsed the sudden decontrol of most parts of the economy in advance. It is true that a majority of West Germans temporarily favored the reintroduction of price controls at the height of the postreform inflation in fall 1948. But the parties of the Bizonal coalition, which backed Erhard, gained the upper hand against the Social Democrats in the elections to the first West German Bundestag in mid-1949. Hence, whatever advantages the state of foreign occupation might have had for

the implementation of an uncompromising currency reform, the thrust of the liberalization package was soon endorsed by the population at large.

Notes

Some of the major points made in this chapter are elaborated in much more detail in Giersch, Paqué, Schmieding (1992).

1. This term was coined by Röpke (1947, p. 57).

2. See Röpke (1951, p. 271). Between mid-1946 and mid-1948, the glass and ceramics industry and the musical instruments and toy industries were by far the most rapidly growing sectors of the West German economy, with employment increasing by 113.5 and 108.4 percent respectively, about five times as fast as overall employment. Ehret (1959, p. 65); the numbers refer to the Bizonal area only.

3. See Krengel (1958, pp. 16, 49–53).

4. For a detailed description of the prehistory of the currency reform and of the measures enacted, see Möller (1976, pp. 433–484), and Buchheim (1988, pp. 189–231); for a survey of how the monetary overhang was eliminated in a large number of countries after World War II, see Dornbusch and Wolf (1990).

5. The respective deposits of public authorities were cancelled altogether.

6. For details, see Möller (1976, p. 455); Müller (1982, p. 137).

7. The first preliminary law on relief for the victims of the war, expellation, Nazi tyranny, and currency reform was, however, not enacted prior to August 1949. The law on the *Lastenausgleich* proper was passed three years later. It provided for a special tax of 50 percent on wealth holdings at the time of the currency reform, payable in annual installments over the next decades. As the valuation clauses were very generous, much less than 50 percent of mid-1948 wealth was eventually redistributed. See Schillinger (1985, pp. 283–290).

8. Wirtschaft und Statistik (1949–50, pp. 12–13, 157).

9. See Buchheim (1988, p. 229).

10. See Gundlach (1987, p. 29).

11. See Buchheim (1988, p. 229).

12. See Ritschl (1985, pp. 140 ff.).

13. Note that housing rents and prices for transport and other services included in the consumer price index were still controlled.

14. Although wages remained under administrative control until early November, the military government had authorized wage increases of 15 percent in late April 1948; Müller (1982, p. 152). This scope was almost completely exploited during the summer so that wages did not lag far behind prices.

15. See, for example, Wallich (1955, pp. 93–95).

16. See Olson (1982, pp. 75–76).

17. See Wallich (1955, pp. 307–310).

18. For the latter point, see Erhard (1954, p. 215).

19. See Abelshauser (1989, p. 94).

20. For a detailed analysis of the EPU, see Triffin (1957) and Kaplan and Schleiminger (1989).

21. See Schmieding (1987), table 6.

22. See Wallich and Wilson (1981, p. 402).

23. See Ehmann (1958, pp. 68 ff).

24. See Erhard (1954, p. 268).

References

Abelshauser, Werner, *Wirtschaft in Westdeutschland 1945–1948*, Stuttgart 1975.

Abelshauser, Werner, "Zur Funktion des Marshallplans beim westdeutschen Wiederaufbau." In: *Vierteljahreshefte für Zeitgeschichte*, Vol. 37 (1989), No. 1, pp. 85–113.

Boss, Alfred, "Incentives und Wirtschaftswachstum—Zur Steuerpolitik in der frühen Nachkriegszeit," Kiel Working Paper No. 295, Kiel, August 1987.

Buchheim, Christoph, "Die Währungsreform 1948 in Westdeutschland." In *Vierteljahreshefte für Zeitgeschichte*, Vol. 36, 1988, pp. 189–231.

Dornbusch, Rudiger, and Holger Wolf, "Monetary Overhang and Reform in the 1940s," Centre for Economic Policy Research, Discussion Paper No. 464, London, October 1990.

Ehmann, Georg, Entwicklung und Erfolg der westdeutschen Außenhandelsliberalisierung, Nürnberg 1958.

Ehret, Rolf G., Der Weg zur Vollbeschäftigung in der Bundesrepublik Deutschland, Winterthur 1959.

Erhard, Ludwig, "Deutschlands Rückkehr zum Weltmarkt," 2nd enlarged edition, Düsseldorf 1954.

Giersch, Herbert, Karl-Heinz Paqué, and Holger Schmieding, "The Fading Miracle. Four Decades of Market Economy in Germany," Cambridge 1992.

Gundlach, Erich, "Währungsreform und wirtschaftliche Entwicklung: Westdeutschland 1948," Kiel Working Paper No. 286, Kiel, April 1987.

Kaplan, Jacob J., and Günther Schleiminger, "The European Payments Union—Financial Diplomacy in the 1950s," Oxford 1989.

Krengel, Rolf, *Anlagevermögen, Produktion und Beschäftigung in der Industrie im Gebiet der Bundesrepublik 1924–1956*, Berlin 1958.

Mendershausen, Horst, "Prices, Money and the Distribution of Goods in Postwar Germany." In *The American Economic Review*, Vol. 39, 1949, No. 3, pp. 646–672.

Möller, Hans, "Die westdeutsche Währungsreform von 1948." In Deutsche Bundesbank (ed.), *Währung und Wirtschaft in Deutschland 1876–1975*, Frankfurt am Main 1976, pp. 433–483.

Müller, Georg, *Die Grundlegung der westdeutschen Wirtschaftsordnung im Frankfurter Wirtschaftsrat 1947–1949*, Frankfurt am Main, 1982.

Olson, Mancur, "The Rise and Decline of Nations—Economic Growth, Stagflation and Social Rigidities," New Haven, London 1982.

Ritschl, Albrecht, "Die Währungsreform von 1948 und der Wiederaufstieg der westdeutschen Industrie." In *Vierteljahreshefte für Zeitgeschichte*, Vol. 33, 1985, pp. 136–165.

Röpke, Wilhelm, "Offene und zurückgestaute Inflation: Bemerkungen zu Jacques Rueffs L'Ordre Social." In *Kyklos, International Review for Social Sciences*, Vol. I, 1947, pp. 57–71.

Röpke, Wilhelm, "Das Deutsche Wirtschaftsexperiment: Beispiel und Lehre." In *Vollbeschäftigung, Inflation und Planwirtschaft*, Schweizer Institut für Auslandsforschung, Zürich 1951, pp. 261–312.

Schillinger, Reinhold, Der Entscheidungsprozeß beim Lastenausgleich 1945–1952, St. Katharinen 1985.

Schmieding, Holger, "How to Fill a 'Dollar Gap?'" Observations on the Liberalisation of West Germany's External Trade and Payments 1947–1958, Kiel Working Paper No. 291, Kiel, July 1987.

Statistisches Amt des Vereinigten Wirtschaftsgebietes, Wirtschaft und Statistik, Wiesbaden, various issues.

Triffin, Robert, "Europe and the Money Muddle, From Bilateralism to Near-Convertibility, 1947–1956," New Haven 1957.

Wallich, Henry C., *Mainsprings of the German Economic Revival*, New Haven 1955.

Wallich, Henry C., and John F. Wilson, "Economic Orientations in Postwar Germany: Critical Choices on the Road Toward Currency Convertibility." In *Zeitschrift für die gesamte Staatswissenschaft*, Vol. 137, 1981, pp. 390–406.

2

The Lucky Miracle: Germany 1945–1951

Holger C. Wolf

In 1945 much of Western Europe resembled an economic shambles: bombed out factories, a largely destroyed infrastructure, and raw material shortages combined with monetary overhangs to yield a glum picture of the economic future. Expert predictions mirrored popular expectations: a recovery to prewar levels of consumption within a decade presented the optimistic end of the spectrum of opinion: "The probable improvements over the next five years, or even in the coming decade, are not likely to bring about a solution of the basic economic problem of Europe—the severe poverty in which the majority of the European peoples live" (United Nations 1948).

The pessimism was misguided—spectacularly: over the subsequent decade growth rates reached record levels. Among the recovering countries West Germany, initially written off as an all but hopeless case, turned in one of the most impressive performances, rebounding sprightly from the postwar depths to reach more then twice the prewar production levels by the end of the fifties while integrating some ten million homeless newcomers from the East in the process. The strong recovery was all the more surprising in the contemporary view since the German government shunned the postwar orthodoxy, adopting policies "that were in many respects the direct antithesis of post-Keynesian prescriptions for rapid growth" (Sohmen 1959). In place of the fashionable Beveridgean demand-side policies, the German model emphasized a peculiar brand of the neo-classical medicine, *ordo-liberalism*, aiming to achieve growth by eliciting a strong primary supply-side response. World opinion gave short shrift to the experiment: "Policies in Germany, it was suggested, were based on obsolete, outmoded economic ideas which had been superseded by those prevailing in enlightened circles in Britain and America" (Hutchinson 1979).

Tempora mutandur. "Economic miracles" à la Erhard are in strong demand today. As the East European economies shed the fetters of planning, the question naturally arises which conversion strategy best lubricates the painful transition. The postwar experience appears to provide valuable insights: many of the maladies haunting Europe in the forties have returned to plague the newly capitalist nations: latent massive unemployment, misdirected production patterns, trade imbalances, and monetary disequilibria are turning in a repeat performance. Faced with the old malady, there is a natural temptation to reuse the old prescription—with a twist. The oddity of the forties has matured into the virtue of the nineties: the new orthodoxy attaches a pivotal role to the creation of competitive markets. The German model in particular has been restyled into a panacea for the childhood illnesses of the transition economies. A solid application of the classical medicine, the argument goes, will do much to revitalize the moribund economies.

I assess the empirical support for the systemic explanation of the German economic miracle. This chapter divides into three sections, starting with a capsule summary of the ordo-liberal development strategy before turning to a filtered recapitulation of the events and policies. Against this background, the third part examines a range of hypotheses put forth to demiraculize the postwar growth spurt. The results are mixed: while the ordo-liberal policies succeeded in fine-tuning the German growth machine, the fuel transforming a potential into an actual miracle was to a significant degree provided by largely fortuitous demand disturbances. One thus has to wonder, following Wallich, whether the true miracle must not be sought in the almost uncanny sequence of lucky turns afforded the German economy in the crucial early years of the transition. This is not to denigrate the importance of the Erhardian reforms—even an abundance of fuel will not transform a Trabant into a Jaguar. Nevertheless, the contribution of the ordo-liberal policies needs to be judged against this extraordinarily favorable background. The finding dampens optimism about the transition economies of Eastern Europe; 1948 vintage miracles require a repeat appearance of Fortuna on an unlikely scale.

1   The Ordo-Liberal Policy Prescription

A prominent strand of research attributes the postwar growth performance of the West German economy to the ordo-liberal policies adopted by the Adenauer-Erhard administration, a set of supply-side measures formulated within a general equilibrium framework: "The potency of liberal policies, of what Lord Keynes has called 'the classical medicine,' has once again been dramatically demonstrated by the recent German events" (Haberler 1949) The ordo-liberal "social market economy," aiming to retain the efficiency properties of competitive markets while mitigating the social nonconcern of traditional laissez-faire policies, indeed presented a marked contrast to the interventionist policies fashionable in most of postwar Europe.[1]

What are the main ingredients of the ordo-liberal view? On the economic front efficiency constitutes the overriding criterion. By default, the attainment of efficient outcomes is to be delegated to competitive markets. The reliance on competitive markets defines the ordo-liberal agenda: Government intervention on economic grounds presupposes market failure. The latter comprises the classical externalities as well as, on a systemic level, the tendency of competitive markets to dissolve into oligopolistic structures: the government is charged with safeguarding competition by creating open markets, most importantly free trade, free choice of occupation, and free entry. The objective of attaining and safeguarding a competitive market economy also restricts the scope for macroeconomic policy: reliable long-term decision making requires a stable price level and predictable fiscal policies; cheap money and fiscal fine-tuning have no place in the ordo-liberal policy armory. The ordo-liberal view thus transcends orthodox laissez-faire: while retaining the Smithian reliance on self-interest, the authorities are not expected to laissez-passer local private sector decisions irrespective of their global implications. "The problem will not solve itself simply by letting economic systems grow up spontaneously. The history of the last century has shown this plainly enough. The economic system has to be consciously shaped" (Eucken 1950).

The social qualifier provides the second distinguishing characteristic between ordo- and paleo-liberalism: societal goals justify efficiency-reducing interventions. Interventions of the latter kind should however be *market conforming*, operating via incentives while steering clear of direct interference in the allocation process: "Government planning of underlying economic structure—yes; Government planning and direction of the economic process—no. To know the difference between forms and process and to act accordingly—this is essential" (Eucken 1949). All policy measures are to be evaluated within an underlying general equilibrium model: "Our fundamental principle consists in viewing individual economic questions as constituent parts of a greater whole. Since all sectors of the economy are closely interconnected, this fundamental approach is the only one which does justice to the subject" (Ordo-Manifesto).[2]

2   Germany 1945–1951

In the popular (ex post) view the German miracle has become inextricably interwined with the spectacular change occurring on the weekend of the

currency reform: the sudden abundance of almost forgotten goods in previously empty shop windows has entered economic lore. The focus on June
1948 renders the contrast with today's reforming economies sobering:
then instant bliss, the overnight transformation of an apparently moribund
economy into a picture of robust economic health, now stagnation, rising
unemployment, and inflation.

A closer look at developments in postwar Germany does much to
brighten the comparative picture, revealing a pattern of repeated setbacks
and confidence crises interspersed with timely interventions of Fortuna,
with a shift toward steady growth not occurring before 1951, some three
years after the initial rebound. The ex post beatification process accompanying the success of the reform measures has forced the quite unspec-
tacular early postreform performance into the background. In the popular
hindsight perspective, the West German miracle thus becomes a hard-to-
replicate immediate transition from stagnation to rapid growth, rather than
the drawn out and uncertain process whose final success was, for a long
time, no more than a hope.

2.1 The Prereform Period 1945–1948

Allied military strategy during the Second World War included a concerted
effort to destroy the Nazi war economy. For the casual visitor to postwar
Germany, the success of strategic bombing in achieving this objective
appeared evident; striking pictures of mile after mile of houses turned to
rubble indeed suggested a devastating destruction. The tourist eye view
is however not borne out by the evidence. The postwar capital stock
substantially exceeded the prewar level, reflecting both the ineffectiveness
of strategic bombing of industrial facilities and the investment boom accompanying the rearmament process: from 1935 to 1939, the capital stock
increased at a net annual rate of 0.89 billion reichsmark (RM), from 1940 to
1945 the growth rate accelerated to RM 3.36 billion per year.[3] The new
investment exceeded the losses due to wartime destruction and demolition;
by 1946, the capital stock was some RM 7 billion above its 1938 level
(table 2.1).

While the overall level of the capital stock was not substantially affected
by the war, a number of key sectors, notably steel rolling mills and ball-
bearing plants, suffered extensive damage and formed bottlenecks during
the immediate postwar period. The emphasis on armaments production
resulted in a shift of the sectoral composition in the direction of heavy
industry and machinery.[4]

Table 2.1
Capital stock (billion RM)

Capital stock 1938	49.3
Plus net investment	25.2
Minus bombing damage	13.8
Minus dismantling	2.8
Capital stock 1946	57.9

Source: Krengel (1963).
Note: In 1950 prices.

Table 2.2
Production 1940–45 (1938 = 100)

	1940	1942	1944	1.1945	5.1945
Raw materials	111	129	116		
Armaments	220	320	625		
Construction	64	36	27		
Investment	109	121	80		
Consumption	95	86	86		
Industrial production	102	106	117	75	ca. 20

Source: Friedensburg (1954), UNECE.

The higher capital stock was matched by an increase in skilled labor: wartime deaths were more than offset by the influx of some three million refugees in the immediate postwar period. The moderate increase in factor supplies was not matched by a rise in output; industrial production plummeted to a fifth of the prewar level (tables 2.2 and 2.3). The decline reflected the collapse of the technological and financial infrastructure. While damage to physical infrastructure remained fairly localized, the low redundancy degree of transportation systems translated local physical damage into sharply reduced global capacity.[5] Concerted repair efforts, however, succeeded in rapidly restoring transportation capacity to near prewar levels and thus removed the main technological constraint on recovery. The continued existence of severe excess capacity predominantly reflected grossly distorted incentives and political risk.

Incentives
The end of the war terminated the Nazi state but left the wartime economic system intact. The new military and civil authorities of the Allied zones inherited a complex system of rigid price controls, resource rationing, and

Table 2.3
The real economy 1936 and 1946 (constant prices)

	1936			1946		
	Employment (million RM)	Production (billion RM)	2:1 (RM)	Employment (million RM)	Production (billion RM)	5:4 (RM)
Agriculture	9	10	1.100	7	5	714
Forestry						
Fisheries						
Industry	12	33	2.800	7.5	10	1.333
Handicraft						
Power						
Trade	6	17	2.800	5	6.2	1.240
Transportation						
Finance						
Services	3	8	2.700	3	4.1	1.370
Household work	1.4	1	700	1.5	0.7	470
Employment	31.4			24		
NNP		69			26	
Depreciation		6			4	
GNP		75			30	
Productivity			2.200			1.083

bilateral clearing agreements, as well as the legacy of ten years of monetized budget deficits, a sizable monetary overhang. The magnitude of the overhang eliminated the possibilities of conversion into interest-bearing assets or gradual elimination via budget surpluses, leaving monetary reform and inflation as options. Reflecting the experience after the First World War, the inflation solution gained few adherents, leaving monetary reform as the only feasible solution.[6] Expecting a fairly rapid agreement on the details of reform, controls were maintained in place. The emerging conflict between the Western Allies and the Soviet Union, however, forestalled a speedy resolution of the outstanding issues; the temporary measures persisted into 1946 and 1947.

Surprisingly, the controls initially held up fairly well. Although a black market began to emerge in late 1946, the fraction of transactions taking place outside legal channels appears to have remained below 10 percent until early 1948 (Mendershausen 1949; OMGUS 1946). The delay in the development of black markets in the presence of a sizable overhang, severe rationing, and the near certainty of an eventual currency reform[7] partly reflected unpopularity,[8] partly the increasing dominance of countertrade and compensation deals in which the official price, while used, played a subordinate role.[9]

While pro forma monetary exchange thus remained the norm, transactions increasingly required the establishment of a double coincidence of wants, reducing the efficiency of the exchange system to that of a barter economy. Lacking current uses for monetary balances and expecting an eventual currency reform, enterprises increasingly limited production to the accumulation of inventories, worsening the supply situation.[10] The resulting danger of political radicalization coupled with the shrinking chances for an Allied consensus finally prompted the decision for a separate currency reform for the Bizone in the fall of 1947.

Uncertainty
While the Damocles sword of the impending monetary reform curtailed production for current consumption, uncertainty about the future shape of the political and economic system discouraged investment in new capacity. Following the capitulation of the Third Reich, the unsettled policy of the Allies, reflected first in the Morgenthau proposal to return Germany to an agricultural economy, later in permanently changing real reparations and restrictions on permissible production in the industry plans, severely restricted the scope for long-term investment planning: "There is evident a general hesitancy to make any decisions at all. The Germans feel them-

selves in the position of a prisoner at the bar who is expecting his sentence and who is not able to make decisions relating to his own future before he knows what the sentence will be."[11] In like vein, Sauermann (1978) argues that "nobody was able to look further than the next day. The courage to envisage a future was almost completely lost..."

While the Kennan telegram and the inclusion of the western zones in the Marshall Plan signaled a turnaround of the Allies' stance, the economic and political shape of the future Germany remained uncertain, with a strong expectation of a quasi-British outcome: the political ascendancy of the Social Democrats, favoring substantial state ownership of resources in key areas,[12] was widely expected.[13] The experience of the thirties, combining rapid growth in the Soviet Union with collapse in the western market economies, forced proponents of market-based reconstruction approaches into hard to defend minority positions.

While the combination of lacking current profitability and dubious future prospects sharply curtailed new investment in the postwar period, the existing capital stock was well maintained and repaired during the years of inaction as workers not needed for current production were shifted toward maintenance.[14] On the eve of the currency reform, the productive capability of the West German economic engine thus considerably exceeded (reported) production, providing the basis for a rapid expansion of output.

2.2   June 1948: The Reforms

Clay: My advisors tell me you are making a severe mistake.
Erhard: Don't listen to them, my advisors tell me the same.[15]

Following preparations, June 1948 witnessed a radical change in the "economic constitution." Although the currency reform has attracted the limelight of attention, the policy package of 1948 consisted of five elements: monetary reform, financial reform, tax reductions, price liberalization, and exchange rate unification. The currency reform proper was conceived as a necessary, but by no means sufficient step: "A currency reform unaccompanied by a change in economic policy would have been doomed to failure" (Erhard 1948). The augmentation of monetary reform by supply-side measures was thus explicitly conceived as a consistent cold turkey shift from Schachtianism to a competitive market economy: "Nothing of the swindle of the past should be allowed to survive—even the last illusion had to be destroyed."[16]

The monetary reform aimed to establish approximate monetary balance by a drastic reduction in nominal balances. The resulting asset gap on the banking sector balance sheet was creatively filled, allowing the reestablishment of a working financial sector.[17] The elimination of the monetary overhang raised the marginal value of money and hence both the price elasticity of demand and the tax elasticity of labor supply.[18] The exorbitant excise and income tax rates imposed to (successfully) ensure budget balance during the immediate postwar years consequently turned into significant disincentives. Reflecting Allied misgivings about the incentive effects of lower tax rates, a compromise combining relatively high base rates with generous deduction allowances for savings and investments was enacted, setting the tone for tax policy over the next decade.[19]

Price liberalization formed the fourth and most controversial pillar of the reform package. The majority view held that price decontrol at this juncture would be premature, risking an inflationary spurt and thereby endangering the success of the currency reform. The ordo-liberal response regarded price decontrol as sine qua non for a successful currency reform: free prices would ensure that the hoarded inventories would be available *at some price* and would thus send the necessary signal to consumers. The final edict presented a compromise, focusing decontrol on those goods most likely to exhibit substantial supply responses, manufactured consumer products and investment goods, while maintaining controls on foodstuffs, rent, and raw materials. Wage control persisted for another five months before being revoked in November. The removal of artificial price limits paved the way for exchange rate unification and moderate trade liberalization: over the months following the reform, multiple exchange rates were gradually unified. The liberalization of foreign trade, apart from a temporary reversal in 1951, proceeded continuously within the European Payments Union (EPU) until full convertibility in 1958.[20]

Two features distinguish in Erhard reform package from the policies adopted elsewhere on the continent. First, it presented an almost purely supply-side-oriented approach toward economic reconstruction. Second, it paid remarkably little attention to equity considerations. In marked contrast to the fashionable welfare state policies, the Erhardian reforms unabashedly favored the Schumpeterian entrepreneur while limiting social concern to the provision of a minimal, though comprehensive, social security net. The option to pursue a deliberately tough reform benefited from Erhard's ability to act as benevolent dictator, backed by the quasi-dictatorial powers of the Allied authorities.[21]

2.3   Postreform: The Short Run

The immediate result of the currency reform was so spectacular as to enter economic lore: "On June 21, 1948, goods reappeared in the stores, money resumed its normal function, black and grey markets reverted to a minor role, foraging trips to the country ceased, labor productivity increased, and output took off on its great upward surge" (Wallich 1955).[22]

The improvement in supplies was matched by an improvement of morale, a shift from the fatalism of the control period to the go-getter attitudes prevailing during the fifties (Klopstock 1949). Erhard's ability to implement and more importantly to sustain the remaining elements of the reform program, in particular the price liberalization and derationing schemes which on their own merit had attracted much less support than the monetary reform, was substantially enhanced by this mood shift toward a "new atmosphere of great expectations" (Lutz 1949). The "almost miraculous effect" (Stucken 1953) of the reform reflected Erhard's all but explicit public insinuations in the months prior to the reform that the authorities would for the time being turn a blind eye toward illegal hoarding, providing enterprises with a tacit warning that the reform was imminent. Reported production and turnover consequently drastically declined in May, boosting not only the statistical impact of the reforms but also providing consumers with a last illustration of the effects of rationing. To ensure the acceptance of the new currency, the prereform hoarding had to be complemented by postreform dishoarding. By holding the initial liquidity of enterprises deliberately low and sharply reducing the availability of short-term credit for the two months following the reform, the authorities actively and successfully encouraged the dishoarding. The domestic supply response was enhanced by increased foreign currency allocations for the import of consumption goods in the months preceding the reform, enabling a targeted release coinciding with the reform measures.

2.4   Postreform: The Medium Run

The initial unconditional success of the reform package did not persist. The disbursement of the second tranche of the per capita money allocation, coupled with a slow release of European Recovery Program (ERP) imports, resulted in excess demand and rising prices. The upward price trend, coupled with stagnant wages and fixed raw material prices, occasioned enterprises to reduce sales, building up inventories in the hope of higher profits down the line. While the central bank countered with sharply curtailed credit in an attempt to enforce a rundown of inventories, the generous initial endowment of commercial banks rendered credit restriction difficult. Enterprises did not experience a sufficient liquidity decline to comply, resulting in renewed shortages. Simultaneously, unemployment sharply accelerated as the creation of new jobs fell short of the continued influx of refugees and released prisoners of war.[23]

The combination of declining real wages, rising unemployment, renewed shortages, the cancellation of 70 percent of the previously frozen savings, and a pronounced sense of inequity tarnished the public image of the promarket policies: the fall of 1948 saw public esteem of Erhard and his policies decline precariously.[24] Following smaller strikes in August protesting higher prices, by November labor unions demanded the reimposition of price controls, a demand underlined by a Bizonal strike in November, following a (defeated) vote no confidence in the economic council. At year end, the survival chances of the reforms, in particular the price liberalization, appeared slim, being held alive thanks more to Erhard's unwavering conviction in the correctness of his view than to either public support or economic results. In a December 1948 survey, 70 percent of respondents supported the reimposition of price controls (Noelle and Neumann 1956).

The price level stabilization in the spring of 1949, and thereby in all likelihood the survival of the Erhardian reforms, partly reflect the contractionary effects of the second money conversion, the emergence of a fiscal surplus,[25] and an exogenous downturn in world demand. More importantly, it resulted from the demand contraction occasioned by falling real wages as wage increases fell short of inflation. Nominal wage constraint reflected both a weak bargaining position caused by the loss of union funds during the currency reform and the continued influx of new workers from the East and a hesitancy to engage in politically divisive action.

The following period until the summer of 1950 saw an uneasy balance between rapidly increasing production and inexorably rising unemployment. Falling unit labor costs, coupled with continued price controls on raw materials, implied large profits for those firms capable of setting their own prices. Reflecting the profit opportunities, both production and investment in these industries expanded rapidly (table 2.4).

During this period (and continuing until the mid-fifties) private savings remained relatively low, reflecting pent-up demand for consumption, low income levels, and the disincentive effects associated with losing a substantial part of savings for a second time within a quarter century (table 2.5).[26] The sluggishness of private savings raised the problem of financing potential investment. Lacking well-developed capital markets, the answer was

Table 2.4
Gross investment ratio

48/II	23.6	51/I	25.7
49/I	23.8	51/II	24.9
49/II	19.8	52/I	25.0
50/I	21.1	52/II	24.6
50/II	22.9		

Table 2.5
Composition of savings (percent of total)

	1950	1951	1952	1953	1954	1955
Private household	17.5	12.1	20.0	23.2	25.6	21.5
Retained earnings	44.3	57.5	48.6	38.2	34.7	38.4
Public household	26.0	25.9	30.5	38.7	39.3	40.9
External finance	12.2	4.5	0.8	−0.1	0.3	−0.9

Table 2.6
Distribution of unemployment

	1948	1949	1950	1951	1952
Average	4.2	8.3	10.3	9.0	8.4
Highest	7.3	21.5	25.2	22.9	19.7
Lowest	1.0	3.3	4.3	3.5	3.4
Spread	6.3	18.2	20.9	19.4	16.3

sought in stimulating retained earnings. The combination of punitive tax rates on profits withdrawn with generous tax credits for retained earnings and equally generous write-off allowances provided the incentive for re-investment of the artifically augmented profits.

While the Erhardian reforms succeeded in stimulating production, the expansion in employment proved insufficient to absorb the continued influx of workers from the East, resulting in an apparently inexorable rise in the unemployment rate from less than 3 percent on the eve of the reform to more than 10 percent by 1950. The resulting political pressures were magnified by extreme regional disparities, comprising almost full employment in the South with unemployment rates last seen during the great depression in the North (table 2.6).

A political conflict regarding the cause of unemployment and the appropriate countermeasures soon developed. The Keynesian view, advocated

Table 2.7
Sectoral growth 1948–52

Total	129
Investment goods	233
Consumption goods	150
Intermediate	130
Foodstuffs	59
Mining	54

by the United Nations Economic Commission for Europe (UNECE) and the Allied authorities, treated the inexorable rise in unemployment as prima facie evidence for the failure of the ordo-liberal approach, advocating the adoption of demand management and investment planning: "Any serious reduction in the number of unemployed in western Germany must start with the adoption by the authorities of an expansionist policy.... It may therefore prove necessary, if an effective employment policy is not to stop halfway—or lead to inflation—to retreat from the liberal principles of economic policy hitherto followed." To overcome the crises the government must "assume considerably greater responsibility than hitherto for directing investment into channels where it can fructify for the benefit of the community.... What is needed is a highly differentiated policy which maintains and even increases the pressure of demand in certain fields and which simultaneously siphons off excess increases in other fields. This is likely to involve a much greater degree of conscious control of the working of the economic system than has been the practice since the monetary reform of 1948."[27] The extent of foreign popular criticism of the ordo-liberal program can be gauged from an anonymous review of Eucken's work in *The Times Literary Supplement*: "[H]e (Eucken) bore a considerable share of the responsibility for the policy of decontrol and deflation pursued in that country which resulted in mass unemployment and a degree of social inequality unparalleled even under the Nazis."[28]

Finding itself exposed to increasingly emphatic suggestions to abandon the free market policies in favor of planned demand management, the German government did not concur in the analysis, attributing the increasing unemployment to structural factors and warning that increased demand would meet inflexible supply, with inflation as the inevitable result. Yet, while adamant in his support of the free market approach, Erhard recognized the force of opposition: "[I]n the summer of 1950 the market economy appeared to be close to ruin" (Erhard 1962).

The political pressure eventually resulted in the adoption of a much-heralded investment program of mid-1950, effectively not much more than a relabeling of programs adopted earlier but providing a soothing outward appearance of expansionary policies. By the time the program took effect, the outbreak of the Korean War had however altered the economic landscape fundamentally. Following full employment policies, most of Western Europe operated at or close to capacity and was thus unable to easily meet the additional demand. Being able to draw on a large pool of skilled unemployed labor, German enterprises stepped into the gap.

The export boom propelled the economy into a second phase of rapid growth, interrupted briefly at the end of the Korean conflict before being refueled by the rearmament drive (Abelshauser 1975). The critical year 1950 also witnessed a turnaround in the growth rate of the labor force as the flow of immigrants and released prisoners of war slowed. Following the peak in early 1950, unemployment continued to decline over the next decade to a low of less then 1 percent.

The West German growth miracle, frequently characterized as an instantaneously popular linear process commencing ab ovo with the 1948 currency reform, is thus better described as a drawn-out process frequently on the brink of disaster, with a shift toward steady growth not occurring before 1951, some three years after the initial reforms. Two aspects are of particular interest with respect to the current transition debate. First, the ordo-liberal policy package, apart from the monetary reform, initially enjoyed at best lukewarm support: "When we changed course in 1948 almost nobody believed in the success of the measures. The statistics, the calculations and all planning considerations suggested incontrovertibly that it would be impossible to introduce, from today to tomorrow, economic freedom in an economy and a market which had nothing left to offer" (tables 2.8 and 2.10).[29] Foreign skepticism matched domestic unpopularity. The international lack of confidence in the new currency found its reflection in a sizable premium on the Zurich exchange persisting into the mid-fifties (table 2.9).[30]

Second, the initial success of the ordo-liberal package in raising living standards beyond the one-time jump following the reform proved to be limited, a broad-based welfare increase had to await the aftermath of the Korean boom, some four years after the initial reforms.

3   The Miracle Explained: Hypotheses

Miracles attract researchers: the unexpected growth performance of the West German economy has motivated an extensive literature attempting

Table 2.8
Instant popularity?

Opinion of Ludwig Erhard		
Date	Good	Not Good
1951	14	49
1952	26	29
1953	37	18
1954	45	13
1955	46	·11
1956	50	11

Source: Noelle and Neumann (1981).

Table 2.9
Deutsche mark/Swiss franc exchange rate

	8.48	12.48	12.49	12.50	12.51	12.52
Free	27.00	22.50	74.50	77.70	85.00	91.20
Official	129.30	129.10	104.10	104.10	104.10	104.10

Table 2.10
Instant prosperity? Are you better off today than a year ago?

	1951	1952	1953	1954	1956
Better off	12	21	24	29	25
Worse off	56	30	19	20	16
No difference	32	49	57	51	59

Source: Noelle and Neumann (1981).

to remove the episode from its lofty stand. We now turn to a discussion of the main hypotheses.[31] Following precedent, we distinguish between the *recovery* and the *growth* phase of the miracle.

3.1 Recovery: The Predictable Miracle

The rapid recovery of output after devastation, whether man or nature made, forms a fairly sturdy feature of economic history, first being remarked upon by John Stuart Mills. Keynes likewise cautions against extrapolating from the immediate devastation at the end of hostilities: "Popular opinion attributes, in my opinion, too much to the war. Fortunately, the accumulations of man's wealth are not in such shape that they can be quickly squandered. War exhausts contemporary effort, but it cannot destroy knowledge, or make an overdraft on the bounty of nature" (Keynes 1922). In a similar vein, Milton Friedman offered a recipe for rapid growth as explanation of Germany's and Japan's postwar growth boom: "Destroy the greater part of a nation's fixed capital in war activity and dislocate the whole economic structure. Eventual recovery from this chaotic state of affairs will be rapid, giving a growth rate of 8–10 percent annually."[32]

The early phase of the German miracle falls well within the Mills-Keynes-Friedman paradigm. The production possibilities of postwar Germany can be modeled as the product of a traditional technological production function $F(K, L)$ and terms A and B capturing the efficiency of the financial and technical infrastructure:

$$Y_t = A_t B_t F(K_t, L_t) \tag{1}$$

The production capacity, conditional on an operational transportation, communication, and financial infrastructure, roughly approximated the prewar level. Upon the capitulation, the de facto technological production possibilities, $BF(K, L)$ remained constrained by the disruption to the technological infrastructure; the reduction in production represented organizational failure rather than physical destruction of plants: "At the heart of our present economic difficulties lies not so much the destruction of productive facilities, but the interruption of economic organization and the absence of genuine interaction between production factors" (Müller-Armack 1946). Reconstruction proceeded rapidly; by 1948 capacity approached prewar levels. The constraint on production shifted from the physical to the financial infrastructure. Once the currency reform reestablished a functioning monetary system, the economy could exhibit a dramatic increase in output at unchanged real factor endowments, bringing forth the "overnight miracle" of June 21, 1948. In contrast, the other European countries commencing reform earlier were forced to repair the technological infrastructure "on the go," reducing the miracle content of their recovery. As table 2.11 reveals, the initial growth spurt of Germany lacks miraculous qualities in the cross-country comparison: until 1951 Germany's cumulative growth rate fell short of the European average.[33]

The initial phase of West Germany's miracle, lasting from 1948 to 1951, is thus well within historical experience.[34] The relatively faster speed of recovery derived from Germany's ability to restore the technical production machine during the prereform episode, thus raising the gap between actual and potential production that could be closed once the remaining brakes were loosened. Furthermore, Germany's recovery commenced when both American financial support and European integration measures were

Table 2.11
Industrial production (1938 = 100)

	1946	1948	1949	1950	1955
Austria	47	92	122	144	226
Belgium	89	122	123	125	156
Denmark	94	120	127	144	164
Finland	70	132	135	145	223
France	85	102	112	120	157
Greece	57	76	89	112	187
Ireland	109	134	140	172	202
Italy	54	102	109	126	195
Netherlands	72	114	129	141	190
Norway	100	124	132	148	198
Spain	125	128	130	145	159
Sweden	102	142	145	152	177
U.K.	105	110	118	124	148
Europe	92	112	120	128	161
Germany	28	51	72	94	167

Source: United Nations, IMF, Mitchell (1978).

already established, providing her with benefits not available to the earlier recuperants.[35]

3.2   Growth

After achieving full employment of capital, the German economy continued to expand rapidly throughout the 1950s, gradually integrating some eight million new workers from the East. We now turn to a selective assessment of the main hypotheses put forward to explain Germany's ability to sustain high growth rates after the recovery phase had come to an end. We begin with a discussion of exogenous causes explaining the boom as the policy-invariant implication of objective conditions facing the German postwar economy before turning to an assessment of the contributions of the policy framework adopted by the German authorities.

Autonomous Effects
Did the miracle happen because of or despite the ordo-liberal policies adopted by the government? An assessment of the role of policy, and thereby of the suitability of the German reconstruction as role model, must attempt to filter out the effect of the environment on the growth process.

We focus on three effects: immigration, "docile" unions, and exogenous demand shocks. Of course, none of these factors is strictly exogenous with respect to the policies adopted; migration and the vigorous response of export industries to autonomous demand shocks partly reflected the incentives provided in the ordo-liberal framework, union behavior was influenced by the observed success of the ordo-liberal strategy. To a non-negligible degree, these features would, however, have also occurred had a more Beveridgean model been adopted, imposing a caveat on the degree to which the miracle can be ascribed to the policy choices.

Immigration   From 1945 to 1953 the West German population increased by some 10 million people, a quarter of the 1945 population in the three western zones. The effect of the inflow of refugees on the absolute and per capita GDP growth rates remains disputed. The availability of labor undoubtedly enabled Germany to react flexibly to new market openings without major consequences for relative wages and inflationary pressures, an opportunity denied to the tight labor market economies of Great Britain and France (Kindleberger 1967). Beyond this aggregate output effect, a number of further links between migration and growth have been suggested:

Hard work: A popular hypothesis attributes a growth effect to the newcomers' desire to reestablish an existence, finding its reflection in "long, hard hours of work." While the hypothesis, first made popular by Wallich (1955) is difficult to test, casual evidence does suggest increased work effort: average weekly hours increased from 39.5 hours before the reforms to 46.3 hours in 1949 and 48 hours in 1950 and remained at very high levels in the international comparison.

Durable demand: The desire of the newcomers to reestablish a material basis also found its expression on the demand side: arriving with virtually no personal property, the gradual accumulation of consumer durables provided a stable domestic source of demand on which to build an export industry.

Human capital: The newly arriving workers, whether coming directly from the GDR or from further East, decided to forego the extensive social security network of the socialist East for the social Darwinism of the West. The selection process implied a preponderance of relatively skilled individuals among the immigrants entering the West German labor market, raising the average skill level and hence productivity of the labor force.

The available evidence indeed points to a very substantial transfer of human capital. Calculations of human and physical capital reported in Krug (1967) suggest an increase in the ratio of around 50 percent between 1938 and 1949. Inter alia, some 20,000 trained engineers and technicians and 1000 academic teachers migrated to West Germany. Abelshauser estimates the total value of the transfer until 1961 at DM 30 billion, five times the value of the ERP aid.

Mobility: The move from war to peacetime production required a substantial reallocation of labor between sectors. By the late fifties, 50 percent of the jobs existing in 1948 had been eliminated. The high sectoral and geographic mobility of the newcomers relative to the (traditionally migration-averse) established workers facilitated the adjustment process and ensured potential investors of the availability of labor.

Docile Labor   The Erhardian reforms attempted to elicit supply responses by raising the return to investment. The success of the strategy depended crucially on the union's acquiescence in the implied deterioration of the income distribution. The apparent willingness of the West German union movement to accept the initially adverse consequences of the supply-side strategy in return for an uncertain future reward has been cited as a major factor in Germany's postwar performance.

The "docile union" argument should not be exaggerated however:[36] virtually from the inception of the West German growth process, the real wage growth exceeded the gains made by the reportedly more militant British unions; from 1949 to 1952, real wages rose by more than 30 percent. While rising rapidly, however, real wages in Germany increased less than productivity. The resulting fall in unit labor cost provided the incentive for additional investment and thus further employment and wage gains, placing the West German unions on a reverse Kouri spiral.

Table 2.12
Income distribution

Group	1928	1950
0–50	23.2	16.0
50–90	39.6	48.3
90–95	10.0	8.7
95–99	14.3	12.4
99–100	12.9	14.6

Source: Wallich (1955).

Exogenous Demand Shocks   The German economic miracle significantly benefited from largely fortuitous external demand shocks. The resolution of the political crisis developing in early 1950 substantially benefited from the sudden strong demand increase resulting from the Korean War. Following the end of the Korean conflict, the rearmament drive took over the role of demand stimulus. The strong external performance during the early postwar period was likewise to a certain degree fortuitous, reflecting to a significant degree the overall expansion of European output and the resulting demand for Germany's classical export goods: high value-added manufactures and capital goods—as well as the advantageous movements in the terms of trade and the stimulus exerted by the Marshall Plan.

3.3   The Role of Policy

The previous section identified a range of exogenous factors contributing to postwar growth. To some degree, these factors were shared across postwar Europe. The *relative* position of Germany in the top growth group thus suggests a potential role for ordo-liberal policy in raising her growth rate above the European average.

By reducing the after-tax real cost of capital, removing the income tax on overtime earnings, and introducing tax benefits for savings, the ordo-liberal package provided extra rewards to investors, workers, and savers. "[I]t was the restoration of incentives which was responsible for the sudden rebirth of economic activity" (Lutz 1949). Sohmen (1959) focuses on the allocative efficiency deriving from competition as the main discriminating variable between the postwar European economies: "With all due respect to all other factors, biological, sociological and metaphysical, the conclusion is nevertheless inescapable that only more efficient resource allocation can explain the difference between West Germany's rate of growth and that of other countries in a comparable state of development... The postwar German experience seems to suggest that it is feasible to intensify competition sufficiently to make an economy perform markedly better than under alternative forms of social organizations."[37]

Sohmen unfortunately offers little evidence supporting his claim of an "intensified" competition in the postwar German economy. Indeed, the case for increased *internal* competition is weak: while decartelization formed part of Allied policy, the implementation remained limited to a few visible cases. The new German government likewise proved reluctant to act upon their rhetorical rejection of oligarchic structures: it took some eight years and the inclusion of extensive loopholes until anticartel legislation was passed in 1957. The tension between theoretical postulate and policy is further illustrated by the response to developing bottlenecks in key sectors. Rather then relying on the price mechanism, an extensive rechanneling of resources was undertaken, including forced investment in key sectors and priority allocation of ERP funds. The bitter taste of the classical medicine was thus mitigated by some Keynesian flavorings: Those "whose principle is 'the freer the better' and who reject any admixture of control as an adulteration cannot claim Germany's success as proof of their doctrine." Whereas the degree of *internal* competition thus did not markedly differentiate the German model from the policies undertaken in other European countries, the ordo-liberal model did, however, provide a partial *external* compensation by an early opening to imports and the initial overvaluation of the deutsche mark.

4 Conclusion

The evolution of ideas:
First Stage: "How absurd; can any sensible person believe such things?"
Second Stage: "These ideas are dangerous; they must be suppressed."
Third Stage: "Of course; everyone knows that; whoever doubted it?"
(Hansen 1947)

In the late forties, Erhard's rejection of the accepted pillars of demand management in favor of the unproven healing powers of the classical medicine invited skepticism. By 1991 the pendulum had swung full circle: the postwar German reform package has been touted as a role model for the transition processes of Eastern Europe. In the present chapter, we tried to season the latter judgment with a grain of salt.

A closer look at the experience does much to dispel the miracle interpretation. The German recovery separates into two stages: an initial expansion from underemployment to capacity production and a subsequent expansion of productive capacity. In contrast to her neighbors, the three-year waiting period until the implementation of the monetary reform afforded Germany with the opportunity to restore her infrastructure and enabled firms to accumulate inventories in anticipation of "Day x." By 1948, the German economic engine was ready to explode into action. Once the remaining braking blocks—price controls and monetary overhang—were removed, Germany could thus experience a very rapid expansion toward full capacity. The miracle epitaph is, however, quite inappropriate to describe this process: most of Western Europe had by 1948 long surpassed their initial capacity levels and approached prewar production, some three years before Germany.

If indeed there is a miracle to be found in West Germany's postwar performance, it must thus be looked for in the second stage, the continued expansion of productive capabilities after the reattainment of capacity output. Yet again a closer look at the evidence disabuses the observer from any miraculous notions she might harbor. A plethora of policy-invariant beneficial factors contributed significantly to the growth performance: Marshall aid, large inward transfers of human capital, favorable terms of trade movements, and strong expansion abroad would have led to a high growth rate even if a more Beveridgean policy framework had been adopted. France and Austria, though following more planning-oriented strategies, experienced growth on the same magnitude as Germany. The ordo-liberal reform package thus did not convert disaster into prosperity, the systemic explanation of the miracle does not hold up to the evidence. While it is tempting to link the (absolutely) impressive West German growth performance to her role as the sole extoller of the virtues of (fairly) unbridled competition, the economic performance of France provides a compelling counterargument. This is not to denigrate the positive role of the reforms: the ordo-liberal focus on the supply side enabled Germany to flexibly respond to the beneficial exogenous developments and thus to reap *incrementally* larger benefits then available to the more interventionist European economies.

What advice can then be given to reforming countries in search of the best system to lubricate the painful transition from rigid planning to markets? The evidence presented argues against the existence of a holy policy grail. In the end, *consistency* may provide a more relevant criterion for judging growth prospects than fundamental philosophies. France and Germany, the two fastest growing economies, adopted opposing but fairly consistently applied growth strategies. The French model provides a case study in the capabilities of intelligent planning implemented by a uniquely qualified civil service; Germany illustrates the growth potential of (relatively) free markets under a stable policy framework emphasizing incentives to the Schumpeterian entrepreneur. Against this background, the negative role model may be provided by Great Britain, illustrating the potential danger of full-employment policies cum pointiliste interventions without the guiding light of a consistent global strategy: "Not the profligacy of policy but its uncoordinated nature accounts for most of our disappointments."[38]

Notes

Prepared for the conference of European Reconstruction 1945–59. Hamburg, 6–7 September 1991. I thank Rüdiger Dornbusch, Anne-Marie Gulde, and in particular my discussants, Wilhelm Nölling and Karl Heinz Paqué, for insightful comments. Financial support by the Center for European Studies, Harvard University, is gratefully acknowledged.

1. See, for example, Oxford Institute (1944, 204): "[A] full employment policy must, in all probability, be accompanied by a number of controls. The first of these is the control of foreign trade.... Secondly, there is the possibility of cumulative price increases ... [due] to pressure for higher money wages. To prevent this it will be necessary to exercise a wide control over prices, either directly or indirectly by means of subsidies. The third control necessitated by full employment is an overall regulation of the total volume of private investment ... to ensure that capital equipment expands in pace with technical progress and changing population.... Finally ... the State must exercise control over the location of industry."

2. Space constraints prevent a more detailed exposition of the ordo-liberal view. The interested reader may wish to peruse Hohmann et al. (1982).

3. Friedensburg (1954) provides a detailed exposition of the German economy during the war years. See also Kaldor (1945) and Balabkins (1964).

4. In some sectors, a substantial proportion of production was devoted to military purposes, posing a reconversion problem. The degree of war orientation differed substantially, ranging from 100 percent in aeronautics to 50 percent in metals and 33 percent in machinery (Friedensburg 1954).

5. An index of railroad capacity shows a decline from 100 in July 1944 to 11 in March 1945, with a likely further decline in the last two months of the war. See Friedensburg (1954).

6. Möller (1961) provides a detailed discussion of the postwar monetary debate.

7. In the three postwar years, a total of more then two hundred reform plans had been published and popularly discussed, suggesting that an eventual reform was regarded as an all but certain event. See Möller (1961).

8. "In Germany, with the exception of Berlin, black market trading does not seem to be as readily accepted as in some other countries and is generally looked upon with disfavor by the population" (OMGUS 1946). I am indebted to Lewis Alexander for making this source available.

9. Buchheim (1989) reports estimates of up to 50 percent of the fraction of all transactions involving countertrade.

10. A survey in Hessia found the level of *raw material* inventories to be twice the level of 1936 and sufficient for one year's production, suggesting unwillingness rather than inability to produce. See Buchheim (1989).

11. Federal Reserve Board Economist Paul Hermberg reporting on a trip to Germany, April 1946, cited in Alexander (1991). See also Kindleberger (1947).

12. Including public utilities, transportation, banks, insurance companies, and key industries. See Domes and Wolffsohn (1979) for a description of the early postwar political landscape.

13. Even the conservative Christian Democrats, in the Ahlen program of 1947, stressed the desirability of public ownership of resources, leaving the potential investor with little hope for capital-friendly policies. Indeed, in the immediate postwar year Adenauer, when asked which British party the CDU most closely corresponded to, chose Labour!

14. A survey conducted in 1946 found that in 10 percent of plants more than a quarter of the labor force was occupied with repairs, in 17 percent of plants between 11 and 25 percent, and in a further 34 percent of firms between 1 and 10 percent (OMGUS 1946).

15. Purported conversation regarding Erhard's (unauthorized) decision to revoke price controls.

16. Ludwig Erhard, cited in Domes and Wolffsohn (1979).

17. Detailed expositions of the monetary and financial reforms are provided in Stucken (1953), Möller (1976), Pfleiderer (1979), and Wankel (1979). Alexander (1991) provides a recent original view contrasting the 1948 and 1990 reforms.

18. Prior to the reform, the main benefit of employment derived from additional ration allocations. The after-tax monetary wage, beyond the amount needed to purchase the ration, was of little importance by early 1948; the average daily wage of RM 10 sufficed to buy a single egg on the black market.

19. Over the period 1949–57, tax deductions for these purposes amounted to DM 28.4 billion, approximately 6.6 percent of total revenues (Stolper and Roskamp 1979). Heller (1949) provides a detailed overview of the fiscal aspects of the reform package.

20. See Wallich and Wilson (1981).

21. In retrospect, Erhard (1962) doubted his ability to implement the 1948 reforms in a parliamentary democracy, a view shared by many contemporary observers, for example, Pfleiderer (1957).

22. Production in expectation of a reform led to an apparent prereform production increase in the spring of 1948. Abelshauser (1975) interprets the timing as evidence against a catalyzer role of the currency reform. Buchheim (1989) and Ritschl (1985) provide a rebuttal.

23. In addition, the sudden return to hard budget constraints eliminated fictitious jobs in the agricultural sector initially created to obtain additional ration allocations.

24. Although announced in 1948, a law to equalize the burdens of the monetary reform between holders of nominal and real wealth was passed only in 1952, some four years after the reform.

25. Tax receipts far exceeded expectations, suggesting that prereform rates might indeed have been counterproductively high.

26. In a survey regarding the intention to save in the future, some 59 percent of respondents answered affirmative before the currency reform, while after the reform the fraction dropped to 49 percent and after the second conversion in October to 32 percent (Lutz 1949).

27. Economic Survey of Europe 1949 and 1950.

28. Cited in Hutchinson (1979).

29. Speech by Erhard on 2 November 1953.

30. See also IFO (1953).

31. As the size of the literature prevents any attempt at comprehensiveness, the focus is restricted to a few aspects of relevance for the East European transition debate. Extensive treatments of the literature can be found in Abelshauser (1975), Ambrosius (1986), and Dumke (1990).

32. Cited in Klein (1961).

33. The comparision is slightly misleading as the German economy in 1938 operated near capacity while the rest of Europe suffered from substantial slack.

34. See Abelshauser (1975), Borchard (1982), and Rohwer (1988) for extended discussions of the reconstruction view.

35. See Milward (1984) on the role of European integration.

36. Hansen (1957). See also Kindleberger (1967).

37. Sohmen (1959, 993–994).

38. Balogh (1949).

References

Abelshauser, W. (1975) *Wirtschaft in Westdeutschland 1945–1948*, Stuttgart.

Alexander, L. (1991) "Radical Economic Reform in Germany, 1948 and ˙1990: Similarities, Differences, and Lessons for the Soviet Union." Mimeo.

Ambrosius, G. (1986) "Die Ökonomie der fünfziger Jahre." *SOWI*, 17–25.

Balabkins, N. (1964) *Germany Under Direct Controls*. Rutgers University Press: New Brunswick.

Balogh, T. (1949) *The Dollar Crisis: Causes and Cure*. Basil Blackwell: Oxford.

Borchard, K. (1982) "Trend, Zyklus, Strukturbrüche, Zufälle: Was bestimmt die Deutsche Wirtschaftsgeschichte des 20. Jahrhunderts?" In K. Borchard, *Wachstum, Krisen, Handlungsspielräume der Wirtschaftspolitik*. Göttingen.

Buchheim, C. (1989) "Die Währungsreform in Westdeutschland 1948. Einige ökonomische Aspekte." In W. Fischer, ed. *Währungsreform und soziale Marktwirtschaft*. Berlin.

Domes, J. and M. Wolffsohn (1979) "Setting the Course for the Federal Republic of Germany: Major Policy Decisions in the Bi-Zonal Economic Council and Party

Images, 1947–49." In R. Richter, ed. *Currency and Economic Reform: West Germany After World War II. Zeitschrift für die gesamte Staatswissenschaft*, vol. 135, no. 3.

Dumke, R. (1990) "Reassessing the Wirtschaftswunder: Reconstruction and Postwar Growth in West Germany in an International Context." *Oxford Bulletin of Economics and Statistics* 52, 2:451–491.

Erhard, L. (1948) "The New Facts." Reprinted in K. Hohmann, W. Stützel, C. Watrin, and H. Willgerodt, eds. *Standard Texts on the Social Market Economy*. Ludwig Erhard Stiftung: Bonn.

Erhard, L. (1962) *Deutsche Wirtschaftspolitik*. Gustav Fischer: Wien.

Eucken, W. (1949) "Die Wettbewerbsordnung und ihre Verwirklichung." *Ordo-Yearbook* 2, 381–398.

Eucken, W. (1950) *The Foundations of Economics*. W. Hodge: London.

Friedensburg, ed. (1954) *Die deutsche Industrie im Kriege 1939–1945*. Deutsches Institut Für Wirtschaftsforschung: Berlin.

Haberler, G. (1949) "Economic Aspects of a European Union." *World Politics* 1, 431–441.

Hansen, A. (1947) "Keynes on Economic Policy." In Harris, S., ed. (1947) *The New Economics*. Alfred A. Knopf: New York.

Hansen, A. (1957) *The American Economy*. McGraw Hill: New York.

Harris, S., ed. (1947) *The New Economics*. Alfred A. Knopf: New York.

Heller, W. (1949) "Tax and Monetary Reform In Occupied Germany." *National Tax Journal*, 215–231.

Hohmann, K., W. Stützel, C. Watrin, and H. Willgerodt, eds. (1982) *Standard Texts on the Social Market Economy*. Ludwig Erhard Stiftung: Bonn.

Hutchinson, T. (1979) "Notes on the Effects of Economic Ideas on Policy: the Example of the German Social Market Economy." In R. Richter, ed. *Currency and Economic Reform: West Germany after World War II. Zeitschrift für die gesamte Staatswissenschaft*, vol. 135, no. 3.

IFO Institut (1953) *Fünf Jahre Deutsche Mark*. Duncker & Humblot: Berlin.

Kaldor, N. (1945) "The German War Economy." *Review of Economic Studies*; 13:33–52.

Keynes, J. (1922) "Reconstruction In Europe: An Introduction." *Manchester Guardian Commercial*, 18.5.1922. Reprinted in *Collected Works* vol. 17.

Kindleberger, C. (1947) "Cleveland-Moore-Kindleberger Memorandum." In *Marshall Plan Days* (1987) Allen & Unwin: Boston.

Kindleberger, C. (1967) *Europe's Postwar Growth*. Harvard University Press: Cambridge, MA.

Klein, L. (1961) "A Model of Japanese Economic Growth." *Econometrica* 29:291.

Klopstock, F. (1949) "Monetary Reform In Western Germany." *The Journal of Political Economy* 57:277–292.

Krengel, R. (1963) "Some Reasons for the Rapid Growth of the German Federal Republic." *Banca Nazionale del Lavoro Quarterly Review* no. 64.

Krug, W. (1967) "Quantitative Beziehungen zwischen materiellem und immateriellem Kapital." *Jahrbücher für Nationalökonomie und Statistik* 143:379–401.

Lutz, F. (1949) "The German Currency Reform and the Revival of the German Economy." *Economica*, May, 122:142.

Mendershausen, H. (1949) "Prices, Money and the Distribution of Goods in Post War Germany." *American Economic Review* 39:646–672.

Meyer, F., E. von Beckerath, and A. Müller-Armack (1957) *Wirtschaftsfragen der Freien Welt*. Fritz Knapp: Frankfurt.

Milward, A. S. (1984) *The Reconstruction of Western Europe 1945–51*. University of California: Berkeley and Los Angeles.

Mitchell, B. (1978) *European Historical Statistics 1750–1975*. Facts on File: New York.

Möller, H., ed. (1961) *Zur Vorgeschichte der Deutschen Mark. Die Währungsreformpläne 1945–1948*. Kyklos-Verlag: Basel and Tübingen.

Möller, H. (1976) "Die Deutsche Währungsreform von 1948." In Deutsche Bundesbank, *Währung Und Wirtschaft In Deutschland 1876–1975*. F. Knapp: Frankfurt/Main.

Müller-Armack, A. (1946) *Wirtschaftslenkung and Marktwirtschaft*. Hamburg.

Noelle, E. and E. Neumann, eds. (1956) *Jahrbuch der Öffentlichen Meinung 1947–1955*. Allensbach.

Noelle, E. and E. Neumann, eds. (1981) *The Germans: Public Opinion Polls, 1947–1955*. Allensbach.

Office of Military Government for Germany (U.S.) (1946) *Appendixes to a Plan for the Liquidation of War Finance and the Financial Rehabilitation of Germany*. Mimeo.

Oxford University Institute of Statistics (1944) *The Economics of Full Employment*. Basil Blackwell: Oxford.

Pfleiderer, O. (1957) "Währungsreform in Westdeutschland (1948)." In *Enzyklopädisches Lexikon für das Geld-, Bank- und Börsenwesen* vol. 2 Fritz Knapp Verlag: Frankfurt/Main.

Pfleiderer, O. (1979) "Two Types of Inflation, Two Types of Currency Reform." *Zeitschrift für die gesamte Staatswissenschaft* 135:352–364.

Richter, R., ed. (1979) *Currency and Economic Reform: West Germany After World War II*. Zeitschrift für die gesamte Staatswissenschaft vol. 135, no. 3.

Ritschl, A. (1985) "Die Währungsreform von 1948 und der Wiederanstieg der westdeutschen Industrie." *Viertel Jahreshefte für Zeitueschichte* 33:136–65.

Rohwer, B. (1988) *Konjunktur und Wachstum. Theorie und Empirie der Produktionsentwicklung in der Bundesrepublik Deutschland seit 1950.* Berlin.

Sauermann, H. (1979) "On the Economic and Financial Rehabilitation of Western Germany (1945–1949)." In R. Richter, ed. *Currency and Economic Reform: West Germany After World War II. Zeitschrift für die gesamte Staatswissenschaft,* vol. 135, no. 3.

Sohmen, E. (1959) "Competition and Growth. The Lesson of West Germany." *American Economic Review* 49.

Stolper, W. and K. Roskamp (1979) "Planning a Free Economy: Germany 1945–60." In R. Richter, ed. *Currency and Economic Reform: West Germany After World War II. Zeitschrift für die gesamte Staatswissenschaft,* vol. 135, no. 3.

Stucken, R. (1953) *Deutsche Geld- und Kreditpolitik.* J. C. B. Mohr: Tübingen.

United Nations. (n.d.) *Economic Survey of Europe.* Various issues.

Wallich, H. (1955) *Mainsprings of the German Revival.* Yale University Press: New Haven.

Wallich, H. and J. Wilson (1981) "Economic Orientations in Postwar Germany: Critical Choices on the Road Toward Currency Convertibility." In R. Richter and F. Stolper, eds. *Economic Reconstruction in Europe: The Reintegration of Western Europe. Zeitschrift für die gesamte Staatswissenschaft* vol. 137, no. 3, 390–406.

Wandel, E. (1979) "Historical Developments Prior to the German Currency Reform of 1948." *Zeitschrift für die gesamte Staatswissenschaft* 135:320–331.

3

Inflation and Stabilization in Italy: 1946–1951

Marcello De Cecco and Francesco Giavazzi

June 1943 marked a turn in the war in Italy. Allied troops landed in Sicily in July. The King removed Mussolini from power, fled to the south to the area liberated by the Allies, and signed an armistice in September. Mussolini, spirited away by a platoon of German paratroopers, went north to found the Repubblica Sociale Italiana under the protection of the German Army. There were now two Italian governments, each with full power over the printing presses in the area where it was established. The main economic events in the five to six years following the landing of the Allied troops in Sicily were: a swift liberalization of prices, a prolonged debate of the merits of a currency reform—eventually stalled by the political deadlock between left and right, two inflationary episodes followed by a surprisingly swift stabilization, and a rapid pick-up in industrial activity and exports.

Some of these developments, and above all the conditions of the Italian economy as it emerged from the war, are reminiscent of what we observe today in the most advanced former socialist countries. For example, the Stanford Research Institute—hired in the forties as consultants to the Italian government on the restructuring of the engineering industry—gave a picture of the sector that is in many ways similar to what we read today about the state of industry in countries such as Czechoslovakia and the former GDR. The banking system during Fascism had performed a function very similar to that performed in socialist countries, accumulating ever larger balances at the central bank, which were not used to make loans to entrepreneurs. After the fall of Fascism, a good part of the population demanded that the fascist leadership, together with their bedfellows from industry and finance, be held accountable for their political and economic misdeeds. But there were as many people interested in a quick return to normalcy. The political forces representing those who wanted to forget and those who wanted to remember were partners in the government coalitions, but they were also pitted against one another in several electoral contests. The resulting heterogeneity made the government coalitions particularly ineffective.

However, the starting point for an analysis of the economic events that took place in Italy in the early postwar period is the state of Italian industry as it emerged from the war.

1   The Italian Economy after World War II

1.1   Italian Industry Immediately before and after World War II

Immediately prior to World War II more than 40 percent of the Italian labor force was still employed in agriculture, whereas no more than 30 percent was employed in industry. In most manufacturing sectors prewar Italy was about half the size of France and 20 percent that of Germany (See table 3.1). Per capita income was about half that for France, and about one fourth the British per capita GDP. Italian exports chiefly went to central and eastern Europe—particularly engineering and chemical products. Trade was, like elsewhere in Europe, organized along the lines of bilateral clearing.

Evaluating the quality standards of Italian industry is more difficult. We have some evidence on the level of mechanization of the textile industry (which accounted for about 20 percent of total industrial employment), said to have reached that of the British textile industry by 1938. Engineering and machine tool production, which was largely a by-product of the rearmament effort, was described in the report of the Stanford Research Institute as being of good quality, and in the early postwar export boom it earned its spurs. The same was said of the chemical industry, which had

Table 3.1
European industry in 1938

	Value of industrial goods (USD)	Production of electric power (Kwh)	Shares of total European production (%)		
			Engineering	Chemicals	Textiles
Germany	9.0	33	38	33	18
U.K.	6.6	24	25	18	28
France	3.0	18	13	12	16
Italy	1.8	15	6.3	8	12

Source: ISTAT, Annuario Statistico Italiano, Serie V, Vol. 1.

Figure 3.1
The Italian engineering industry: value of per capita production in 1938 in various Italian regions
Source: A. Jacoboni, *L'industria meccanica italiana*. Roma: Centro Studi e Piani Economici (1947)

greatly expanded its most modern factories in the 1930s for strategic reasons.

The bulk of Italian industry survived the war largely intact.[1] As vividly illustrated in figure 3.1, most potential industrial targets were in the north and had therefore escaped the early bombing that was concentrated in the south where the Allies were to land.[2] The large FIAT works in Turin were left unscathed, for example. Power-generating plants were also left untouched by the Germans and the Allies. In 1946 the production capacity of hydroelectric plants was 18 percent higher than in 1938. In Italy hydroelectric plants provided the bulk of electric power (90 percent of the total); moreover, since these plants only need mountains and rain, the availability of electric power was not at the mercy of imported raw materials. The new steelworks in Genoa were dismantled by the German troops, who carted off the mostly German-made machinery. Nevertheless, steel production was back to prewar standards as early as 1947, thanks to the availability of electric power and scrap in the form of millions of tons of Allied war equipment given to the Italians.

The railway network was left in disarray from the German retreat. Bridges had been blown up as the German troops went north, and rolling stock was lost through removal or by Allied bombing. However, as elsewhere in Europe, reconstruction took less than a year, and by the end of 1946 the network was almost back to normal, with the production of carriages and locomotives exceeding that of 1938 by 50 percent.

In textiles (which after the war accounted for 20 percent of total exports) capacity had not been reduced by the war, as opposed to what had happened elsewhere in Europe (see table 3.2).

Table 3.2
Capacity in the textile industry in 1948 (index numbers, 1938 = 100)

	Wool industry		Cotton industry	
	Spindles	Looms	Spindles	Looms
France	95	102	87	90
U.K.	102[a]	94[a]	96	80
Italy	123	105	103	94
Germany	63[b]	n.a.	62	69
Europe	n.a./99[c]	n.a./103[c]	91/95[c]	80/80[c]

a. 1947
b. western zone only
c. including Germany/excluding Germany
Source: United Nations, E.S.E., 1949.

Although industrial capacity was available (and often of relatively good quality), there was an absolute dearth of raw materials and semifinished products. Italy had no serious coal production; the coal that was produced was of extremely low quality. (Better-quality coal used to be mined in Istria, a region that had been given back to Yugoslavia.) Raw materials were normally imported, but since Italy had sided with two countries, Japan and Germany, that were also deficient in raw materials, supplies could hardly be obtained within the Axis. Coal had been supplied by Germany but only when there was enough to spare. Supplies of raw materials dwindled as the war proceeded. Moreover, the considerable merchant fleet that Italy had built up in the interwar years had been decimated by the British navy. Thus, starting in 1942, industrial capacity was gradually made idle by a lack of raw materials and by a lack of a means to deliver them.

The state of Italian industry before and after the war is summarized in figure 3.2. By 1947 industrial capacity was 37 percent higher than in 1938, but industrial production was 43 percent lower.

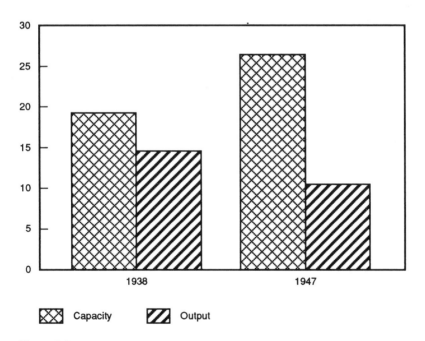

Capacity   Output

Figure 3.2
The Italian engineering industry: capacity and production 1938 and 1947 (in billions of 1938 lire)
Source: ISTAT, Annuario Statistico Italiano, serie V, vol. 1

Supply conditions are important to understanding the inflationary episodes of 1946–1947. The quality and composition of manufacturing output was such that Italian firms were ready to meet an increase in foreign
demand. Capacity was available; raw materials were the critical bottleneck.

1.2   Public Finances during the War and the Buildup of a Monetary
Overhang

The Italian budget had been running a constant deficit since World War I,
with the exception of the stabilization years (1923–24 to 1930–31). The
Ethiopian War of 1936, the Spanish Civil War, and finally World War II all
shaped the growth of the deficit (see figure 3.3).

During World War II the budget deficit rose from 9 percent of national
income in fiscal year 1937–38, to over 17 percent in 1939–40. By 1943–
44, only 16 percent of expenditure was financed by tax revenue, and the
deficit had risen to over 64 percent of national income.

No more than 60 percent of the deficit was financed through public debt
issues; the rest was monetized. Between 1938 and 1943, public debt increased from 90 to 120 percent of national income, and its maturity short-
ened: the share of floating debt, purchased mostly by banks, went from 30
to 70 percent of the total. In this five-year period, monetary circulation

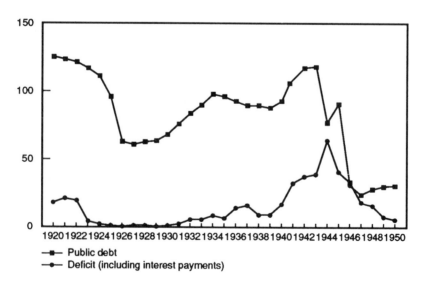

Figure 3.3
Italy: debt and deficits (percent of GDP)
Source: Ministero del Tesoro, *Il Debito Pubblico in Italia: 1861–1987*, Roma (1988)

increased 2.5 times[3] and bank and post office deposits nearly doubled. By contrast, wholesale prices rose by only 52 percent and retail food prices by 85 percent, while wages lagged behind, rising only 50 percent (see figure 3.4). Inflation was curbed by strict wage and price controls, particularly by resorting to the so-called monetary circuit that was aimed at keeping newly created money strictly out of public reach. Money was created and spent by the state; it reached the banking system and was then reabsorbed by the state through special deposit accounts at the central bank where banks had to place the liquid resources they came to possess. The banking system thus came to perform a function very similar to that performed in socialist countries. Its role was no longer that of intermediating between savers and investors—in fact, the production and consumption circuits were kept completely separate. Banks accumulated larger and larger balances at the central bank, which they could not use to make loans to entrepreneurs. A monetary overhang had thus formed by 1943.

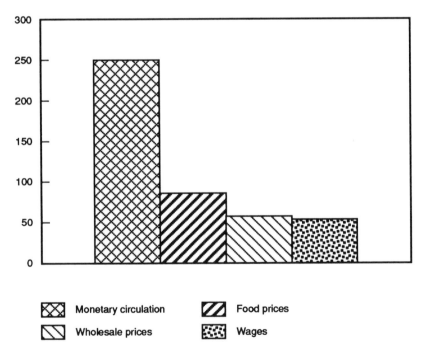

Figure 3.4
Italy 1938–43: the monetary overhang (percent increase)
Sources: Banca d'Italia, *Annual Report*, various issues, and ISTAT.

2.   Inflation and Stabilization

2.1   The First Phase of Open Inflation, the Deadlock over a Currency
Reform: 1943–46

In 1943 and 1944, most of the money printed went to satisfy the demands
of the Allied forces in the south and the German forces in the north.[4] In this
period, neither of the two Italian governments could think of selling debt
to the public, nor were taxes easily extracted from the population while the
country was engaged in a civil war.[5] Nevertheless, there was a big difference in the policy measures adopted in the two halves of Italy. In the north,
the Germans exacted from the Fascist government a war tribute of 184
billion lire (L). The Fascist government, for its part, spent about L 170
billion, only 50 billion of which it obtained through taxation An additional
L 300 billion of claims on the state were thus created—mostly in the form
of more blocked balances, which the banking system held at the central
bank, and of treasury bills banks were forced to keep in their portfolios.
The seeds of inflation were thus sown in the north, and the inflationary
potential was placed in the hands of the banking system.

In the south, monetary circulation increased by L 80 billion, almost all of
it printed for the Allied Military Government.[6] However, no serious monetary overhang arose in southern Italy; inflation was allowed to rage openly.
The south accounted for a small fraction of total production, both agricultural and industrial. Cut off by the frontline from the production centers in
the north, and faced with an additional 400,000 consumers (the number of
Allied soldiers who landed in Italy) well-supplied with paper money, both
the supply potential and the price controls were overwhelmed. Further fuel
was added to the flames when the Allied Chiefs of Staff decided that the
exchange rate for the lira be fixed at 100 lire per dollar, and 400 lire per
pound sterling. In the previous year (1942) the exchange rate on the dollar
had been officially held at 19.7, while that on sterling was held at 77.8. An
attempt to calculate the purchasing power parity for the lira using wholesale prices yields about 40 lire per dollar. It was said at the time that the
rates were fixed at the request of the British Treasury, which had already
established a 480 lire rate for sterling in the former Italian colonies it had
occupied. It must be added, however, that free market rates for Italian
banknotes in Switzerland and Portugal were quite near the rates adopted
by the Allied Commanders. Whatever the true explanation, it is clear that
the exchange rate was established with the intention of extracting from the
local population resources for the Allies' use, and that it was completely
out of line with the Italian price levels—which gave the Allied troops a

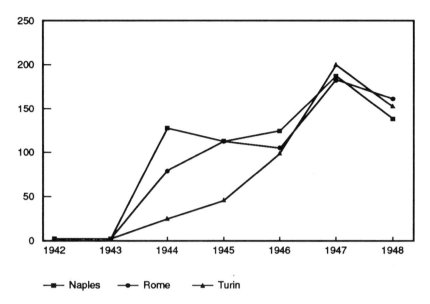

Figure 3.5
Retail price of bread (lire per kg), Naples, Rome, and Turin
Source: ISTAT, Annuario Statistico Italiano, serie V, vol. 1

very high purchasing power. The results could only be inflationary, as contemporary observers such as *The Economist* immediately recognized.[7]

Thus between the summer of 1943 and the winter of 1944, the first spate of inflation occurred in the liberated areas of southern and central Italy. The Wholesale Price Index rose from 2.3 times its 1938 level in 1943 to over 8 times in December 1944.

After the liberation of northern Italy, in April 1945 the inflationary process began to move north (as figure 3.5 clearly shows), but in a few months prices stabilized throughout the country. This pause in inflation lasted almost a year. Not only did prices level off but food prices fell considerably, from a peak of approximately 40 times their 1938 level to about 25. The printing presses slowed down as well, and the stock of currency in circulation remained stationary until the end of 1946. The free price of gold sovereigns also declined, as well as that of dollar banknotes.

The inflationary spiral seemed to have run its course. Public confidence in the currency was restored to the point that money hoarders started preferring Italian notes over foreign currency. The government began replacing currency issues with issues of public debt. A very large loan was floated (*Prestito Soleri*): the terms at which it was floated (5 percent fixed interest five-year bonds maturing in 1950), the prices at which it was sold

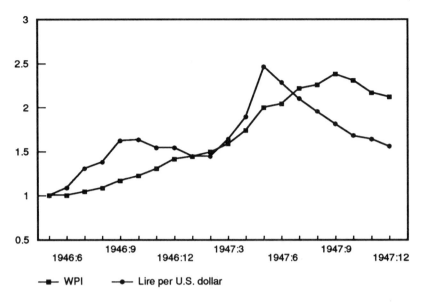

Figure 3.6
The free-market exchange rate and wholesale prices (May 1946 = 1.0)
Source: Banca d'Italia, *Annual Report*, various issues

(97.5 in the south, and 99 in the north), and the amount sold (L 109 billion) all indicate that public confidence had returned. The exchange rate also stabilized, and in the autumn of 1946 the price of U.S. dollars and pounds sterling actually started to fall (see figure 3.6). Between September and March the free market price of the dollar fell 10 percent; between September and December the stock market fell 17 percent. Even the rise in stock market prices stopped in the summer of 1946, and for a few months prices fell.[8]

This would have been the right moment to soak up the monetary overhang still in the hands of commercial banks with a currency reform. In fact, the Italian government, like others in Europe, began to consider a currency reform. But in the end, Italy was the only European country besides Britain not to carry it out.[9] The reason for this failed currency reform lies in the troubled politics of postwar Italy. A currency reform would have taxed war profits, hurting black marketeers and currency hoarders. The latter, who were reckoned to hold 25 percent of currency outstanding, were largely farmers (the traditional electoral base of the Christian Democrats) and small merchants.

This was a very troubled time for Italian politics. The country was just emerging from a short but violent civil war, as well as from twenty years of dictatorship. There were as many people interested in a quick return to normalcy as there were who feared that the preceding twenty years would be forgotten, if the fascist leadership, together with their industrial and financial accomplices, were not held accountable for their political and economic misdeeds. A grand coalition of six parties, which included socialists and communists, was running the government. The treasury was in the hands of Epicarmo Corbino, a conservative economist who saw the currency reform as confiscation and was opposed to all forms of state interference in the free working of the resource allocation system. On the contrary, the Ministry of Finance was the fief of the left, and it drafted and leaked out tax and currency reform proposals that scared the middle classes.

Although it was eventually not carried out, currency reform was discussed so widely that its anticipation started feeding expectations. Thus the chance of stabilizing prices was lost.

A currency reform would have required that the government sterilize the liquid claims commercial banks had at the treasury and at the Bank of Italy, converting them into longer term instruments—precisely as a past treasury minister, Alberto de Stefani, had done in 1925 to stop the post-World War I inflation. Corbino, as well as the governor of the Bank of Italy, Luigi Enaudi, entertained a different view of the world. They both believed in fast and complete liberalization of markets and prices. Corbino fought against currency reform, while Einaudi did all he could to liberalize the banking system.

Because of generalized bankruptcy in the 1930s, the largest Italian banks had been rescued by a state buy-out and had been run as a close-knit cartel ever since. Their independence had formally survived, but the "monetary circuit" had meant that they had very little freedom to run their balance sheets as they saw fit: the Banking Law of 1936 had placed commercial banks under the control of the central bank and of the Inspectorate for Credit and Saving. After he was appointed governor, Einaudi saw to it that the banks were restored to a situation in which they could compete with one another. He gave them leeway on the opening of new branches and left them free to rearrange the structure of their assets and liabilities.[10] Consequently, he was naturally opposed to a preemptive strike against the inflationary potential that was in the banks' balance sheets. Rather than keeping their assets frozen, he allowed, and even incited, them to unfreeze them. All that was required to transform the liquidity glut into a demand boom was the firms' willingness to borrow. This came from the combination of a boom in exports and an industrial capacity available to satisfy foreign demand.

2.2   1946–47: The Threat of Hyperinflation

The second phase of Italian inflation was thus ushered in in the second half of 1946, and it was almost completely a bank-dominated episode. The government's oscillating behavior in some important fields of economic management in those crucial months was the springboard of inflation. It was the government's eagerness to abolish all controls on stock exchange transactions, and all taxes on them, that upset the stability of the stock market and fueled an extraordinary stock exchange boom that raged for a whole year, from spring 1946 to May 1947. Stock prices rose 7 times in one year and, even more important, they rose by 2.5 times between April and August 1946. In September 1946 the Treasury had had to come to terms with a second large reconstruction loan. In order to attract savers and discourage them from the stock market, it decreed that there be a compulsory revaluation by industrial and commercial firms of the value of their plants, buildings, and other property, and that 25 percent of it be devolved as a tax to the state. This punctured the boom, but a few weeks later the market was rising again. The bubble eventually burst in May 1947 when a property tax was announced, which scared the well-to-do into liquid assets—although the tax in the end was so watered down that it yielded the state only a minimal amount of revenue.

Another episode that stoked the fire of inflation occurred in May 1946 when the price of wheat for the compulsory sales to the government was increased by 300 percent. This made the government many friends among the farmers, but it sent a very powerful signal to the rest of the population. Wheat prices were now more than twenty times their 1938 level. This meant that the government had lost all hope to stabilize prices at the level of 8 to 10 times their 1938 level, at which most officially fixed prices had been kept until then. The price of bread, however, was kept fixed. The difference was effectively paid for by the Bank of Italy and thus resulted in direct creation of new money.[11]

If the government directly stoked the fires of inflation, an additional impulse was provided by international demand for raw materials and industrial products. As we noted in section 1.1, Italian industry had survived the war largely unscathed. Productive capacity was intact in the most important sectors, but production had dwindled to very low levels because of a severe shortage of raw materials. As the world returned to peace, international trade revived and demand for industrial products became buoyant. Italian industry was ready to join the fray, if only it could lay its hands on raw materials, which Italy could import only through the Allies. Italian industry lobbied very hard to convince the government to ask the Allies for permission to import industrial raw materials, especially cotton, wool, and coal, which were to be transformed into manufactures for export.

Italy regained access to raw materials imports *before* the Marshall Plan facilities were created. As documented by Foa (1949, 35), between September 1943 and December 1947 international and U.S. assistance to Italy amounted to $2 billion: this allowed coal imports, for example, to recover by June–July 1947, the prewar level of 900,000–1,000,000 tons per month.[12]

It is essential to understand the role of the textile industry, and particularly that of its export boom between 1945–47, in order to get a satisfactory explanation of Italian inflation and stabilization. In the 1920s Italian textile producers had played an important role in the world textile boom occurring at the end of World War I. By contrast, during the 1930s this sector lay low, first because of the depression and later due to sanctions that deprived Italy of all imported cotton and wool. The revival of world demand in 1945 found Italian textile producers as near-monopolists in Europe, due to the temporary disappearance of Germany and Japan and to full employment and labor unrest in Britain. In the years immediately following World War II, textiles came to represent as much as almost 40 percent of total Italian exports.

The revival of Italian industry was thus preeminently export led and highly sectoral.[13] However, foreign demand was met with a severe shortage of raw materials and with bottlenecks in the labor market. Commodities' wholesale prices were rising very fast in the United States and in other markets. The labor market, although industry as a whole was hiding surplus labor, experienced local shortages, and wages, which until then had lagged behind prices, began to rise.

Italian prices were thus pushed up by rising international commodity prices, and, paradoxically, by Italy's own industrial potential. All that was required to transform the potential export boom into a real one was an accommodating stance on credit, import, and exchange rate policies.

The government had the means to prevent the banks from supplying industrialists and speculators with the loans they needed to buy commodities on the foreign and domestic market. The Banking Laws of 1926 and 1936 gave monetary authorities very powerful weapons to control credit. To cite one example, there was a rule imposed in 1926 and brought up-to-date in 1946 according to which each bank had to keep in a special account with the Bank of Italy its deposits exceeding 30 times its own capital. Since the capital base of the banks had not kept up with inflation—which had swollen nominal deposits—this rule would have been extremely restrictive, but nothing prevented the authorities from modifying it in order to control credit without at the same time throttling the economy. Einaudi, however, ignored it; he believed in bringing monetary policy back to the traditional role of controlling the cost, rather than the quantity, of credit. He allowed the banks to fight for borrowers, transforming their balances with the central bank and their stocks of government debt into loans. Contango loans showed enormous jumps both in 1946 and 1947. The loan/deposit ratio of Italian banks (see table 3.3) rose from 41 percent in March 1946 to 75 percent in September 1947. In eighteen months Italian banks achieved a loan/deposit ratio higher than the ratio their U.S. counterparts spent the next twenty years returning to from their equally depressed wartime level.

Table 3.3
Bank loans and bank deposits

Monthly growth rate of demand deposits: 1947*

	Raw data	Seasonally corrected
Feb	4.0	5.8
March	7.0	6.8
Apr	6.0	6.3
May	8.8	10.2
June	4.3	4.5
July	4.1	2.9
Aug	0.7	1.1
Sept	2.2	0.9
Oct	0.2	0.4
Nov	−1.3	−2.2
Dec	4.1	1.7
Ratio of loans to deposits:		
March	1946	.41
Dec	1947	.60
March	1947	.64
June	1947	.71
Sept	1947	.75
Dec	1947	.71

Source: Banca d'Italia, *Annual Report*, 1947.
*Seasonal factors to correct the individual components of the Italian money supply in that period are published in the *Annual Report* of the Bank of Italy for 1954 (p. 358) and are also used in Baffi (1958).

In the meantime, while industrial capacity was available to satisfy foreign demand, the supply situation for food and other essential products was not improved. Agricultural production had been compromised by the severe winter of 1946–47, and the import allowances Italy obtained from the Allies had been partly used up to import raw materials for the textile industry. Although Italian total imports showed huge increases in 1947, most consisted of raw materials for the export industries and did nothing to relieve the domestic shortage of food and other essential products. Food prices were still controlled, but farmers took advantage of the buoyant demand for their products and avoided selling them at these official prices. A very active black market developed, and a very large differential between the prices ruling in it, and the official prices opened up.

While a classic case of credit inflation was developing, Einaudi seemed to be concerned only about the government deficit, which was fueling the monetary base through wheat subsidies in particular. This was not an inconsiderable problem by any means, but, as Amedeo Gambino reminded the governor in an article published in mid-1947, the banks' power to create deposits, and the fact that they were doing exactly that, could not be overlooked as a force in the inflationary spiral.[14] In fact, throughout 1946 and until the summer of 1947 deposits increased much more than currency (see figure 3.7). Einaudi, however, did not seem to worry about banks being able to increase the velocity of circulation of high-powered money.

2.3   Stabilization

In the end inflation was stopped by acting precisely on the banks' ability to create deposits. Early in June 1947 a new government was formed by De Gasperi that excluded Communists and Socialists. Einaudi became deputy prime minister and budget minister. Del Vecchio, another eminent economist, was appointed treasury minister. One of the first decisions of the new cabinet was to reinstate the Ministerial Committee for Credit Control, which in its first meeting decided to introduce a system of compulsory reserves for the banking system. The new system was to take effect in September. The news of the cabinet's proposed financial program was enough to cool off the boom on the stock exchange: by the end of July stock prices were 30 percent lower than in May. The price of the dollar on the free foreign exchange, which had risen 30 percent during the month of May, fell 7 percent in June and 7 percent in July. The growth of wholesale prices stopped accelerating: the monthly rate of increase fell from 6 percent

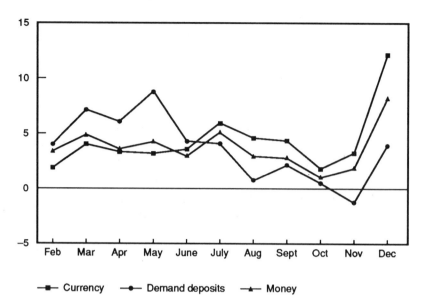

Figure 3.7
Money growth in 1947, raw data (percent per month)

in June to 3 percent in July. In October the price level started to fall (see figure 3.6).

Einaudi swallowed his laissez-faire principles and reverted to credit controls because by the summer of 1947 Italy was on the verge of a liquidity and foreign exchange crisis. Banks could not have proceeded very far in their lending as the public had started to get hold of currency again, and the balances banks had at the central bank were almost exhausted. The sharp depreciation of the lira was taken as a very clear signal by the public to get rid of bank deposits, get hold of currency, and try to spend it as fast as possible.

Through its policy of premature liberalization, the government achieved an export boom. But exporters were doing all they could to keep export proceeds in foreign currency, possibly in Swiss bank accounts, as the lira continued to depreciate. Italian dollar reserves were almost exhausted, and sterling balances were unusable. International assistance was sought but could not be secured for several months. A run on the banks could not be discounted. It would have stopped credit inflation, but it would also have meant another traditional Italian episode of generalized bank insolvency accompanied by industrial and commercial failures.

It is difficult to say whether inflation stopped in anticipation of the credit squeeze announced for the autumn or simply because the government had

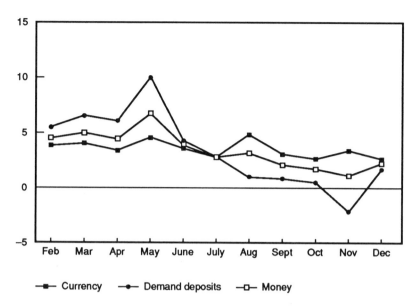

Figure 3.8
Money growth in 1947, seasonally adjusted (percent per month)
Source: Banca d'Italia, *Annual Report*, various issues. For seasonal factors see table 3.3.

changed and the new coalition was the first in the postwar period to exclude communists. Casella and Eichengreen (1992) dismiss the view that the imposition of reserve requirements on commercial banks was enough to explain the disinflation. They point instead to the election results and to the announcement (also made in June 1947) of the Marshall Plan: the combination of these two factors allowed resolution of the war of attrition between different interest groups that was at the core of the hyperinflation.

Yet, the credit squeeze did occur. The seasonally corrected monthly growth rate of bank deposits fell from 10 percent per month on average in May, to − 2.2 percent in November (see table 3.3). Total money supply fell less than bank deposits because currency circulation kept growing. As correctly pointed out by Casella and Eichengreen, circulation kept growing because "the new reserve requirements diverted loans to business from the commercial banks to the central bank, which extended loans to enterprise through the public sector." The government intervened to mitigate the effects of the credit squeeze on industry. It raised the endowment of IRI (the state industrial holding company) and created a special fund for the engineering industry. Total disbursement for these two programs added L 20 billion to public expenditure—20 percent of the year's deficit (see Banca d'Italia *Annual Report* 1947). The total deficit for the second semester of

1947 amounted to L 98 billion and was entirely financed by drawing on the treasury's account at the central bank.

Figure 3.7 shows the monthly growth rates of the money supply and of its components (currency and demand deposits) in 1947. The top graph was created using the raw data; the bottom one uses the seasonally adjusted data.[15] The seasonally adjusted growth rate of the total money supply fell from 5 percent per month on average in the spring to 1.7 percent in the last three months of the year. In December, the growth rate of money accelerated again, in part probably reflecting an increase in money demand after inflation expectations had stabilized.

Once applied, credit controls worked extremely fast. In the last three months of 1947, wholesale prices fell by almost 20 percent. Imports dwindled to a trickle, while exports maintained and even increased their levels, thus showing that most imports had been of a speculative nature.

The cut in the supply of credit further deflated stock exchange prices. It also found most industrial and commercial entrepreneurs with a very lopsided balance sheet. Expecting inflation to continue, they had invested all their liquid resources in new equipment and in inventory accumulation, while they had borrowed as much as they could, hoping to repay the debt with inflated money. The credit squeeze left them cut off from their supply of new liquidity and owing a great deal to banks. They reacted by pushing up exports, stopping speculative imports, and repatriating the foreign balances they had accumulated in Swiss banks, using them to lighten the burden of their lira debt to banks.

On November 28 it was decreed that the 50 percent of export proceeds exporters had to sell to the government would no longer be exchanged for lire at a fixed rate but at a rate that followed the free rates ruling on the month before the sale. The foreign exchange market was thus effectively unified, and a parity was established with the dollar which, after the small readjustment following the devaluation of sterling in 1949, was to remain unchanged until 1971. Black market activity dwindled, and the parallel rate for the lira in Switzerland showed no difference from official rates.[16]

2.4   The Stabilization Crisis

Italy, which had preceded all other belligerent countries into reconstruction, and had been pushed by the policy of early liberalization toward two bouts of serious inflation, also preceded other countries into recession, when inflation was belatedly but effectively stopped. Industrial unemployment mounted as firms tried to restore their balance sheets to more normal times. Industrial production stagnated well into 1949.

While the credit squeeze was taking effect, the government also managed to restore its own budget—a task made relatively easy by the fact that inflation had wiped out the public debt. After a last spending spree, clearly linked with the elections of April 1948 when the opposition was routed, the budget deficit was drastically cut in 1949 and 1950 (figure 3.3).

Along with the credit squeeze came a fall in foreign demand for Italian exports. As of 1948 other major suppliers of industrial goods were gradually reappearing on the world market, and the immediate postwar boom experienced by the United States rather abruptly came to a halt. By 1949 the United States was in a recession.

The Italian economy was thus subjected to a contemporary drop in both domestic and foreign demand, just as Marshall Aid became available to the countries of Europe. But the Italian authorities used the aid more to increase foreign reserves than to import Marshall Aid goods. Foreign observers were astonished to note that, while other countries used Marshall Aid to boost production and foreign trade, Italy did not show the absorption capacity to use all the aid it was entitled to—a fact that invited extensive criticism from Marshall Aid administrators and independent foreign observers. While the rest of the world complained about the "dollar gap," Italy was busy accumulating dollars and gold, using for this purpose even the Counterpart Funds of Marshall Aid imports. Italian sterling balances mounted as well and were the cause of much bickering between the Italian and British governments. Foreign critics asked themselves how on earth Italy could spurn Marshall Aid while her industrial capacity was idle and unemployment was alarmingly high. Other countries, like France and Germany, were using all the aid they could get their hands on to augment industrial capacity and infrastructure.

The fact is that Italian industry had been geared toward exports: the return of other industrial producers to the market had made it much less competitive and much less profitable than it had been in 1946 and 1947. Foreign demand is not always easily replaced with domestic demand, especially when the structure of exports is such that they consist, as Italian exports did in 1946 and 1947, of as much as 40 percent textile products and another 20 percent engineering products. To generate a level of domestic demand high enough to absorb the capacity of those two sectors, personal incomes would have to make a giant leap, and this the authorities thought could only happen with another massive injection of liquidity, which they were not willing under any circumstance to provide.[17]

Having suffered no great damage, and having quickly repaired what damage had been caused by war, the Italian economy could absorb foreign aid only in the form of food and raw materials. It had a surplus capacity of its own in the capital goods sector and a surplus capacity in light industry as well. It could only be rescued by an increase in world demand.

Thus, the end of the stabilization crisis had to wait until the end of the American recession and the explosion of the Korean War boom, at which point Italian industry was once again ready to exploit the rise in world demand.

3 Concluding Remarks on Italy's Postwar Experience

3.1 The Limits of Italian Postwar Liberalism

What we have said so far would seem to portray the Italian governing classes as completely permeated, at least since the earliest postwar times, with the spirit of free trade and free enterprise. Having an efficient export industry at the very end of the war meant that the authorities were subjected to very strong pressure to liberalize foreign trade and credit to private enterprise, even when that meant giving free way to raging inflation and, in due course, to harsh stabilization measures. This view of Italian economic policy is, however, rather considerably obscured by the attitude the same authorities, and the political body as a whole, maintained throughout the early postwar period about state-owned industry.

As we have mentioned, Italian banks and large-scale industry had been bankrupted by the world depression of the thirties. In order to rescue them, the state had first to rescue the banks and form a state holding company (IRI) to own them as well as the industrial companies the banks owned. The Banking Law of 1936 separated the banks from industry but maintained state ownership for both. All firms—both industrial and banking—remained joint-stock companies and IRI owned most of their shares.

At the end of the war the Allies, especially the Americans, tried to convince the Italian government to privatize state-owned banks and industries. But, in spite of the efforts of Einaudi, Corbino, and others, IRI remained firmly in state hands, and the state-owned oil company, ENI, resisted all efforts to disband it. The fact is, the greatest part of the state-owned firms did not make any money and were saddled with hard-to-fire excess labor. Much of it was in engineering, where fascist war requirements had swollen production by 50 percent between 1938 and 1943, and a painful task of reconversion had to be faced. There were not many private entrepreneurs who were entertaining any desire to lay their hands on state-owned industry when their own firms faced excess capacity. As to banks, they could be sold back to the private sector only through the financial market, as there was not enough concentration of capital in the country to buy them privately. The Italian stock exchange was certainly not capable of absorbing the shares of public banks. While stock prices were rising, the market was overcrowded with new issues by private companies. When prices fell, there were no investors eager to go into stocks.

In addition, large public banks, in spite of being owned by the state, had maintained excellent relations with the main private industrial entrepreneurs. And, with the possible exception of the steel industry, the same was true of publicly owned industrial companies.

As a result, no private entrepreneur was really interested in seeing the end of IRI. The latter was, moreover, endowed with very able managers, often technically and always politically superior to their counterparts in the private sector. They were able to fend off early threats by the Allies and to convince them of the benign nature of Italian state ownership. They also managed to get themselves adopted by the left wing of the Christian Democratic Party, which protected them against all threats.

3.2   Lessons from the Italian Postwar Experience

Through their policies, the Italian authorities helped Italian industry to seize the opportunity it had at the end of the war of supplying the rest of Europe and the world with the industrial goods it was in a special position to produce. Very high profits were accumulated that later helped to cushion the impact of the credit restriction measures introduced in the autumn of 1947.

The Italian experience thus confirms that profitability (and an undervalued currency) are key ingredients for economic success. Italy was to repeat the experience two decades later in the aftermath of the first oil shock. In 1976–78, just before Italy joined the European Monetary System, currency depreciation and high inflation were instrumental in producing a profit boom that helped Italian industry survive the costs that would result from the decision to peg the lira to the deutsche mark. (For an account of that experience see Giavazzi and Spaventa 1989.)[18]

Another lesson is that economic dogmatism is important to establish credibility, but it should not prevent economic pragmatism from taking over when necessary. Einaudi was a staunch free marketeer, but he did not hesitate when his policies backfired to slam on quantitative credit controls and to restore a dirigistic insitution like the Cabinet Committee on Credit Control, which had been abolished in the earlier phase of liberalization enthusiasm.

If one very large difference is to be detected between the Italian postwar experience and that of the former socialist countries of today, it is the early availability of a foreign market starved for goods of all kinds, and of a deep-pocketed supplier of cheap or even free raw materials, the United States.

Another difference is represented by the possibility of selling competitive goods on the free market and less competitive goods, like engineering products, on bilateral clearing arrangements. The Italian textile industry, which was fully competitive, could reap all the benefits of its near-monopoly position in the early years, while its ability to cut costs and absorb reduced profit rates enabled it to survive even in the low phases of the international cycle. The capital goods industry went through a process of painful reconversion that lasted almost ten years. But its pains were reduced by the chance it had of selling, on bilateral clearing arrangements, to countries in Eastern Europe and Latin America, and to the Sterling Area.

Notes

This paper was presented at the conference on "Post–World War II European Reconstruction" in Hamburg, 6–8 September 1991. We thank conference participants, and in particular Barry Eichengreen, for comments.

1. Agriculture was in a much sorrier state, especially because of lack of fertilizers, because factories had been converted to war production, as well as because of the large-scale slaughter of cattle and sheep by the hungry population and by the invading troops. Mobilization of the male population to fight the war had also drastically decreased the amount of labor available in agriculture in the war years.

2. The shares of industrial capacity damaged by the war were: 11.8 percent in the north, 88 percent in the central regions, and 50 percent in the south.

3. Part in the form of cashier's checks, which played the role of nonexistent high-denomination bank notes.

4. Two thirds of the total money printed on behalf of foreign troops was for the Germans, one third was for the Allies.

5. For a careful analysis of Italian monetary developments in the postwar years, see Baffi (1958).

6. In the south, the government found another way to finance itself. The Bank of Italy offered commercial banks to take in deposits at 4.5 percent. This opportunity was seized by the banks, which received back the notes printed for the Allies and spent them in transactions with the Italian population.

7. See also Foa (1949), Harris (1957), and Baffi (1958).

8. The exchange rate series shown in figure 3.6 is the price of U.S. dollars on the free foreign exchange market established in March 1946. Until then, all trade and foreign exchange transactions had been strictly regulated. Italian exchange controls dated back to 1934. Following the demise of the gold standard by Britain in 1931, Italy, like all countries that had scarce gold reserves (and thus could not resort to a buffer-stock system to manage the exchange rate), introduced strict exchange rate controls, declaring a state monopoly over foreign exchange. This regime of fixed rates and complete exchange and trade regulation lasted more or less until 1946. Following the war, the clauses of the armistice concluded on September 8, 1943, precluded Italy from having a commercial policy. All that Italy could export in that period, and in general all foreign exchange receipts, was paid into a postliberation account. It was only at the start of 1945 that Italy obtained from the Allies the permission to engage in a limited policy of foreign trade negotiations with neutral countries, which took the shape of bilateral clearing agreements. In March 1946, the first free market for foreign exchange was established.

According to the new system, exporters were allowed to keep 50 percent of the foreign exchange they received in payment for their merchandise and could use it either to pay for imports, or to sell on the free foreign exchange market, with the provision that the foreign exchange would be used exclusively to import goods described in a list supplied by the government within ninety days from the day the foreign exchange was sold. This treatment was reserved only to so-called export currencies (the dollar, sterling, escudos, Egyptian pound, Swiss franc). There were thus two exchange regimes, a free regime applying to certain goods and currencies, and a clearing regime for other goods and currencies.

In special cases the authorities allowed particular industries to sell more than 50 percent of export proceeds on the free market. A case of this was shipping. Italian shipowners who had purchased foreign ships could keep all they earned in foreign currency as freight charges. Another case was textile producers, who were allowed in July 1947 to keep 75 percent of their export proceeds, a benefit later extended to Italian ship operators who hired foreign ships. On January 20, 1947, all foreign transactions yielding free currencies to Italian citizens were allowed to the 50 percent regime.

In March 1946, after the opening of the foreign exchange market, prices rose substantially. The dollar rose to L 364 within twenty days, with a depreciation of 38 percent. Sterling went to L 1446, and the Swiss franc to L 98 (a depreciation of 48 percent). The rise in the price of foreign exchange continued until October 1946 for the dollar and pound (which rose above double the official rate) and even later for the Swiss franc, which rose until December 1946. Prices stabilized during the winter, and quotations actually started to fall.

9. For a review of European currency reforms in the immediate postwar period see Dornbusch and Wolf (1991).

10. See Baffi (1958), DeCecco (1972).

11. Wheat stockpiles were paid for by the government with wheat bills, which growers exchanged at banks for ready cash. Banks, in turn, discounted those bills at the Bank of Italy, which could not refuse them.

12. Thus the finding reported in chapter 8 by De Long and Eichengreen, this volume—namely that in 1948, in the absence of all Marshall-Plan financed imports of raw materials, Italian industrial production would have fallen by only 7 percent—is not surprising. Italian imports of raw materials recovered before Marshall Plan aid had become available. By late 1947 the Italian economy was entering into its first postwar recession.

13. Apart from textiles, it involved traditional Italian exports of luxury goods, which were requested by overseas markets like Argentina, and some sections of the engineering industry.

14. See Gambino (1947).

15. Constructed using the seasonal factors described in the note to table 3.3.

16. External convertibility for the lira, however, was not reestablished until the late fifties. And internal convertability had to wait much longer, until July 1990.

17. Similar considerations had been made by the British Treasury and by the Bank of England in the interwar period, when Britain had experienced a slump in the demand for its export industries. As in the British case, the argument was sound, but it was used in Italy to exclude even a modest dose of government-induced reflation.

18. In the fifty years following the mid-1920s, Italian industry underwent four episodes of large restructuring. The two we mention in the text, 1945—46 and 1976—78, were accompanied by currency depreciation and high inflation. They should be contrasted with the "restructuring with tears" of 1926—27 and 1963—64, both of which took place in a strong-currency, low-inflation macroeconomic environment.

References

Baffi, P. (1958), "Monetary Developments in Italy from the War Economy to Limited Convertibility," Banca Nazionale del Lavoro *Quarterly Review*, no. 47, December.

Bank of Italy Annual Report 1947, Rome: Bank of Italy.

Casella, A. and B. Eichengreen (1992), "Halting Inflation in Italy and France after World War II," in Bordo M. and C. Forrest (eds.), *Monetary Regimes in Transition*, Cambridge: Cambridge University Press.

De Cecco, M. (1972), "Italian Economic Policy in the Reconstruction Period", in Woolf, S. J. (ed.) *The Rebirth of Italy*, London: Longman.

Dornbusch, R. and T. H. C. Wolf (1991), "Monetary Overhang and Reforms in the 1940s," mimeo, MIT.

Foa, B. (1949), "Monetary Reconstruction in Italy," published for The Carnegie Endowment for International Peace, New York: King's Crown Press.

Gambino, A. (1947), "Recent Developments in Banking Activity in Italy," Banca Nazionale del Lavoro *Quarterly Review*.

Giavazzi, F. and L. Spaventa (1989), "Italy: The Real Effects of Inflation and Disinflation," *Economic Policy*, No. 8.

Harris, C. R. S. (1957), "Allied Military Administration of Italy 1943–45," Her Majesty's Stationary Office, London.

4   Economic Reconstruction in France: 1945–1958

Gilles Saint-Paul

Macroeconomic theory can be divided into two branches: the first deals with short-term fluctuations and stabilization, the second studies the dynamics of long-term capital accumulation and growth.

In most social sciences, theory can learn a lot from pathological cases, for they are the nearest thing to a controlled experiment. In this respect, wars provide an interesting experiment for the two branches of macroeconomic theory. Because they are associated with destruction of the capital stock, they imply an unambiguous deviation from steady-state growth. Because they are associated with difficult budgetary problems, they are often followed by high-inflation periods, thus providing one or more case studies in stabilization.

In this chapter we will analyze French postwar reconstruction, using the following question as a guideline: What can macroeconomic theory learn from such a period?

After having reviewed the course of events in section 1, section 2 analyzes how the immediate postwar inflation was stabilized and how Marshall aid was instrumental in this process. Section 3 discusses how the theory of long-term growth can be useful in thinking about reconstruction. Section 4 analyzes the dynamics of investment during the period and confronts them with the theoretical analysis sketched in section 3. Section 5 reviews the main factors for the high rate of productivity growth during the period.

1   A Brief Historical Reminder

The two main characteristics of the French economy during the 1945–1959 period are, first, the persistent climate of political and economic instability: governments were rotating at a dizzying pace, budgetary and balance of payments crises were recurrent, inflation was rarely controlled, and

Table 4.1
Estimation of some war losses

Railways	
Tracks	6%
Stations	38%
Engines	21%
Hardware	60%
Roads	
Cars	31%
Lorries	40%
Roads	8%
Rivers	
Navigable waterways	86%
Canal locks	11%
Barges	80%
Ports	
Waterfront length	79%
Docks and warehouses	47%
Handling hardware	59%
Merchant navy	
Oil tankers	78%
Cargos	64%
Buildings	
Dwellings	1,229,000
Agricultural	278,000
Industrial	246,000

Source: INSEE (1949).

so forth; and second—this was a novelty compared to the prewar period —the major involvement of the state in all sectors of the economy, in particular in the financial sector and heavy industry.

On June 6, 1944, General de Gaulle constituted the first French government of the postwar. As shown in table 4.1, the French economy had suffered substantial damages during the war. Although France had lost fewer lives than during the First World War, a large share of the capital stock was destroyed: 25 percent of the housing stock, 60 to 70 percent of transportation infrastructure, and so forth. Industrial production was less than half its (low) 1938 level, that is, only 30 percent of the 1928 level. Whereas the private capital stock may have suffered less from direct destruction than its public counterpart, it suffered from depreciation and lack of maintenance during these four years, so that it was probably substantially below its prewar level; therefore, it seems reasonable to assume that the aggregate capital stock was 20 to 35 percent below its prewar value.

The de Gaulle government (which included members of the Communist Party as one of the three main political parties from the Résistance) started a series of nationalizations, including coal mines, the Bank of France, the main car manufacturer, the main four deposit banks, the insurance system, and public utilities. It created a large number of active public agencies, in particular the Commissariat Général au Plan, which had a lot of influence in managing the reconstruction tasks.

As a result, the French economy was organized on a basis quite different from that which prevailed in the prewar period, when free-market principles were more influential: 25 percent of the workforce was employed in the public sector—about twice the prewar figure. The most important sectors of the economy were now under state control: banking, transportation, and energy. The few large firms that remained private in these sectors (in particular in the oil sector) were in fact heavily regulated and had little independence. The influence of the state also prevailed through price and wage controls: most prices and all wages remained administered some time after the end of the war, and for others like energy prices or the minimum wage, controls remained throughout the whole period. The state also played an important role in the restructuring of the agricultural sector.

The three years following the liberation were a period of painful recovery amidst a climate of very high inflation and permanent budgetary problems (see tables 4.2 and 4.3). Rationing was still prevalent, work duration had reached forty-seven hours a week, the government controlled wages and most prices—and yet it was unable to control inflation.

The poor production level of 1938 was achieved in 1948, but with a longer working week, and the last restrictions were only lifted in 1949.

Not surprisingly, there was a large balance of payments deficit, and reserves were eroding quickly while external debt was sharply rising. The process peaked in late 1947, early 1948, with a balance of payments crisis. In January 1948, the franc was devalued by 50 percent and the quarterly rate of inflation reached a peak of 30 percent.

On the political side, the climate had deteriorated: major strikes in the public sector followed the exclusion of the Communists from the government in 1947.

Then came the first Marshall aid and a period of relative stability: the Marshall aid allowed the government to reduce its deficit, to rebuild foreign exchange reserves, and to stabilize external debt. Along with it came a sharp reduction in inflation. Furthermore, the new exchange rate of the

Table 4.2
National accounts data

	(1)	(2)	(3)	(4)
1946	16.0	4.4	14.5	28.0
1947	6.3	6.6	13.3	26.5
1948	13.2	7.8	11.3	47.8
1949	6.2	10.6	11.2	4.8
1950	6.0	12.2	10.9	8.6
1951	6.0	13.1	11.5	23.0
1952	3.4	11.5	11.2	3.1
1953	3.1	11.4	11.1	−0.6
1954	6.8	12.3	11.0	1.1
1955	5.2	12.7	11.4	2.5
1956	5.7	11.3	12.7	5.0
1957	6.1	11.4	12.8	7.9
1958	2.9	11.7	12.2	9.1
1959	3.5	12.2	11.7	5.9

1. GDP growth, annual, %
2. Exports/GDP ratio, %
3. Import/GDP ratio, %
4. Inflation rate, annual, %
Source: Laroque et al. (1989).

Table 4.3
Devaluations of the French franc during the period

Date	Magnitude (%)
December 25, 1945	50
January 26, 1948	50
September 20, 1949	40[1]
August 1957	20[2]

1. Following the sterling devaluation on September 17.
2. *De facto* devaluation, which will be made official in June 1958.
Source: INSEE (1959).

franc was competitive enough to restore the balance of payments. The franc was devalued again at the end of 1949 to match the devaluation of the sterling.

At the same time, along with other Organization for Economic Cooperation in Europe (O.E.C.E.) countries, France engaged in a program of exchange liberation in order to progressively restore convertibility. "Free markets" for some currencies were created.

However, with the burst of the Korean War, military expenditures doubled, leading to a new rise in inflation in 1951, although at a more reasonable level than before 1948. This led to a new balance of payments crisis, which was followed by a suspension of all previous exchange liberation measures.

The crisis was stabilized by Antoine Pinay, who was appointed prime minister in the middle of 1952. This was surprisingly successful, in light of the short time he stayed in power and the lack of tangible stabilization measures in his program. He essentially cut public investment programs, which had little impact on the *current* deficit, did not raise taxes, did not devalue, and borrowed more; his year of power is a record deficit year. Despite this, inflation dropped to a reasonable level (but this may well be due to the recession that followed). In short, the Pinay stabilization is a striking example of how confidence may have first-order effects in economics, although one should not forget that maintaining high nominal interest rates did part of the job.

The 1954–55 recovery was a period of marked stability, with practically no inflation, despite a policy aimed at encouraging investment and a decline in the trade deficit due to the numerous export subsidies and import taxes that the Edgar Faure government established in order to avoid a devaluation. This allowed the exchange liberation process to start again.

This was not to last forever, since the Suez crisis in 1956 and the difficulties in financing the Algerian War generated a new burst in inflation, a new balance of payments crisis, and the need for a new devaluation. Again, all measures of trade liberalization were suspended, and the process only resumed after de Gaulle returned to power.

It is convenient to date the end of this period in 1958, when de Gaulle returned to power. The sixties were a decade of sustained expansion, with much more political and economic stability than the previous period.

2   American Aid and Stabilization

One of the most well-known features of this period is the Marshall Plan. The first aid from the Marshall Plan was distributed in early 1948. The plan lasted more than four years, and then military aid took over, so that American support of various forms lasted until 1956. The conventional view is that the Marshall Plan was instrumental in providing France with the necessary capital goods it needed for reconstruction. This view is supported by the amount of the aid, which was roughly 30 percent of France's total imports. It is generally held that the Marshall Plan helped to build up a "large program of investments."

In this section, we argue that this conventional wisdom is somehow misguided. The main reason is that most vital imports took place *before* the Marshall Plan and that we do not observe a sharp rise in imports when the plan was introduced. In fact, France's trade balance was almost in equilibrium in 1948 and *exports*, not imports, grew after the start of the plan (see table 4.2). This pattern is reinforced if one confines oneself to exports and imports of manufactured goods, of equipment goods, or goods from the Dollar zone. However, one has to be cautious in interpreting this pattern because there was a devaluation at the beginning of 1948: its size was such that a rise in exports was hardly surprising. In fact, this suggests that the 1948 devaluation was somewhat excessive: if American aid was to be used to finance imports, a more favorable exchange rate had to be aimed at. Instead, France chose to rebuild its reserves and to stabilize external debt, probably at the expense of investment. In any case, the fact that it was able to do so proves that imports from abroad were not so desperately needed.

Another piece of evidence can be obtained by looking at investment: according to the "traditional view," investment should rise when the Marshall Plan is introduced, since it finances capital goods imports. But as we will argue, investment was relatively depressed during this period and remained so after the first American aid was received.

This is not to say, however, that the Marshall Plan was unneeded or played no role in France's reconstruction. The first role of the Marshall Plan was the stabilization of external debt. As table 4.4 shows, external debt was rapidly rising until the plan was introduced. It is not obvious whether this path was sustainable: some painful adjustment measures would have been needed in the future. This should not, however, be overstated: the external debt/GDP ratio was far from critical at this point. Given that the trade balance recovered in 1948–49, the rise in external debt that would have been observed in the absence of the Marshall Plan seems quite tolerable. Nothing warrants, however, that the French economy would have followed the same course in the absence of the aid, and we argue it would not.

Second, foreign aid played a key role in the stabilization of inflation. Until the middle of 1948, France was trapped in a high-inflation equilib-

Table 4.4
Budget data, % of GDP

	(1)	(2)	(3)	(4)	(5)
1946	2.64	8.33	82.82	8.30	0.00
1947	3.37	11.18	73.25	6.74	0.00
1948	0.27	15.00	54.38	6.26	2.39
1949	0.13	15.40	50.89	2.25	3.91
1950	− 1.09	14.70	47.20	2.82	1.93
1951	0.00	11.43	39.06	2.89	1.36
1952	0.12	10.13	38.11	5.02	1.10
1953	1.75	9.44	41.20	3.57	0.97
1954	−0.46	7.98	40.24	2.29	1.16
1955	−0.73	6.82	38.87	3.00	0.70
1956	−0.42	5.72	38.88	4.54	0.29

1. Credits from the Bank of France to the treasury
2. External debt
3. Public debt
4. Fiscal deficit
5. American aid
Source: INSEE (1959).

rium, with annual rates of 20 to 50 percent and a peak of 25 percent the first quarter of 1948, due to the devaluation. Inflation then dropped to a substantially lower level and never reached these heights again. This drop coincided with the first inflows of Marshall aid.

Inflation had been initiated by the large monetary overhang that agents held after the shortage period of the war. These shortages helped to finance the large burden of "occupation fees" while price controls kept inflation at a moderate level. Furthermore, part of the private sector's excess wealth was held in the form of government debt, which was relatively high, and had been issued by a government considered illegitimate. Therefore, the temptation was strong for the new government to let inflation erode this stock of public debt. The inflationary process was subsequently reinforced by the difficulties encountered by the government in financing the budget deficit by other means than money creation. First, expenditures were practically incompressible, due to the magnitude of the reconstruction task. Second, the inflationary environment made it difficult for the government to issue public debt (see INSEE 1959): either indexation or coercive measures were needed to convince the public to buy new government bonds. Third, there is a presumption that inflation was adding to the budget deficit through fiscal lags (the Tanzi-Oliveira effect). In particular, people who held an import license had access to a de facto credit from the government at a zero nominal interest rate (see Laroque 1981). These effects were reinforced by the lack of an appropriate fiscal infrastucture: the Direction Generale des Impots, the main administrative body for collecting taxes, was only established in 1948. Special accounts of the treasury were a way of disguising deficits that jeopardized the credibility of a potential stabilization; they were suppressed at the beginning of 1948.

All these factors explain why the government repeatedly used money creation to finance its deficit (see table 4.4), along with "exceptional taxes," and increases in public sector prices, which also contributed to inflation (as a matter of fact, credits from the central bank ceased in the spring of 1948, which coincided with the first inflows of American aid). The 1945 devaluation added to the process.

The Marshall aid was a natural tool for the government to get out of this vicious circle by reducing its deficit, since the franc value of the aid automatically appeared as a receipt on the government balance sheet. In fact, most of the aid was used to finance public expenditures and/or to reduce various forms of public debt. For example, Parodi (1971) reports that only 15 percent of the aid was used as loans to the private sector, whereas 45 percent was directed toward public enterprises, which held a large amount of public debt. A sizable share of this aid was thus used to retire public debt. This role is evidenced in table 4.4. American aid coincides with a large drop in the deficit/GNP ratio.

In order to illustrate how an external transfer can help stabilize inflation, we find it useful to analyze a small model, close in spirit to those that have been used to describe the link between high inflation and budget deficits (see Bruno et al. 1988).

The model is summarized by the following equations:

$$x = m - p = -\beta i \tag{LM}$$

$$y = -\gamma(i - \pi) \tag{IS}$$

$$\pi = \dot{p} = \alpha(y - \bar{y}) \tag{AS}$$

$$\dot{x} = D(\pi)/e^x - \pi \tag{MC}$$

where $D' > 0$, at least over a range.

The first three equations are the familiar LM, IS, and AS (aggregate supply or Phillips) equations. Here m is the log of nominal money, p the log of the price level, y the log of aggregate demand, $\bar{y}$ the "natural rate," i the nominal interest rate, π the inflation rate and x the log of real money balances.

The last equation determines how money creation affects the evolution of real balances. More specifically, if uppercase letters denote levels, one has:

$$\dot{M}/P = D(\pi)$$

where $D(\pi)$ is the part of the budget deficit that is financed through money creation. We assume that $D'(\pi) > 0$ over at least a range: this may be due to the burden exerted by fiscal lags on the budget, or to the fact that it is simply more costly to issue debt at higher inflation rates, because of risk premia, indexation costs, and so forth; hence the government will print more money to finance its deficit. We assume that over this range these effects dominate other effects, like the alleviating effect of inflation on the interest burden of nonindexed debt.

This equation implies:

$$(\dot{M}/P) = D(\pi) - \pi M/P$$

Dividing this by M/P and recognizing that $x = \log(M/P)$ yields:

$$\dot{x} = D(\pi)/e^x - \pi$$

Hence, equation (MC).

To solve the model, one first eliminates i and y from the first three equations, getting:

$$\pi = [(\alpha\gamma/\beta)x - \alpha\bar{y}]/(1 - \alpha\gamma).$$

We assume the usual stability condition $\alpha\gamma < 1$. This defines a locus PP in figure 4.1. The XX curve is the $\dot{x} = 0$ locus given by equation (MC). As drawn, the XX curve has an upward sloping portion. Along this portion, an increase in inflation must be compensated by an increase in real balances: perverse effects are so strong that the losses in tax receipts are higher than the gains from an increased inflation tax (per unit of real balances), so that the government must increase real balances.

The model highlights how a strong fiscal lag effect can lead to multiple equilibria: in the long run, the economy may end up either at point E, a low-inflation equilibrium, or at point F, a high-inflation trap. If the inflation rate is artificially maintained at a low rate π_0 for a certain period, for example, through shortages, then the economy will accumulate a large monetary overhang and end up at a point like G. Immediately after World War II, the French economy was at a point like G. When price restrictions are lifted, the economy jumps from G to H and eventually reaches the bad equilibrium F.

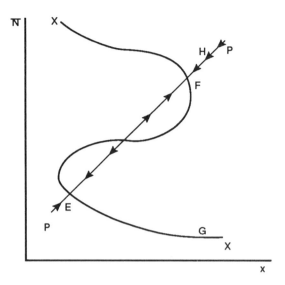

Figure 4.1

Figure 4.2 illustrates how the Marshall Plan helped to stabilize inflation: the inflow of funds eased the government budget constraint and made it possible to finance the deficit with a lower level of money creation. As a result the XX locus shifted to the left, so that the bad equilibrium disappeared; the economy proceeded toward the (new) good equilibrium E′, and ended up at E after the end of the aid, instead of reverting to F. The interesting point is that even if the aid is temporary, the economy will never reach the high-inflation equilibrium again.[1]

2.1   Other Possible Linkages

While this story certainly captures part of what was going on in this period, other phenomena may have been important in the stabilization process. The rise in external debt may have indirectly fueled inflation through expectations: if people were expecting a stabilization program in the future, including a large fiscal contraction, this should have a positive impact on aggregate demand through lower long-term interest rates, thus adding to the inflationary process (see, for example, Blanchard 1981). American aid removes this effect by making fiscal contraction less likely. It is however dubious whether rational expectations are a sound description of the pub-

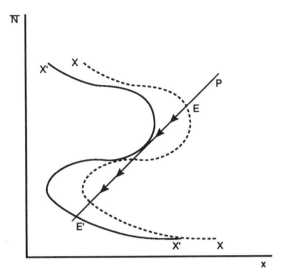

Figure 4.2

lic's behavior in this period: a striking fact is that there is no "announce-ment effect" associated with Marshall's Harvard speech: the stabilization of inflation only occurred after the aid actually took place.[2]

After examining the reconstruction period from the point of view of short-term stabilization, we now study it from the point of view of long-term capital accumulation. In order to do so, we first ask how growth theory can be useful in order to analyze the dynamics of a recovery follow-ing a destruction of the capital stock.

3   Reconstruction and Growth Theory

In order to assess what we can learn from such periods, it is necessary to ask what we should expect to observe. Growth theory can give us some elements of an answer, although new developments in this area are likely to lead to a multiplicity of answers. In the last five years, many endogenous growth models have been proposed (see Lucas 1988, Romer 1990), and their predictions sharply differ from those of neoclassical growth models. In this respect, reconstruction periods provide a real world experiment in the form of a massive destruction of the capital stock, so that there is no doubt that the economy has deviated from its previous steady state. Therefore, looking at the dynamics of growth in the postwar period may help discriminate across various hypotheses. In order to do so, we first present three models of growth that have strikingly different implications for the behavior of the economy in reconstruction periods. We then use them as benchmarks to analyze the behavior of investment during the period.

3.1   The Ramsey Model

One standard tool to analyze the dynamics of investment in a reconstruction period is the open-economy Ramsey growth model (see Blanchard and Fischer 1989). It provides us with a useful benchmark for what should happen in a constant-returns world. The two main characteristics of this model are (i) a representative agent who has access to world capital markets and (ii) finite investment flows due to the existence of installation costs. In such a world, the marginal product of capital is equalized across countries in steady state. If a region experiences a destruction of its capital stock, the marginal product of capital increases in this region, and so does Tobin's q. As a result, investment rises in this region, while consumption falls only moderately because the income loss of the region's inhabitants is smoothed over the whole future. Therefore one should expect a capital inflow from the rest of the world toward this region and a large balance of payments deficit. As the adjustment proceeds, the return to capital progressively goes down, as does investment and the capital flow. Because of the interest payments on cumulated debt, the trade balance surplus is eventually higher than before the destruction occurred. The transitional dynamics of output and investment are illustrated in figure 4.3. Note that if installation costs are not too important, the adjustment process should be quick so that the return to capital in this country should not exceed the world interest rate by a large amount for a long period of time. Some elements may slow down the adjustment process without altering the basic properties of the model: in particular, productive externalities if they are not strong enough to generate constant returns to capital.[3]

To summarize, destructions are followed by a catch-up process during which the economy invests more and grows faster until the previous level of the capital stock is reached.

The Ramsey model is the most traditional, and we use it in the next section as the starting point of the discussion. This sort of model typically predicts large capital inflows due to the very high investment rate that follows massive destructions (see Blanchard 1983).[4]

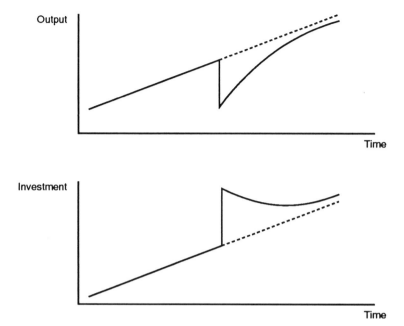

Figure 4.3
The Ramsey model

3.2   The Constant Returns Model

The implications of endogenous growth models are in general quite different from those of neoclassical models. Most of these models rely on a form
of constant returns to capital at the aggregate level. (A pioneering contribution is Uzawa 1965.) The simplest way of getting this is to assume an
externality such that the *private* production function has the form:

$$Y = BK^a L^{1-a}$$

while in fact $B = AK^b$, with $b = 1 - a$. Such a world is quite different from
the neoclassical world. First, because of constant returns, growth opportunities through capital accumulation are never exhausted: the economy
may grow endogenously in the long run, even in the absence of technical
progress. Second, the private marginal product of capital does not depend
on the capital stock: it is a constant equal to aA. These features have strong
implications for the response of an economy to a destruction (this is illustrated in figure 4.4). Because the marginal product of capital does not rise

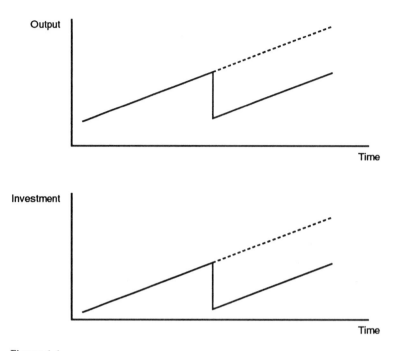

Figure 4.4

after a destruction, there is no incentive for a higher investment, and therefore there is no capital flow from the rest of the world. From the point of view of private agents, total factor productivity *drops* by a percent amount proportional to the drop in the capital stock. The economy proceeds at the same growth rate and the upfront loss from destruction is never made up. In the end, the economy is permanently poorer than if the destruction had not happened. This model will hereafter be referred to as the *constant returns model*.

3.3   The King-Robson Model

King and Robson (1989) proposed an endogenous growth model with multiple growth paths. The main feature of their model is an externality in *investment* instead of the capital stock as in the previous model. This type of externality may lead to multiple growth paths because there is a positive mutual interaction between investment and the return to capital. Furthermore—and this is of great interest to us—an initial destruction of the capital stock may well shift the economy toward a *more favorable* growth

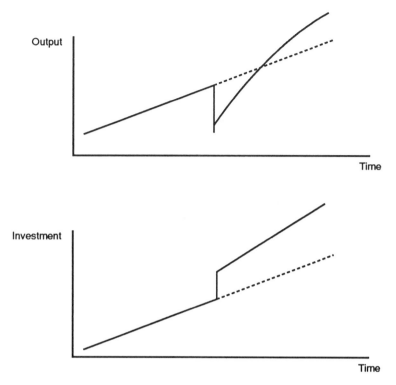

Figure 4.5
The King-Robson model

path: the initial drop in the capital stock generates a rise in the return to
capital, thus inducing investment to rise. But in their model, contrary to the
Ramsey model, this process is not just an adjustment back to the previous
growth path. Because of the externality, the high rate of investment prevents the return to capital from going down, so that the investment rate
does not eventually decline: the economy finds itself on a higher growth
path instead of reverting to the previous one.

The dynamics of reconstruction are thus indicated in figure 4.5: the
economy *overshoots* the previous path. Investment and the return to capital
are permanently higher than before the destruction occurred. The economy
first behaves similarly to the Ramsey economy, but instead of catching-up,
it eventually overtakes its previous growth path. This, King and Robson
argue, may explain the economic miracles experienced by Continental
countries after World War II, while countries like the United States and the

United Kingdom, which suffered less from damages during the war, had a period of relative stagnation.

4   Why Was Investment Low?

In this section, we look at the behavior of investment during the postwar period and try to compare it with the predictions of the theories we just mentioned.

Table 4.5 depicts the behavior of the investment/output ratio from 1946 to 1959. A striking feature is that contrary to what the standard neoclassical model would tend to predict, investment was relatively low. Although

Table 4.5
Investment rate, % of GDP

	(1)	(2)	(3)	(4)
1924			16.7	
1930			20.8	
1938			13.4	
1946	11.0	15.3		13.4
1947	12.7	17.1		14.4
1948	15.4	20.2		14.3
1949	15.7	18.8	19.7	14.5
1950	15.4			14.0
1951	18.4			14.0
1952	18.2		17.8	12.6
1953	16.9			11.9
1954	18.1		18.5	12.5
1955	19.5			13.4
1956	21.2			14.5
1957	22.2			15.0
1958	21.7			15.3
1959	20.4			13.8
1957–60			21.2	
1963			22.7	15.6
1966			24.1	15.8
1969			25.0	16.6

1. Source: Bournay and Laroque (1979)
2. Source: Gavanier
3. Source: Dubois, Carr, Malinvaud (1972)
4. Source: Laroque et al. (1989), excludes public investment

the investment rate was substantially higher in 1949 than in 1938 (a very recessionary year), it never exceeded the values of the late 1920s until 1956 and was below the values of the sixties. Furthermore, it does not exhibit the progressive decline from high initial levels that the standard Ramsey model tends to predict. In fact, the opposite occurred: the investment rate started from a very low level in 1946 and progressively rose to become larger than 20 percent only in 1956. The rise in investment went on into the sixties to reach 25 percent in 1969. Hence, the "investment miracle" is much more a story of the late 1950s and the 1960s than the reconstruction period.[5]

What are the factors that may explain this discrepancy between observed behavior and what standard theory predicts? One can think of four hypotheses:

Hypothesis 1   The open economy assumption of the Ramsey model is not valid. The closed economy assumption is a better description of the French economy during this period. In such a case, investment must be equal to saving, which had to be low and could recover only progressively: income was so close to the subsistence level that the savings rate could only be very low.[6]

Hypothesis 2   The decreasing returns to capital assumption is not valid. In fact, positive externalities imply constant returns to capital at the aggregate level. Therefore, the constant returns model is more appropriate. Hence a destruction of the capital stock implies neither an increase in the return to capital, nor in investment. The subsequent rise in investment was due to other factors: technical progress, openness, etc.

Hypothesis 3   Political and social instability was prevalent during the period; there was considerable uncertainty on whether property rights on capital were going to be enforced. This drove a wedge between the *ex ante* return to capital and its *ex post*, observed value. As a result investment was low and recovered only progressively as uncertainty disappeared.

Hypothesis 4   Financial markets were not functioning well. This drove a wedge between the return to financial investment and the return to physical capital. As a result the supply of funds to the French financial system was low, thus constraining investment to be too low.

Of course, these four hypotheses are not mutually exclusive and may more or less contribute to the observed behavior of investment. In order to assess the relative importance of each factor, it is necessary to document each hypothesis more closely.

Hypothesis 1: Lack of Openness
The fact that France's openness was relatively limited during this period should not be denied: exchange controls prevailed, imports were severely restricted, the market for foreign exchange was severely regulated and segmented.[7]

The question is, how binding was this constraint? Typically, exchange controls are aimed at limiting capital *outflows*, not inflows. But the model predicts a large capital *inflow*. Therefore, one may doubt whether exchange controls impeded investment.

More specifically, the rules specified that *new* foreign investment, along with the profits and capital gains it generated, was completely convertible (see, for example, De Lattre 1963). However, *old* foreign assets could not be repatriated but had to be either reinvested or spent (tourism) in France. Furthermore, foreign loans to French firms were severely restricted. Short-term credit from abroad was essentially prohibited, although available. Long-term credit mainly consisted of bonds issued by public enterprises on foreign capital markets.

These rules may have a negative impact on investment for two reasons. First, the distinction between old and new capital is dynamically inconsistent. That is to say, there may be a strong suspicion that such a measure may be repeated; the mere fact of implementing it signals that the French government is of the type likely to do so, and therefore undermines its credibility.[8] Although this is a side effect of capital controls, it is logically connected to hypothesis 3 (expropriation of capital) rather than hypothesis 1 (quantitative restrictions on capital flows). This channel is certainly relevant since the government effectively reneged on its commitments during the 1951–1952 balance of payments crisis.

Second, the potential return on a loan to a French firm may be greater than the return to direct foreign investment, because domestic firms are endowed with all the intangible capital (knowledge about interior markets, etc.) necessary to undertake production and distribution. Restricting loans may thus have a disruptive effect on investment even though foreign investment is still allowed.

These two factors certainly played a role, but if one assumes, as the neoclassical model implies, a large increase in the return to capital, it is hard to believe that they explain most of the low level of investment.

We conclude that exchange controls left enough room for foreign capital to come in, so that their effect explains the low level of investment only to a partial extent.

Hypothesis 2: Production Externalities
The main thrust of hypothesis 2 is that a major destruction of the capital stock does not imply a rise in the marginal product of capital. In order to assess the validity of this hypothesis, we compute a rough estimate of the (gross) return to capital by dividing capital income by an estimate of the capital stock. This was done for France using national accounts data from Bournay and Laroque (1979) and for the United States, using Denison's (1974) data. This yields the following result: the estimated return to capital was 25 percent in 1949 and 15 percent in 1959. By contrast, we obtain an estimate of only 9 percent for the United States, and the figure is the same in both years. While this very simple method can certainly be criticized on several grounds, the results are striking enough to make us confident. The return to capital was much higher in France than in the United States in both 1949 and 1959. While it did not move in the United States, it declined in France, suggesting that decreasing returns were important. The gap suggests that a much higher capital flow should have been observed. In particular, the current account should have been in deficit during the whole period. All this did not happen, but not because there was no differential in the return to capital.[9]

Another way to eliminate this explanation is to estimate a simple investment equation in which investment is positively affected by productivity. Consider for example the simplest Jorgenson-type investment equation:

$$I_t = \lambda(K_t^* - K_t) \tag{1}$$

Where K_t^* is the desired capital stock, that is, with a Cobb-Douglas production function:

$$K_t^* = (\alpha A_t/\theta)^{1/(1-\alpha)} L_t$$

Where α is the capital share, A_t total factor productivity, and θ the required rate of return. Using $\alpha = 0.25$, it is possible to calibrate a series for A_t using a Solow residual-type technique, and to estimate equation (1) by regressing I_t/L_t on $A_t^{1/0.75}$ and K_t/L_t. This has been done for the 1960–1989 period, getting plausible significant coefficients (-0.01 on the capital/labor ratio using quarterly data). The main point is that this equation overpredicts investment during the reconstruction period (see fig. 4.6). This not only gives us a benchmark for our claim that investment was too low but also controls for total factor productivity, whether truly exogenous or due to externalities.

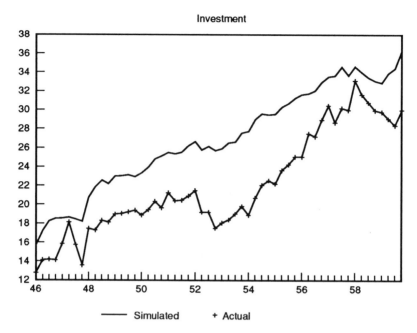

Figure 4.6
Simulated and actual values

This is not to say, however, that externalities played no role in the process; for example, Carré, Dubois, and Malinvaud (1972) estimate total factor productivity to be 10 percent lower in 1945 compared to 1938.[10] Clearly, knowledge is embodied in people and machines, and both suffered from the war.

It is thus difficult to believe that one of these two hypotheses explained the slow recovery of investment. This suggests that there must have been a wedge between the perceived financial return to investment and the observed real return.

Hypothesis 3: Uncertainty about Property Rights
Was there, therefore, uncertainty as to whether property rights would be defended? We argue that this was the case. The main contributing factor to this uncertainty was the Communist party. It played a key role in the Résistance, so that its participation in the government was unavoidable. It left the government in 1947 when the cold war burst. Not surprisingly, given that the party controlled the main trade union, this was followed by

Table 4.6
Major postwar strikes

Date	Sector	Comment
Nov. 1947	Mining	Following the end of communist participation in the government; violent incidents
Oct. 1948	Mining	Lasted four months
Feb—Mar. 1950	Various sectors	
Mar. 1951	Metallurgy Public service	
May 1953	Merchant navy	
Aug. 1953	Public services, Transportation	
Aug. 1955	Shipbuilding	
Oct. 1957	Various sectors	

Table 4.7
Votes for the Communist party

Election year	Votes (%)
1936	15.3
1945	26.0
1946 (June)	26.1
1946 (Nov.)	28.6
1951	25.6
1956	25.7
1958	18.9

Source: Ellenstein (1976).

numerous strikes, particularly in public enterprises: as table 4.6 indicates, large waves of strikes were customary until 1953.

The political support of the Communist party was considerable in France during this period, as table 4.7 indicates. The prospects for a communist government were thus quite real. The political support of the Communist party during the sixties was around 20 percent, significantly lower but still high; more importantly, there was much more consensus on the other side than during the fifties.

Another contributing factor, related to the previous one, was the numerous nationalizations that the government undertook in 1945—46: the largest industrial firms and almost the whole banking sector were nationalized. These nationalizations were due to several factors: retaliation for collaboration with the Vichy government, concessions to the Communist party, and the Colbertian belief, expressed in the Monnet plan, that the government was more competent to manage the huge task of economic reconstruction.

Other factors can be included in this category; in particular, "exceptional" discretionary taxes were commonplace until 1948, thus possibly creating the fear of a capital levy. In this respect, American aid might also have indirectly favored private investment by alleviating the budget deficit.

Clearly none of these circumstances were likely to encourage private investment. Although this seems obvious, it is not often recognized in the historical literature.

A natural way to corroborate this hypothesis is to look at the stock market. Although rates of return on stocks are difficult to interpret, in particular because a large share of profits was reinvested rather than distributed, there is some evidence that the rate of return was abnormally high, and securities values depressed, for some years after 1947. As table 4.8 shows, rates of return started rising steadily after the ousting of the Communists from the government; they started declining again, at a rather slow pace, after 1954. As an example, Moreau-Néret (1957) reports that the 3 percent perpetuity was selling 40 percent below face value in 1949, whereas it had been above par in 1945.

Hypothesis 4: Inefficiencies of Financial Markets
Various pieces of evidence corroborate the hypothesis of ill-functioning financial markets. Some of them are linked to the previous hypothesis

Table 4.8
Rates of return on bonds (%)

1945	2.37
1946	4.07
1947	5.17
1948	6.47
1949	7.50
1950	6.64
1951	6.66
1952	6.14
1953	6.09
1954	5.91
1955	5.34
1956	5.39

Source: Moreau-Néret (1957).

because they contributed to the belief that property rights on capital were not going to be fully enforced: for example, when exchange controls were established right after World War II, holders of treasury bonds were no longer anonymous. Some institutions inherited from the Vichy government had similar effects: for example the C.C.D.V.T (Caisse Centrale de Dépôts et de Virements de Titres), created in 1941 on the Austro-German model of the Kassenvereins, a compulsory "clearinghouse" where securities had to be deposited, was widely regarded as a potential tool of expropriation. It was suppressed only in 1949.

More generally, budgetary problems were such that there was a constant incentive for the government to interfere with the functioning of financial markets in order to finance its deficit at a preferential cost. Through the nationalization of the main deposit banks and the creation of the Conseil National du Crédit and the Caisse des Dépôts et Consignations, the state controlled the bulk of the allocation of saving. In fact, as late as 1956, 70 percent of saving was directed toward the public sector. By contrast, this figure oscillated between 25 and 40 percent in the sixties, which was also, interestingly, the most prosperous period for the French economy.

Publicly controlled financial institutions, in connection with the regulatory environment, contributed to divert savings away from private investment toward financing the public deficit. For example, public deposit banks had to hold a minimum share of their assets in the form of treasury bills. This was also true for pension funds and insurance companies. Issuing private bonds was subject to an agreement from the administration. Short-term bonds could only be issued by public institutions and there was no secondary market for them. Taxation was more favorable for holders of public bonds, and so forth.

While this system certainly created a lot of inefficiencies, it should not be forgotten that a great share of reconstruction expenditures was initiated and/or financed by public institutions, which partly justifies the large share of savings directed toward the public sector. It is difficult to evaluate how good a job these institutions were doing in targeting the most efficient investments. The presumption is that it may have biased investment toward large-scale, visible projects; for example, in 1949 the production of energy was 32 percent above its 1929 level, while production of other industrial goods was still 11 percent below its 1929 level. One may wonder where all this energy has gone, or why 1949 techniques were consuming so much of it compared to 1929![11]

Table 4.9
Issues of securities on the French financial market

	% of GDP
1913	9.2
1924	7.5
1929	6.9
1930	9.6
1938	3.2
1949	2.4
1954	2.8
1959	3.6
1964	3.7

Source: Carré, Dubois, and Malinvaud (1972).

Another piece of evidence can be obtained by looking at the stock market. As table 4.9 (borrowed from Carré, Dubois, and Malinvaud) indicates, the stock market was much less developed during the reconstruction period than during the interwar and pre-World War I periods. This is obviously related to the previous argument: all the savings absorbed by the newly created public credit institutions were no longer available to the financial market. However, this might have affected its efficiency: in a thinner financial market, the law of large numbers does not operate so well, so that its performance in terms of diversification is not as good. (This argument was first developed by Pagano (1985).[12] In fact, some firms may be discouraged from participating in the stock market, thus creating a "thin market" externality such that the market may be stuck at a low, inefficient equilibrium. Furthermore, given the distortions to which they were subjected (see the previous paragraph), public institutions were not a perfect substitute for the stock market as a source of funds.

As a result, self-financing was a major source of funding for most firms. It was no less than 64 percent during the reconstruction period, being above 70 percent during most of the period, and reaching a peak of 88 percent in 1953. By comparison, it never exceeded 70 percent in the sixties, oscillating between 58 and 69 percent. It is thus reasonable to believe that liquidity constraints were a serious limit to investment.

To conclude this section, how do we assess the relative contributions of these factors to the relatively low level of investment? Externalities seem to have been the less important factor, whereas exchange controls may have worked essentially because they created doubts about the possibility

Table 4.10
Government and housing investment (% of GDP)

	(1)	(2)	(3)
1946	1.6		
1947	2.1		
1948	1.6		
1949	1.9	1.7	2.7
1950		1.6	2.7
1951		2.0	4.1
1952		2.0	4.1
1953		2.1	4.6
1954		2.3	4.9
1955		2.2	4.7

1. Government investment computed using budget data
2. Government investment
3. Housing investment
Source: INSEE (1959).

of repatriating profits in the future. On the other hand, the two other factors seem to have been strong enough to significantly depress investment.

How does this highlight the validity of the three basic models we discussed in the previous section? First, it seems that productive externalities are not strong enough to generate the type of effects one gets in the constant returns model: the physical return to capital was very high as suggested by the Ramsey model, and went down as the recovery proceeded. Second, the French postwar experience suggests that the short-run environment plays a more important role in capital accumulation than is usually assumed in growth models: these factors impeded the investment boom predicted by the Ramsey model to occur, thus considerably slowing the reconstruction process. The same can be said about the regulatory environment and other institutional factors that contributed to drive a wedge between the physical and perceived return to capital.

The four factors we emphasized—lack of access to foreign financing, productive externalities, fear of expropriation, and inefficient financial markets—are likely to affect private investment more than public investment. Therefore, it is natural to assume that public investment evolved more in accordance with the predictions of the Ramsey model during this period, that is, one should observe a progressive decline from initial high levels. Various factors should reinforce this pattern: first, public capital was destroyed more than private capital, second, the Monnet Plan (1947–52) supposedly boosted public investment.

However, as we see in table 4.10, public investment evolved very much like private investment: it progressively rose during the period, starting from relatively low levels. The highest levels of the period are reached *after* the Monnet plan. This either casts doubt over the efficiency of the government in managing the reconstruction tasks or suggests that the financial difficulties of the early years prevented a higher level of public investment.

5 Why Was Growth High After All?

Given the relatively dim performance of investment, one may wonder how the French economy managed to achieve the high growth rates we see in table 4.1. This must be, of course, because total factor productivity growth was high, which is what Carré, Dubois, and Malinvaud find in their book. The question is, why? The King and Robson view—that is, an externality coming from the high rate of investment—does not seem to be the right explanation, since, as we argued above, investment was not particularly impressive during this period. Another popular explanation, namely that increased openness favored productivity growth, should be taken with caution. As table 1 shows, there is no trend toward more openness during this period: the import/GDP ratio is surprisingly stable from 1945 until 1959, as is the export/GDP ratio after the first years of large trade deficits. Rather, what happened was a change in the structure of trade: intra-European trade progressively replaced trans-Atlantic trade.

Therefore, what are the main factors behind this good performance of total factor productivity growth?

First, the mere restarting of economic activity played an important role in these high growth rates. Clearly, the 50 percent drop in output due to the war is much larger than what the observed drop in the capital stock (around 25 percent) suggests. This explains large growth rates in the first years of the war, say until 1947, but not after.

Second, migrations from agriculture to industry proceeded at a much higher pace during this period than before the war: between 1949 and 1954, a five-year period, the share of the labor force employed in the agricultural sector dropped by 3 percent from 29 percent to 26 percent. By contrast, it only dropped by 5 percent in the sixteen-year period from 1913 to 1929. Carré, Dubois, and Malinvaud (1972) estimate that these migrations contributed to 0.5 percent a year of total factor productivity growth. If productive externalities are important, the contribution should be larger than that. These migrations accelerated even further in the late fifties and in the sixties, so that in 1968 only 14.6 percent of the labor force remained in agriculture. It should be stressed that the early postwar figures are quite high compared to countries like Germany and Britain: there is a sense that France started its industrial revolution only after 1945.[13] Clearly, wars, by breaking all sorts of ties, contribute to these migrations. However, given that France had practically been at war on a permanent basis since the Revolution, this hardly explains anything.

Third, vintage effects must have played an important role: the capital stock was already outdated in 1938, and the war did not improve this situation. The magnitude of this effect is hard to quantify.[14]

Fourth, the government, in spite of the disruptive effects we discussed above, may well have played a positive role through two factors: first, by providing the economy with modern infrastructure: it is now recognized that public capital is an input in the aggregate production function and that public investment plays an important role in the growth process (see Barro 1990). Second, by coordinating the agents on a "good equilibrium" where resources are located in high-productivity, increasing returns sectors rather than traditional and agricultural sectors (see Murphy, Shleifer, and Vishny 1989). This "big push" may well have been the most significant contribution of French planning to the late industrialization of the economy.

6   Conclusion

The performance of the French economy in this period was relatively poor, both compared to the sixties and compared to what one should expect from standard economic theory. If a miracle is to be celebrated, it is the long overdue industrialization of a rural country. Whether public policy had an impact on this industrialization remains a matter of speculation. The rest of the picture is a mix of financial instability, financial repression, repeated balance of payments crises, social conflicts, external conflicts, mediocre investment, and high inflation.[15]

Our analysis casts light on a number of myths: there was far less of an investment boom than is usually believed, and it does not seem that the Marshall Plan had a tremendous impact on either imports or investment. The "general rise in world trade" does not seem to have affected the French economy: due to the repeated trade restrictions that were established following the balance of payments crises, there was no trend toward more openness during this period.[16] And whether the celebrated plan had tangible positive effects remains to be established.

It is difficult to evaluate the extent to which the performance could have been better. It seems pointless, for example, to claim that social conflicts could have been avoided if a corporatist system of social consensus had been established: nothing warrants that this would have been possible in a country far more heterogenous than Sweden or Austria.

In this respect, several questions have been brought up: one may wonder, for example, whether the Marshall aid might have been used in a more productive way. As we argued above, a more favorable exchange rate should have been aimed at if the aid was to finance capital goods imports rather than financial recovery. However, given the impediments to private investment, the efficiency of foreign aid in fostering reconstruction may well be much lower than its efficiency in inducing financial stabilization. This suggests that to be productive, this policy should have been accompanied by a complete reform of the financial sector. Such a reform was to be initiated only in the eighties.

Another very important question is whether the state's involvement in the economy was excessive or not. We repeatedly pointed out the distortions it created. On the other hand, we suggested that it might have played a positive role in coordinating the country's industrialization and providing key infrastructure to the economy. Therefore, it is difficult to know if another strategy would have been more successful. What is clear is that the impressive achievements of French planning are largely a myth, at least during this period, and that Germany, which opted for a market-oriented strategy, did better.

Other factors are beyond the scope of this chapter but played a great role. Colonial wars were probably a luxury that France could not afford, as was the Franc zone: the persistent balance of payments and trade deficits of the Franc zone countries vis-à-vis France led to money creation and diverted resources that could have been used for reconstruction at home. More generally, there was a discrepancy between an ideal of grandeur (strong currency, military power, colonial empire), and the dim reality of a weakened country.

Last, the French reconstruction experience suggests that recently fashionable endogenous growth models should not be taken literally, at least in their simplest form based on constant returns to capital. Externalities were far from strong enough to impede a catching-up process that, although slowed by the impediments to investment that we discussed, was nevertheless real: the physical return to capital was both high and declining during the period.

However, the war period was short enough not to affect "the culture of capitalism": entrepreneurial behavior, the drive for innovation, and all the institutional infrastructure that make a market economy work were still here after the war. While it is true that they developed along with economic activity (the sort of feedback endogenous growth models usually emphasize), it is not true that a destruction of the capital stock and a temporary disruption of economic activity destroy this intangible capital to a comparable extent.

Therefore, it is dubious whether this optimistic conclusion can be extrapolated to the more recent reconstruction problem faced by Eastern European countries: by its nature, and because it lasted much longer, communism has destroyed many more components of a market economy than German occupation. In this case, the dim implications of endogenous growth models may well be relevant.

Notes

This paper was prepared for the Center for Economic Performance conference on reconstruction, Hamburg, September 6–7, 1991. I am grateful to Olivier Blanchard, François Bourguignon, Guy Laroque, Jacques Mélitz, Carlos Winograd, and Charles Wyplosz for helpful comments and suggestions.

1. This model has the unpalatable feature that real balances are higher in the high-inflation equilibrium than in the low-inflation equilibrium. This is because in this model nothing pins down real rates since there are no alternative assets. This feature would disappear if one introduced, for example, foreign bonds or stocks. While this is a serious limitation to the applicability of the model to other countries, we believe it is not too bad an assumption in the case of France. Given the magnitude of exchange controls and the prominent role of the state in the financial sphere, savers had indeed little access to alternative assets. And nominal rates were indeed higher after the stabilization occurred than before. The evidence on real balances is less clear-cut, since there seems to have been a shift in money demand after the stabilization, which suggests that inflation itself, or inflation uncertainty, may enter the money demand function as an autonomous variable.

2. This point should be qualified on two grounds: first, regression analysis shows a positive residual in the consumption function in the second quarter of 1947, when Marshall made his speech. This is however not very robust to specification changes. Second, there was a general belief before the 1948 devaluation that the franc was overvalued; expected depreciation may have fueled aggregate demand, and hence inflation, through the public's attempts to get rid of French assets. This effect may well outweigh a possible announcement effect of the Marshall speech.

3. A popular view is now the "0.8 option": productive externalities are strong enough to generate decreasing, but near-constant returns to (all forms of) capital (see Mankiw, Romer and Weil (1990)). This implies convergence at a relatively slow rate (around 2 percent a year, see Barro and Sala-i-Martin (1990)).

4. It should be noted that the labor input did not drop due to human losses during the war. Several factors tended to compensate these losses: first, the high unem-

ployment rates of the great depression had ended; second, work duration had increased compared to the prewar period; third, women's rate of participation had risen; and fourth, an average of 400,000 German "war prisoners" added to the available pool of workers (this figure reached a peak of 700,000 at the end of 1945 and was still above 300,000 at the end of 1947). Therefore, it is reasonable to expect a rise in the physical return to capital.

5. Considerable uncertainty is associated with the measurement of investment before 1949, and this is reflected in the wide divergences across sources that we observe. Some sources (like Bournay and Laroque (1980), which we use in table 4.5), give a very low level of investment until 1948, and therefore imply a jump in the investment rate when the Marshall Plan is introduced. Others, like Gavanier (1953), give a high investment rate of around 20 percent, implying no effect of the Marshall Plan but a pattern more in line with the Ramsey model.

6. The fact that capital movements across countries are not as large as economic theory would predict is well documented (see Feldstein and Horioka (1980), for example). But this may well be due to the fact that in normal times rates of return do not differ very much across countries.

7. France had a complex system of multiple exchange rates, and several "free" markets with floating rates existed. The supply of funds to these markets was regulated according to the origin of these funds; for example, exporters could sell a certain share of their foreign exchange on the free market.

8. This is by now a standard discussion in economics; see Kydland and Prescott (1977), Barro and Gordon (1983).

9. It should be noted that these figures tend to understate the return to capital in France. It is because the estimate of the capital stock for 1945 was obtained using a conservative estimate of war damages, while subsequent real investment was cumulated using a (rather low) 4 percent depreciation rate.

10. Caballero and Lyons (1990) provide evidence on external increasing returns in Europe.

11. To be more complete, one should also say that both tails of the size distribution of firms benefited from these funds: as Mélitz (1991) reports, small trade and agriculture, as well as large public firms were helped by the Caisse des Dépôts et Consignations.

12. Other mechanisms may intervene: for example, the lack of an appropriate financial infrastructure may have an adverse impact on technological choice and may keep the economy in a low equilibrium where the returns to financial development are perceived to be low; see Saint-Paul (1992).

13. According to Deane and Cole (1962), the share of the workforce employed in agriculture in England was 11 percent in 1891—less than for France in 1968!

14. Carré, Dubois, and Malinvaud (1972) estimate the contribution of these effects to be 0.3 percent a year. Surprisingly, it is lower in 1951–1957 than in following periods.

15. This picture does not disappear in a cross-country exercise. For example, Wolf (1992, table 10) reports the growth rates of industrial production for fourteen countries between 1938 and 1955. France is ranked twelfth, with Belgium a very close thirteenth and Britain last. Note that Finland and Spain, which did not benefit from the Marshall Plan, did better.

16. Although Kindleberger's (1972) data give a slightly more optimistic picture, they imply that France was one of the countries with the lowest growth in the export/GDP ratio.

References

Barro, R. (1990) "Government Spending in a Simple Model of Endogenous Growth," *Journal of Political Economy*, XCVIII, S103–S125.

Barro, R. and D. Gordon (1983) "A Positive Theory of Monetary Policy in a Natural Rate Model," *Journal of Political Economy* 91, 4, 589–610.

Barro, R. and X. Sala-i-Martin (1990) "Economic Growth and Convergence across the U.S." NBER Working Paper.

Blanchard, O. (1981) "Output, the stock market, and interest rates," *American Economic Review*, 71, 1, 132–143.

Blanchard, O. (1983) "Debt and the Current Account Deficit in Brazil," in Aspe, P. et al, eds. *Financial Policies and the World Capital Market: The Problem of Latin American Countries*, U. of Chicago Press.

Blanchard, O. and S. Fischer, *Lecture Notes on Macroeconomics*, MIT Press, 1989.

Bruno, M., G. Di Tella, R. Dornbusch and S. Fischer, eds. (1988) *Inflation Stabilization*, MIT Press.

Bournay, J., and G. Laroque, *Comptes trimestriels 1949–1959*, les collections de l'INSEE, C 70, March 1979.

Caballero, R. and R. Lyons, (1990) "Internal vs. External economies in European Industry," *European Economic Review*, 34, 4, 805–826.

Carré, J. J., P. Dubois, and E. Malinvaud, *La croissance Française, un essai d'analyse économique causale de l'après-guerre*. Editions du Seuil, 1972.

Deane, P. and W. A. Cole (1962) *British Economic Growth 1688–1959*, Cambridge U. Press.

De Lattre, A. *Les Finances Extérieures de La France*, Presses Universitaires de France, 1970.

De Lattre, A. *Politique Economique de la France depuis 1946*, Institut d'études Politiques de Paris, 1963.

Denison, E. (1974) *Accounting for US Economic Growth*, Brookings, Washington.

Feldstein, M. and C. Horioka (1980) "Domestic savings and International Capital Flows," *Economic Journal*, 90, 314–329.

Ellenstein, J. (1976) *Le Parti Communiste*, Grasset, Paris.

Gavanier (1953) "Le Revenu National de la France: Production et Disponibilités Nationales en 1938 et de 1946 à 1949," *Statistiques et Etudes Financières*, 20.

INSEE (1949) *Mouvement Economique de 1938 à 1948.*

INSEE (1959) *Mouvement économique en France de 1944 à 1957.*

Kindleberger, C. (1972) *Europe Post-war Growth*, Harvard U. Press.

King, M., and M. Robson (1989) "Endogenous growth and the role of history," NBER WP #3151.

Kydland, F. and E. Prescott (1977) "Rules rather than Discretion, the Inconsistency of Optimal Plans," *Journal of Political Economy*, 85, 3, 473–492.

Laroque, G. (1981) "Conjoncture économique de l'immédiat après-guerre," *Economie et Statistique 129*, January.

Laroque, G., P. Ralle, B. Salanié, and J. Toujas-Bernate (1990) "Description d'une base de données trimestrielles longues", INSEE, mimeo.

Lucas, R. E. (1988) "On the mechanics of economic development," *Journal of Monetary Economics.*

Mankiw, N. G., D. Romer, and D. Weil (1991) "A contribution to the Empirics of Economic Growth," mimeo, Harvard.

Mélitz, J. (1991) "Monetary Policy in France," CEPR discussion paper, #509.

Moreau-Néret (1957) *Les Valeurs Françaises*, Sirey, Paris.

Murphy, K., A. Shleifer, and R. Vishny (1989) "Industrialisation and the Big Push," *Journal of Political Economy* 97, 5, 1003–1026.

Pagano, M. (1985) *Market Size and Volatility in Stock Exchanges*, M.I.T Ph.D. Thesis.

Parodi, M., *L'économie et la société Française de 1945 à 1970*, Armand Colin, 1971.

Romer, P. (1990) "Endogenous Technological Change," *Journal of Political Economy* 98, S71–S102.

Saint-Paul, G. (1992) "Technological choice, financial markets and economic development," *European Economic Review* 36, 763–781.

Uzawa, H. (1965) "Optimal Technical Change in an Aggregative Model of Economic Growth," *International Economic Review* 6, 18–31.

Wolf, H. (1992) "The Lucky Miracle: Germany 1945–51," chapter 2 this volume.

5

Reconstruction and the U.K. Postwar Welfare State: False Start and New Beginning

Patrick Minford

The Second World War was fought by Britain under what was largely a command economy. Hayek (1988) has commented that socialism has its attraction because it reminds us of our tribal roots, and it is essentially the organizational mode of the tribe. Britain during the war was organized on tribal lines. The chiefs in Whitehall allocated resources to the war machine and then to private consumption with a virtually universal rationing system; what was not rationed was taxed heavily by the inflation tax, which fell on the large government bond issue (which eventually reached 300 percent of GDP) as well as on money. Production was directed to "the patriotic war effort," with unions induced to cooperate by a combination of threats (of action for treasonable behavior) and promises (of postwar rewards, not clearly specified, though the government coalition included Labour, whose aims were clear). Finally, mass democratic mobilization was underwritten by a similar implicit promise: that after the war, the masses would be looked after.

It is perhaps no wonder that after the war, with no external force able to override these institutions or implicit commitments (as in Japan, for example), the British establishment set about running a peacetime economy along socialist lines. A Labour government was voted in, but only because it was in tune with the popular and intellectual mood of the times. The Civil Service and the rest of the establishment shared the general view that they could do as good a job of running the peacetime economy as they felt they had of the war machine. Having "won for freedom," they also shared the general view that men and women of goodwill must build the good life that so many lives had been sacrificed to make possible.

It was in such an atmosphere that many intellectuals felt that "Joe" Stalin was rather a good chap, and some of them—their antecedents having fought in the Spanish Civil War on the communist side—sold him security secrets, most often out of idealism.

For example, Priestley in "Letter to a Returning Serviceman" (1945) wrote: "Whatever their faults, the Bolsheviks had put their hand to the great task and were trying to lift the load of want, ignorance, fear and misery from their dumb millions, while the Americans—as they fully admit now—were living in a fool's paradise of money-for-nothing and martinis, and we were shuffling and shambling along, listening to our Tory politicians talking their old twaddle."

In a similar vein, A. J. P. Taylor, in a broadcast after the 1945 election, announced that "nobody in Europe believes in the American way of life—that is, in private enterprise; or rather, those who believe in it are a defeated party which seems to have no more future than the Jacobites in England after 1688" (quoted in Howarth 1985).

Nor was the Conservative party of the day immune from the atmosphere, though it did remain attached to a highly diluted and pragmatic market philosophy. Churchill and Rab Butler made no attempt to reverse the institutions of the welfare state put in place by the Atlee Labour government of 1945—51. They gradually eliminated rationing, but this was something that the Labour government had started and would have continued. They did bring down taxes. But in many other ways they were merely a less doctrinaire group of interventionists and so gave rise to the phrase "Butskellism," the composite interventionist economic philosophy of the two chancellors, real and shadow, Butler and Gaitskell.

From the viewpoint of what we know today about the efficient operation of modern economies, it is hard to understand the naive utopianism of this postwar era. This is why I have spent a few paragraphs attempting to conjure up the spirit of the age. Those who disbelieve me should read Tom Howarth's *Prospect and Reality* (Howarth 1985), a book that quotes amply from the thinkers of the day, themselves products of the Fabian movement and the Webbs.

The key theme of this chapter is that after the war Britain—out of intellectual error—took a wrong turn and that it needed three and a half decades of stumbling incompetence to induce it to make a new beginning in 1979. The reason that Britain's experience is of so much interest in Eastern Europe lies precisely in this curious history. They see close parallels between the decay induced by Britain's socialist experiment and that in their own economies, and they desire to understand how that can be reversed, as so much of it was by the governments of Margaret Thatcher.

Another theme of this chapter is that economic decay and success depends crucially on the institutions that create or eliminate incentives for the people to employ their native wit and energy. Sheer investment of money in such things as infrastructure and manufacturing capital are necessary but not sufficient conditions for success: it is useless building roads and subsidized factories for a lethargic people, but an energized people will induce the roads and factories they need through rising tax revenues and profitable industries.

The "new growth" literature stresses economies of scale, especially in the returns to human capital. But before new growth processes can get to work, there must be the institutions that permit the bright and innovative to obtain rewards. Without them government can cram as many of such people it likes into a given space and nothing much will happen—the example of Sweden, full of brilliant and well-trained people directed by an all-wise government, illustrates how little indeed can be achieved when taxation removes effective rewards.

In what follows we take a look, one by one, at the key institutional developments of the postwar era. In the spirit of institutional analysis rather than history, the historical details will be blurred, in a way that would not please a proper historian. My excuse must be that I am no historian and that I trust the rather different exercise I have in mind will be of interest.

After a short historical sketch, we proceed to analyze these developments under three main headings. Government spending is the first, and is the driving force of the second, taxation. Benefits could be considered under spending or under taxation; since they have both income and substitution effects, we will consider them under both. Finally, we will look at the paraphernalia of regulation and control, whether of labor and unions, credit and currency, housing, trade, or industry.

A Brief Historical Sketch of Postwar Recovery

Britain's financial position after the second world war it had fought this century was ruinous. Having entered WWI with net private overseas earnings (from property and other assets) equal to 9.4 percent of GDP, and WWII with them still equal to 3.9 percent, by 1945 they had dwindled to 1 percent and were dwarfed by the enormous (and largely unquantified) lend-lease debt to the United States. This was later written off except for $650 million of goods in the pipeline.

In current terms, the position was one of large deficit, both in the public accounts and the external. The public deficit, including the huge off-budget military program, was 27 percent of GDP. The balance of payments deficit on current account was 10 percent of GDP.

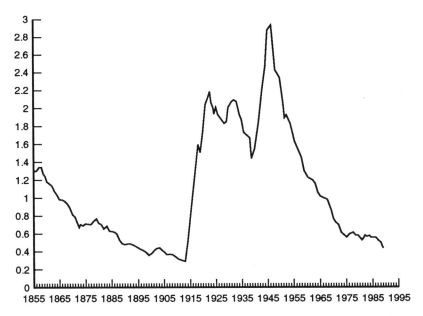

Figure 5.1
The U.K. debt-income ratio, 1855–1989
Source: *Public Debt Management: Theory and History*, ed., R. Dornbusch and M. Draghi,
Cambridge, 1990

To the Whitehall planners of the time this state of essential bankruptcy,
both internal and external, was the key problem to be dealt with. They had
little time and gave little thought to issues of incentives; meanwhile the
Labour government's plans to construct a welfare state must have been a
highly unwelcome distraction from the stabilization problem.

The economic history of 1945–1951 therefore proceeds on two parallel
tracks: the financial reconstruction together with the physical redeploy-
ment of resources away from military use, and the building of the welfare
state.

On the financial side, the internal debt (fig. 5.1) was partly dealt with by
a rapid return to budget surplus through military rundown. Emergency
military spending of 46 percent of GDP was rapidly eliminated—a record
peace dividend. The overhang of debt, an extraordinary 300 percent of
GDP, was brought down by inflation, none of it dramatic (the average rate
in the six postwar years was 5 percent) but sufficiently different from the
zero inflation at which prewar longterm debt was issued and the similar
terms on which war debt was compulsorily acquired, to cut its value by a
quarter by 1951.

More intractable in the planners' eyes was the external debt. The British government was expecting generous treatment from a grateful United States. In the event, Congress returned rapidly and unsentimentally to business as usual: lend-lease was cut off in 1945, though as we have seen the existing debt was also largely written off. A new loan was finally ratified by 1946 on strict conditions that the United Kingdom introduce full convertibility (which it did in mid-1947 but immediately revoked).

Cheated of large grants or interest-free loans, the planners could see no market-led way to curb the balance of payments deficit, much of it with the United States, as the only unravaged supplier. The sterling-dollar rate was not felt to be a factor: the prevailing view was one of elasticity pessimism and disillusion with interwar rate flexibility. Consequently devaluation was ruled out. In its absence, import controls were kept on rigorously and a "dollar gap" was proclaimed.

Other European countries were enlisted to reinforce this unfamiliar non-market concept on an impatient United States. The result, as is well known, was the Marshall Plan. Though small in relation to GDP or the size of the peace dividend, this aid was large in terms of foreign exchange and the gap. It therefore permitted Britain and other European countries to proceed with the dismantling of wartime controls, as desired by the Americans, without the excuse for delay provided by insuperable external liquidity problems. Ultimately, these led to a general European devaluation in 1949, of which Britain's at 30 percent was one of the largest. But arguably in the intellectual atmosphere of the time such a devaluation would not have come in time to avert severe dislocation, in the absence of Marshall Aid.

By 1951 the external deficit was much reduced and the onset of the Korean War, with renewed Allied cooperation, financial as well as military, pushed it into the background. With the war over, the deficit had essentially disappeared. The stage was therefore clear for the elimination of the control economy. As we shall see, this opportunity was grasped by the new Conservative government of 1951 but with an uncertain and tremulous hand.

The parallel creation of the welfare state was, considering this background of financial crisis, a remarkable achievement, whether one approves or disapproves of its objectives. Driven by the political forces of Nye Bevan and Ernest Bevin, the Transport and General Workers' boss, the program went ahead at full steam, despite the occasional protest from Dalton and Cripps at the treasury. By 1948 the welfare support system of pensions and other national insurance benefits (unemployment, sickness, disability, etc.) and the National Health System (after a determined campaign of opposition from the doctors—who in the 1980s have more determinedly opposed its internal market reforms) were all in place. The 1944 Education Act, under the wartime coalition, had already raised the school-leaving age to fifteen (to become sixteen as soon as resources permitted), with universally free provision and streaming from eleven. By 1951 the nationalization program had been completed.

Thus the pragmatic Clement Atlee had in six short years transformed a mostly private economy with a growing but spotty welfare system essentially based on the Liberal theorizing of Asquith and Lloyd George, into a mostly state-controlled economy with a private sector restricted to the less commanding heights of manufacturing and services and even there corraled by mighty unions and/or minimum wage and other regulations.

The incoming 1951 Conservative government, which won the 1951 election after pushing Atlee to a bare majority in the 1950 election, was to enjoy power for thirteen years. But the new generation of Tory leaders—Butler, Macmillan, Eden, indeed Churchill himself—was in economic matters uncommitted to free market ideas. True to time-honored Tory principles, they regarded it as more important to govern than to pursue ideology—that was for Liberals, Labour, or Whigs. Nevertheless, among them were true liberals, such as Enoch Powell and Peter Thorneycroft. They had no chance in the prevailing intellectual atmosphere of achieving the sort of market freedom they espoused. Had the Labour government's program collapsed in economic chaos, they might well have had; but Marshall Aid prevented that—like so much aid, it succeeded in propping up the government policies of the day. Labour had pulled it off and the Conservatives decided to go with the tide and keep the basic Labour inheritance, merely modifying it cautiously in a liberal direction.

From 1951 to the early sixties there was accordingly a discreet program of liberalization within the welfare/nationalized state ground rules set out by Labour. Rationing gradually went, import controls were eased and had effectively gone by 1960, taxes were cut (but not on the rich, and the burden of income tax on the average earner steadily rose), steel was denationalized with much controversy, and there was an attempt at decontrol of private rented housing. The mixture in the mixed economy moved only slightly in the direction of the private sector.

With price controls and rationing gone and external and internal stabilization completed, attention turned to the conduct of monetary policy. The orthodoxy of the times was of course fixed exchange rates under Bretton

Woods. Under Atlee the overvalued pound required stringent credit restriction to survive; this was achieved by direct credit controls and other forms of direct resource allocation—import controls, foreign exchange controls, and so forth. In the 1950s formal credit controls were dropped, foreign exchange convertibility introduced (but with continued stringent foreign exchange controls), and import controls abandoned. Domestic credit expansion (DCE) was limited by informal directives to the banks.

Monetary policy was in fact given a limited role, with fiscal policy and infrequent devaluation (if absolutely necessary) being seen as the principal instruments for controlling demand and the balance of payments. This subordinacy of monetary policy was given the academic imprimatur of the Radcliffe Committee in 1959; it and its principal author, Professor R. S. Sayers of the London School of Economics (LSE), argued that money could not be usefully defined because of the many assets that closely substituted in providing "money services" and that instead liquidity should be controlled in a discretionary way by interest rates and credit restrictions.

In practice this meant that from time to time a credit squeeze was implemented to help finance a current account deficit or as an emergency means of slowing demand when fiscal policy was not working fast enough. This can be seen as the rudiments of a DCE control system.

Unfortunately, such a hands-off approach to money creates problems when short-run monetary independence is as great as it was until the world capital market integration of the seventies. Excessive money supply growth, even with the exchange rate fixed, will drive up domestic prices—inflation in the fifties was higher than the OECD average (figure 5.2); and the correction from falling reserves will only gradually occur, as the current balance goes into deficit with reduced competitiveness and capital flows responding little if at all. Britain had at this time a large if declining monopolistic position in many manufactured markets, so that the response to higher prices was slow in coming.

Eventually the economy is forced either to reverse policies ("stop-go") in an attempt to force relative prices back down or to devalue, validating the previous price shift. The competitive boost of the enormous devaluation in 1949 (30 percent) was probably not eroded until the middle sixties. By 1967, when the cumulative price shift had pushed the current account into permanent deficit at normal employment levels, the case for another devaluation appeared overwhelming, given the difficulty of driving wages and prices down.

We now turn to the three themes of the postwar evolution—spending, taxation, and regulation.

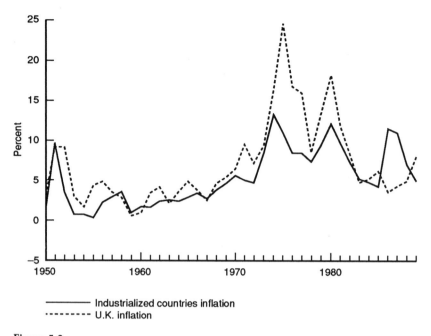

Figure 5.2
Inflation in the United Kingdom and industrialized countries
Source: International Financial Statistics, I.M.F. and the C.S.O

Government Spending

Labour inherited a machine for wartime control and government spending in 1945, just as the Conservatives did in 1918. In 1918 it was assumed that this should be dismantled. In 1945 Labour assumed that it should be built upon.

The three key areas to be built up were in health, education, and welfare benefits. In education, there was a general commitment by all parties to public provision, as already put in place by the 1944 Education Act: Labour at this stage gave no priority to radical change in the system, contenting itself with substantially increased spending.

Health and welfare were another matter. The National Health Service "nationalized" the doctors and hospitals, and provided their services free or at minimal charge to the populace.

A national network of benefits and pensions, to be paid for out of National Insurance, was also introduced. The loss of wages due to such "social" contingencies as illness, old age, and unemployment were now "socially insured" and refunded at least to some degree by the state.

Thus were proclaimed the three pillars of the Welfare State. An explosion in civil state spending resulted between 1945 and 1951. Total real civil government spending excluding debt interest increased in this period at 18 percent per year; as a percent of GDP it rose 8 percent. Of the overall increase in this spending 12 percent was accounted for by education, 4 percent by pensions, and 40 percent by health and other insurance benefits.

Between 1951 and 1960 the Conservatives, who regained power in 1951 and kept it for the next thirteen years, pursued a policy of containment but acceptance of the welfare state Labour had created.

Indeed in education they proved to be adept at spending, building up the grammar schools, grant-aided schools for the academically able children, while expanding the secondary moderns which were to cater for the rest. There was a commitment to provide further technical schools, which were to have a less academic syllabus, but these barely materialized.

The net result of Conservative continuation of Labour policies was that the growth of spending was held, at 1.9 percent, only slightly below the growth of GDP for the decade. But then in this period of recovery GDP was itself growing at a—for Britain—rapid 2.4 percent per annum.

Within this total, the growth in spending on health was held down, remarkably, to only 1.8 percent per annum, whereas education surged at 5.6 percent per annum and current grants, which were partly driven by demand and demography, grew only just less, at 5 percent per annum. The National Insurance benefits within this grew at 6.2 percent per annum, almost entirely accounted for by pensions and widows' benefits.

So Labour put in place an engine of welfare that the Conservatives unquestioningly fueled throughout the sixties. That they succeeded in holding health spending down as successfully as they did no doubt owes much to the ethos and old-fashioned administrative methods of the dedicated staff they inherited from the pre-NHS system. Later, when the NHS came to be reformed in the early seventies (by a misguided Conservative government), with a new administrative structure, much of this system was destroyed.

During the sixties there was little questioning of the new structure. Politicians assumed that this new framework was "what the people wanted" and even those on the right therefore took it to be their democratic duty to deliver this in as efficient a manner as possible. For example, Enoch Powell, who was minister of health in the early sixties, has stated as much publicly in respect of the NHS (speech to BIM/Civil Service annual conference, Cambridge, 1989, author's recollection).

Though there were the usual complaints, and in particular Labour grumbled that secondary moderns and the associated "eleven-plus" selection exam at eleven years old were divisive, the school system worked well in delivering good academic education for the able and in producing literacy elsewhere, while the NHS—in the undemanding spirit of the times—was perceived as doing an effective job. The people were pleased with the social insurance aspects too; in the aftermath of war, it seemed right to look after the old and sick, just as in war the wounded and disabled were cared for. There was negligible unemployment and so "dole scrounging" was not an issue.

Had the welfare state been able to freeze itself in that condition, with dedicated medical staff and schoolteachers and an undemanding population grateful for release from the rigors of war, this chapter would have a different tone and history a different course.

But inevitably this would change, though it was not until the sixties that this process began in a serious way; and even before this it had to be financed, naturally by raising marginal tax rates, and it was accompanied by a philosophy of widespread control. Together these inevitably ensured that the hopes of the war generation for the good life within a loving collective tribe would be frustrated.

Taxation and Its Interaction with Benefits

Prewar (central government) tax was 22 percent of GDP. By 1945 this had risen to 34 percent, falling back a little by 1950 to 29 percent. (Figures for total taxation including local government run in parallel and are to be found in figure 5.3 with corresponding figures for total government spending in figure 5.4.) There was only slight scope for tax-cutting in this period. Even though military spending fell from 53 percent of GDP to only 7 percent, a deficit of 29 percent of GDP had to be eliminated (at the least, given the huge debt burden; in fact there was a shift to surplus of 4 percent of GDP), and room made for the big rise in the civil program (by 8 percent of GDP). During the 1950s when the share of (central) government spending in GDP fell modestly (from 24 percent to 22 percent of GDP), the tax share also declined further to 24 percent; this was assisted by a run-off in the budget surplus, from 4 percent to a borrowing requirement of 2 percent of GDP, under the Keynesian policies of the time. A further contributing

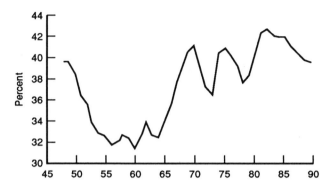

Figure 5.3
Tax receipts (as a percent of GDP)

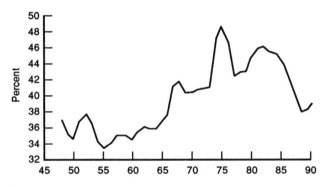

Figure 5.4
General government expenditure (as a percent of GDP)

factor was the fall in the debt interest burden by 0.6 percent of GDP. Nevertheless, up to the end of the sixties it cannot be said that—certainly by more recent standards—the marginal tax rates paid by the average citizen were particularly high, even if, as figures 5.5 and 5.6 show, the income tax and National Insurance burden on the average wage earner was steadily rising and marginal tax rates were significantly higher in 1960 than in 1938. One must look elsewhere for the principal incentive problems that beset the British economy.

Public debt had reached 300 percent of GDP by the end of the war. The Labour government felt it right to budget for a surplus to begin paying it off. Marshall aid generated further capital resources between 1948 and 1951, totaling £696 billion, about 5 percent of 1950 GDP. However the

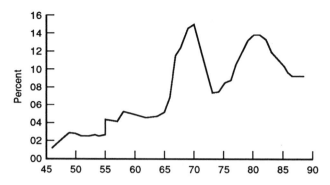

Figure 5.5
Employers' national insurance contributions (percent)

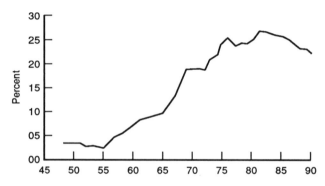

Figure 5.6
Average amount lost in taxes and NI for head of household and two children

lion's share of debt liquidation was performed by inflation that had written off nearly half of the postwar debt's face value by 1960. By then the debt-GDP ratio had fallen to 160 percent of GDP.

The effectiveness of the inflation tax had diminished substantially by then, since long-term interest rates had risen to 5 percent to give some compensation for expected inflation (actual inflation had averaged 4 percent over the 1950s).

Another way of putting this is that out of the enormous increase of the GDP available for civil use between 1945 and 1960, only a third was put into private consumption; although civil-use GDP nearly tripled, growing 7.1 percent per annum over the fifteen years as a whole, consumption grew only 2.4 percent per annum. Approximately 30 percent of the overall increase in civil GDP was devoted to public civil consumption and another 30 percent to general investment (public and private). A tenth of the increased GDP flow was devoted to paying off foreign debt. This compression of private use was achieved by the capital levy of the inflation tax and by reducing tax rates only slowly. The enormous peace dividend was largely appropriated by the state.

The burden of ordinary taxation was felt mainly in income tax (including the new National Insurance contributions that chipped in a regular 4 percent of GDP from their inception), whose share had risen from 45 percent of the total in 1938 to 56 percent by 1950 and was still 53 percent by 1960. The standard rate rose from 27.5 percent in 1938 to 45 percent in 1945–1950. By 1961 it had been cut back to 30 percent. However, the top rate on earned income, which had reached 97.5 percent in 1949, was still 80 percent in 1959 and 70 percent in 1961, after Selwyn Lloyd's supposedly reforming budget of that year.

Capital taxation also became confiscatory after the war. The top rate of estate duty rose from 34 percent in 1938 to 70 percent in 1949–50. The rates were kept at these levels throughout the 1950s and the yield of this and other capital taxes dropped from 2.3 percent in 1949 to around 1 percent by 1960. Unearned income was treated worse than earned, in a similarly confiscatory spirit, that did not change with the Conservatives, who maintained an unearned income surcharge of 19 percent after the Lloyd reforms.

Thus it was with higher earners and better-off savers that the culture of high marginal tax rates began in the postwar period. When one turns to the marginal tax rates produced by the tax/benefit interaction at the bottom end of the income scale, one finds that the seeds of today's poverty and unemployment traps were sown but had not grown much by 1960. The unemployment benefit was in principle generous at 70 percent of net wages for a lower quartile married wage earner with two children. But it was fiercely "work-tested" according to the Beveridge principles embodied in the law and there were few unemployed. In-work benefits (National Assistance) were only available on a selective basis to those able-bodied workers in need, as established by National Assistance boards. Later, work-testing was to fall into disuse and National Assistance became a means-tested right.

With the top rate of income tax and inheritance tax down to 40 percent today, it is hard to conjure up the nightmarish tax world for higher earners of the 1950s (in the 1960s it was to become still worse, as the peace dividend was not there to offset the new spending demands from the Labour program after 1964). The Beatles discovered they "would tax your feet," but economists—many of whom had been civil servants, few in any sort of business—made little fuss. Even such a robust and intelligent commentator as Ian Little dismissed incentive effects of high tax rates routinely in 1962, remarking that "the empirical evidence available strongly suggests that there is no significant connection between either marginal or average tax rates and the amount of effort on the part of wage earners and lower salaried workers. So far as higher-income earners are concerned, there is no quantitative evidence of any disincentive effect of marginal tax rates" (Worswick and Ady 1962, 282). In an earlier age when "evidence" was less available and economists trusted their instincts more, Little had written more nervously in 1950, after running through the potentially dangerous long-term consequences for effort, evasion, and emigration: "It can hardly be denied that a reduction in marginal tax rates might prove highly desirable" (Worswick and Ady 1952, 182). In econometrics, as in all else, a little knowledge is a dangerous thing. Little Mark 1 is the superior of Little Mark 2 ten years later. Recent work of Lindsey (1986) for the United States and Minford and Ashton (1991) for the United Kingdom suggests that high earners respond strongly to incentives; the latter work on the 1980 General Household Survey (GHS) estimates the substitution elasticity for annual labor hours of high earners at around unity, and replication with the 1982 GHS gives still higher elasticities.

In retrospect it seems incredible that apparently responsible governments, of both left and right, took such risks with confiscatory marginal taxation. They did so with the connivance of the economics profession in the United Kingdom, who used the excuse of "lack of evidence." One might as well have said, before the arrival of carbon dating, that Schliemann's Troy showed no evidence of significant age. Economists had pathetically weak empirical tools and yet spoke pompously of evidence, forgetting their intellectual inheritance.

Regulation and Controls

We turn last to the web of controls spun around economic activity by the Atlee government as it inherited the wartime panoply of interventionist powers. Given their plans to raise such high marginal tax rates, controls were a logical reinforcement. Disgruntled savers and entrepreneurs could take nothing out of the country, could obtain no credit for nonapproved

Table 5.1
Snapshots of central government finances, 1945–60 (£m.)

	1944/45	1950/51	1960/61
Government spending total	6174	3417	5590
Debt interest	435	515	858
Noncivil	5257	990	1765
Civil	482	1912	2967
Education	85	253	215
Pensions	40	93	609
Health and other insurance benefits	229	835	1209
Taxes total	3355	4157	6016
Income and property	1390	1525	2424
Death duties	111	185	227
Profits	510	268	262
Indirect and other	1344	2179	3103
Balance	−2819	740	426
Memo items	1945	1951	1960
Public debt (excl. floating)	21509	26125	27937
GDP	9831	14433	25522
GDP (civil use)	4574	13443	23761
Real GDP (1945 = 100)	100	109.7	139.8
Real civil GDP	100	204.0	279.9
GDP deflator (1945 = 100)	100	133.8	185.7

purposes that might deprive the tax collector of his swag, could not pay workers in unusual ways without falling foul of the union-employer bodies bargaining collectively around him or the prices/incomes freezes (1948) or restraints (1949), could find no lodgings for wandering workers because of rent controls, could obtain foreign exchange only by approval for an inconvertible pound, and so on.

Only the euphoria of recovery from war could explain the substantial resurgence of production in such a suffocating climate. As it was, even the muddled Conservatives of that time could not wriggle out of an attempt to loosen and occasionally eliminate controls. The spirit in which they did so is summed up by the prime minister, Sir Anthony Eden's ignorant disingenuousness in a note to his chancellor of the exchequer over import controls: "As to the question of imports, I should be most reluctant to contemplate any return to licensing and government controls ... Is it not, however, possible to get something of the same results by other methods?

Cannot the banks, for instance, be given some indication from time to time that such and such materials are those for the import of which we should be most reluctant to see money advanced?" (Eden, 1960, 322)

Labour not merely preserved but also built up the wartime control regime. Nationalization was their most famous policy, taking in coal, all transport (road, rail, and air), electricity boards, gas, iron and steel, all telecommunications, and the Bank of England. Some bodies such as British Overseas Airways Corporation, had already been nationalized in or before the war, in a spirit of pragmatic control that later characterized the Conservative approach post-Labour.

The fact remains that this was a remarkable extension of government control over industry; it represented about a fifth of British GDP. It was reinforced by Labour's links with a highly unionized labor force in private manufacturing (see figure 5.7—the 9.25 million union members in 1950 represented 53 percent of the employed labor force outside the armed forces, but public and private nontransport services with 35 percent of employment were barely unionized, implying 80 percent or higher unionization in industry and transport). Where unionization was negligible, Bevin introduced minimum wage laws (the Wage Council Acts of 1945 and 1948) that extended union-equivalent protection to 4.5 million workers. One way or another, therefore, the government exercised controls, either through unions, management, or direct labor market intervention, on virtually the whole of the economy's production.

Control over production was buttressed by comprehensive financial controls—on bank credit, hire purchase, and foreign exchange—and controls on imports.

Finally, there was effective control over mobility by the government ownership of much rented accommodation and control over the private remainder of the rented sector. The market in rented housing was subsidized and distorted through these means so that a worker wishing to move would both lose his or her sitting tenant rights and have to rent expensive uncontrolled (furnished) accommodation in the chosen new location.

The Conservatives therefore confronted in 1951 a population and industry held in thrall by the government. The only concession toward decontrol Labour had made was in the removal of much rationing, though food rationing was still in force. The Conservatives' reaction however was considerably less radical in practice than the free market rhetoric of their election campaign might have suggested.

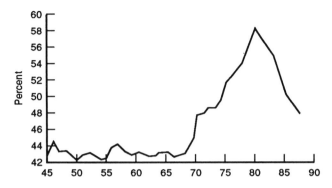

Figure 5.7
Unionization rate (percent)

They retained all Labour's financial controls and union/minimum wage laws. Though they made no formal use of incomes or price controls during the fifties, there was all the usual exhortation and joint Trade Union Congress (TUC)-industry-government consultation; and in 1961 Selwyn Lloyd was to reintroduce formal wage controls.

Apart from abolishing rationing, the only concessions the Conservatives made to free market ideas was to abandon formal import controls (but as we have seen retaining informal controls through credit and foreign exchange controls) and to bring in a half-hearted Rent Decontrol Act in 1957—and even this was soon to fall victim to popular outrage over the practices of Rachman, a notorious landlord. The pound also became convertible at the official fixed rate on the foreign exchanges, which meant that foreigners at least could use it freely at this rate (previously there was de facto a dual exchange rate, a freely floating one for foreigners and a fixed one for controlled residents). However, residents continued to be subject to exchange controls.

It is therefore in the controls, the politicized incentives of nationalized industry managers, and the strong powers of government-encouraged unions that one finds the factors most depressing to the incentives of ordinary people during this time. The British working man became the character later immortalized by Peter Sellers in *I'm All Right, Jack,* and the British manager was bound to feel—and did—that the main goal was to keep the workers happy so as to keep production running after a fashion and then go cap in hand to government if layoffs threatened.

Bringing the Story Up To Date

This cursory account of the building of the postwar welfare state and its associated taxes and controls must suffice. We now consider subsequent developments before reviewing the implications of the experience for others, especially Eastern Europeans.

With minor interruption, the regime we described for the end of the fifties continued throughout the sixties and seventies. There were of course changes of detail, but apart from a brief interlude when Mr. Heath's Conservative government came into office in 1970 pledged to restore free markets, only to reverse direction within twelve months, nothing was done to alter the basic philosophy of intervention, high and rising government spending, and taxation. The steady deterioration in the environment is well known. Mischief was afoot and it took its course.

The effects of these trends on the British economy were visible to the most casual observer by the end of the seventies. Britain was "the sick man of Europe," the butt of jokes at economic assessment conferences across the world. Its economy and even its social fabric fell into ruins in the final months of the Labour government in 1978–79, with the "winter of discontent," the explosion of wages and pent-up inflation after the collapse of yet another incomes policy and the descent into severe recession as corrective monetary policy was applied.

The causal connections between the policies described here and this ultimate collapse are essentially simple, the systemic suppression of incentives acting to erode proper economic behavior, but the details are complex and a matter of much econometric detective work. Parts of the picture defy proper analysis in the time-series domain at least.

A number of authors have attempted an assessment of "Thatcherism" and by implication its preceding opposite—for example, Layard and Nickell (1989), Matthews and Minford (1987), Maynard (1988), and Walters (1985). Then there is work on housing and labor mobility—Hughes and McCormick (1984), Minford et al. (1987), and Muellbauer and Murphy (1988). On privatization, Veljanovski (1987) and Yarrow (1986) have made useful assessments. In the central labor market, there have been studies of classical and Keynesian "wage pressure" effects (Layard and Nickell 1985, Minford 1983); more recently studies of hysteretic and insider effects—Lindbeck and Snower (1986), Blanchard and Summers (1986); and studies of union effects on performance (Blanchflower, Millward, and Oswald 1991; Machin and Wadwhani 1991). And there is much more—on high marginal tax rates (see above), health, education, and dependency—as well as macro issues.

Rather than attempt to go over this ground one more time, it seems more useful—since in spite of much disagreement on details, there is a substantial body of agreement about general incentive effects—to set out the evidence of this relative failure that emerges from the basic macroeconomic measures of performance.

The Relative Performance of the U.K. Economy

Clearly one could look at many detailed measures of performance and attempt an in-depth analysis of the effects of these policies. However, this would be beyond my present scope. Instead we examine two measures: overall GDP per capita and productivity in manufacturing (where it can reliably be measured). Productivity measures the performance of those in work and total per capita GDP adds in the extent of labor participation. For a comparison, we use Germany, because in the postwar period it pursued a very different, free ("social") market path of reconstruction (the German concept of the social market embraces strong unions, bargaining for high productivity, and high employment with strong employers' federations; while clearly different from the orthodox model of a competitive labor market, the outcome of such evenly balanced bilateral bargaining could generate a similar result, as explained by McDonald and Solow (1981)). Comparisons of growth over different time periods for the United Kingdom alone do not convey much because they do not control for the differing circumstances of the times (interwar depression and protection, postwar liberalization and expanding world markets for example).

The comparisons are set out in figures 5.8 and 5.9. The first set show the trends in per capita income. In the period from 1913 to 1980, the postwar period up to 1979 stands out as one in which Germany massively outstripped the United Kingdom. This had not been true of the interwar period when the two countries had a rather similar performance. From 1979 the trend of relatively high German growth also ceased.

It has been widely argued that Germany outperformed Britain in growth from around 1870 merely because it was able to catch up a technological lead, Britain having been the home of the industrial revolution and Germany being late in achieving the necessary national identity and stability (e.g., Kennedy 1988). It might be possible to extend this argument, whatever its merits, into the 1950s, but it seems implausible. The process would seem to have run its course by the thirties, judging by figure 5.1. In any case Germany's per capita income exceeded Britain's by 1958. It then continued to grow faster for nearly two decades. This seems clearly to

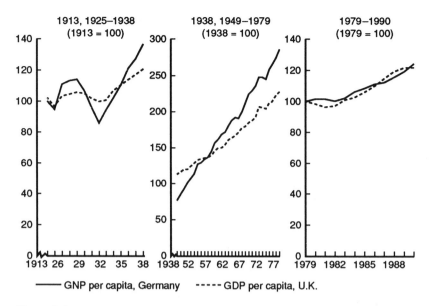

Figure 5.8

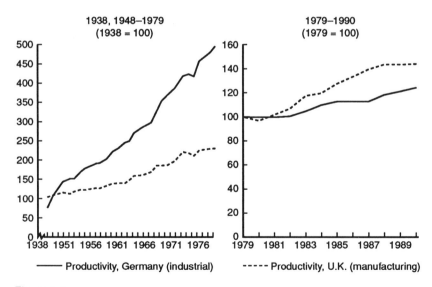

Figure 5.9

indicate that deeper forces were at work, of the sort described in this chapter.

As for the reversal from 1979, while it may be possible to point by now to the potential for Britain to catch up, the fact that the process began at all, let alone in 1979–82, points clearly to the causal role of the large-scale reforms of the Thatcher government.

We turn next to relative productivity, where data only since 1938 is available. Here the turnaround in relative performance is even more startling. Between 1938 and 1979 German productivity growth was 3.9 percent per annum, Britain's 1.8 percent. Between 1979 and 1990, Germany's was 1.5 percent, Britain's 3.1 percent per annum; in each period, growth of one is double the other's, but the roles are reversed between periods.

These facts appear to support the conclusion that Germany set out on a relatively free market course postwar and prospered while Britain chose interventionism and underperformed, whatever absolute gains may have come its way from general postwar prosperity and rapidly expanding world trade. Belatedly in 1979 Britain began (painfully) to copy the German free market example and over the next decade ultimately reaped some initial rewards. An irony may well be (Davis and Minford 1986) that by the late seventies Germany was actually copying parts of the British "social" model, and some of the turnaround could be due to this negative factor. The point about the importance of relative incentive systems is thereby only further underlined.

Conclusions

Let me conclude by summarizing the lessons as I see them for the behavior of the British and hence other economies.

The first point is that of interactive complications. Medical people are familiar with the way a body weakened by a serious disease contracts numerous associated ailments, which cumulatively destroy it and may be hard to combat even when the original main disease has been tackled. So with economies. A serious and fundamental distortion, such as penal marginal tax rates on low—and high-paid workers, will cut back labor performance, with a series of add-on effects—for example, on tax revenues, on the incentive to inflate, and on the propensity to introduce controls that further worsen micro performance. Once unemployment takes hold, it will tend to become long-term; once long-term it will produce deterioration in skills and motivation among the unemployed (hysteresis effects) and it will strengthen the defensive attitudes of insiders who fear deeply for their own exposure to such risks. It is interesting to note the general absence of these effects in a well-functioning labor market such as that of the United States.

The second point follows from the first. From a policy viewpoint the path of corrective reform for such a weakened economy is hard to prescribe and depends crucially on the politics of the country and situation. Should everything be changed at once in a big bang (New Zealand, Poland)? Or should a step-by-step approach be followed (Thatcher's United Kingdom is the classic example, another is China)? No doctor would attempt a prescription without considering the patient's whole situation, and it seems that the same is true here. The account I gave in 1988 of Mrs. Thatcher's reform program—though clearly her luck ran out in her third term, for reasons there is no space to go into here—can still stand for the achievement of a largely irreversible reform of British institutions (Minford 1988). And at the time of writing the overwhelming evidence is in favor of step-by-step strategies and against the big bang.

Finally, it appears that monetary assistance is the least of the necessary inputs. Marshall aid was as liberally available to the United Kingdom as to Germany; yet Germany forged ahead on the basis of a reconstructed free market system while Britain wallowed in stultifying controls. Japan benefited little from monetary aid, yet after the MacArthur free market reforms and destruction of the old cartelized, semifeudal, restrictive networks, Japan built up a competitive industry without equal. One could go further, as argued by Kostrzewa, Nunnenkamp, and Schmieding (1990): Marshall aid to the United Kingdom may well have scuppered the chances of a free market policy by buttressing and subsidizing the policies of the Atlee government. Disheartened that their prophecies of Labour collapse failed to come true, the Tories threw in the free market towel and signed up to pragmatic interventionism.

What is certainly clear is that free markets must be the end, without compromise or ambiguity, even if they are deliberately not all freed overnight. The Soviet example seems to make that very clear: where people sense a lack of direction, they will not trust themselves to the risky business of business.

In the end, what Britain lacked was the excuse to have a General MacArthur sort us out. Instead we got Marshall aid and polite American tut-tuts as they powerlessly watched us drift away on a flood of socialist emotion. Would-be reconstructors of Eastern Europe should seek out not money but MacArthurism.

Notes

I am grateful to Bruce Webb for research assistance, and to Assar Lindbeck and other participants at this conference, and also to David Worswick, for their comments on earlier drafts. The usual disclaimer applies.

References

Blanchard, O. and L. Summers (1986) "Hysteresis and the European unemployment problem," in S. Fischer, ed., *NBER Macroeconomics Annual*, MIT Press.

Blanchflower, D. G., N. Millward, and A. J. Oswald (1991) "Unionism and employment behaviour," *Economic Journal*, 101, July, 815–834.

Davis, J. and P. Minford (1986) "Germany and the European disease," *Recherches Economiques de Louvain*, 52, pp. 373–398.

Eden, Sir Anthony (1960) *Full Circle: Memoirs, 1951–57*, Cassell.

Hayek, F. A. (1988) *The Fatal Conceit—the errors of socialism*, Routledge.

Howarth, T. E. B. (1985) *Prospect and Reality—Great Britain 1945–55*, Collins.

Hughes, G. and B. McCormick (1984) "Do council housing policies reduce migration between regions?" *Economic Journal*, 91, 919–932.

Kennedy, P. (1988) "The Rise and Fall of the Great Powers," Fontana.

Kostrzewa, W., P. Nunnenkamp, and H. Schmieding (1990) "A Marshall Plan for Middle and Eastern Europe," *The World Economy*, March, pp. 27–49.

Layard, R. and S. Nickell (1985) "The causes of British unemployment," *National Institute Economic Review*, 3, Feb., 62–85.

Layard, R. and S. Nickell (1989) "The Thatcher Miracle?" LSE Centre for Labour Economics Discussion paper no. 343; shorter version in *American Economic Review*, 79(2), pp. 215–219.

Lindsey, L. (1986) "Individual taxpayer response to tax cuts 1982–4 with implications for the revenue-maximizing tax rate," NBER Working Paper No. 2069.

Lindbeck, A. and D. J. Snower (1986) "Wage setting, unemployment and insider outsider relations," *American Economic Review*, Papers and proceedings.

MacDonald, I. M. and R. M. Solow, "Wage bargaining and employment," *American Economic Review*, vol. 71, 1981, pp. 896–908.

Machin, S. and S. Wadwhani (1991) "The effects of unions on organisational change and employment," *Economic Journal*, 101, July, 835–854.

Matthews, K. G. P. and P. Minford (1987) "Mrs. Thatcher's economic policies, 1979–87" *Economic Policy*, 5, October, 57–101.

Maynard, G. (1988) *The economy under Mrs. Thatcher*, Blackwell.

Minford, P. (1983) "Labour market equilibrium in an open economy," Oxford Economic Papers, 35 (supp.), 207–244.

Minford, P. (1988) "Mrs. Thatcher's economic reform programme" in R. Skidelsky (ed.) *Thatcherism, Chatto and Windus*, London, pp. 93–106.

Minford, P. and P. Ashton (1991) "The Poverty Trap and the Laffer Curve—What can the GHS tell us?" *Oxford Economic Papers* 43, 245–279.

Minford, P., M. Peel, and P. Ashton (1987) *The Housing Morass—regulation, immobility and unemployment*, Hobart Paperback 25, Institute of Economic Affairs.

Mitchell, B. R. (1988) *British Historical Statistics*, Cambridge University Press.

Muellbauer, J. and A. Murphy (1988) "House prices and migration: economic and investment implications," Shearson, Lehman and Hutton Securities research report.

Veljanovski, C. with M. Bentley (1987) *Selling the State*, Weidenfeld and Nicholson.

Walters, A. A. (1985) *Britain's Economic Renaissance: Margaret Thatcher's economic reforms, 1979–84*, Oxford University Press for the American Enterprise Institute.

Worswick, G. D. N. and P. H. Ady, eds. (1952) *The British Economy 1945–50*, Oxford University Press.

Worswick, G. D. N. and P. H. Ady (1962) *The British Economy in the Nineteen-fifties*, Oxford University Press.

Yarrow, G. (1986) "Privatization in theory and practice," *Economic Policy*, 2, 323–364.

6   A Perspective on Postwar Reconstruction in Finland

Jouko Paunio

The literature on the problems of transition in the economies of Eastern Europe and the Soviet Union—hereafter called Eastern economies—is growing, like mushrooms overnight. The enormous complexity of the economic, social, and political issues involved as well as the different initial conditions in the countries concerned pose a great challenge to economic analysis and policy advice. The conventional viewpoint of mainstream economics is obviously not broad enough to encompass the whole spectrum of elements in the transition process. As I interpret the current state of the art, we do not have at our disposal well-developed theories or models about the transformation of the former centrally planned economies into decentralized market economies. The emerging new literature offers a bewildering diversity of approaches that reflects the lack of consensus as to the most appropriate path of transformation. The search goes on. The topic of this conference provides one of the many directions open to this search process.

An interpretation of the problems faced by Eastern economies is presented in the first part of this chapter, followed by a few comments on West European economies after the war. Against this backdrop, Finnish postwar reconstruction is discussed. The chapter ends with concluding remarks on the relationship between the Finnish postwar experience and the current problems in Eastern economies.

1   Gloomy Outlook in Eastern Economies

In early 1990 the short-term growth prospects in Eastern economies in the East were not on the whole very encouraging. But there was a general optimism about their medium and long-term development outlook. The setback during 1990 was, however, much more severe than expected. The UN secretariat estimates that in Eastern Europe and the Soviet Union the output decline was about 6 percent in 1990 (World Economic Survey 1991). Now there is a fair amount of agreement among experts that a protracted period of austerity is to be expected with either sharp downward adjustments or at best stagnation in absorption and output. As many of the intended reforms have not been implemented, there is now also a widely shared pessimism about formulating and carrying out credible economic reforms in the Eastern economies.

It has recently become better understood in the West that the transition process will involve difficult and painful changes. The burden of the costs of transition will mainly be borne by the countries themselves notwithstanding the expected foreign assistance. For the people, the transition process must also be painful because there is no guarantee that reforms will succeed.

I find the following description by the United Nations Economic Commission for Europe (ECE) secretariat of the broad conditions for economic transition very much to the point (ECE 1991, chap. 4):

• Political consensus: Without unambiguous political agreement on decision-making by consensus, a credible reform program is all but impossible. The key question is the degree to which political agreement on reform will obtain wider political support.

• Social consensus: Once most of the political difficulties of economic transition have been overcome, a broad social consensus needs to be reached on the steps to be taken. Even if such social agreement is attained initially, there is no guarantee that such a consensus can be maintained once the costs of the adjustment begin to emerge.

• Market economy consensus: All Eastern countries have now committed themselves to some type of market-oriented reform. Once the political leadership has firm popular support for moving ahead with the transformation process, the next problem is the formulation of a clear-cut blueprint for the introduction of a full market system (see, for example, Portes 1991).

It is still open to question whether these conditions have been at all fulfilled.

The very poor investment performance lately (the volume of gross investment fell by more than output in 1990) makes matters worse for Eastern economies. No general upsurge in fixed investment is in my view to be expected as long as the major building blocks of the economic reforms are not in place. It is hoped that improvements in efficiency of resource allocation and use may eventually contribute to the achievement of desirable rates of economic growth with more modest rates of investment than were previously attained in these economies. For the present, since investment is the major instrument of economic change and transformation, the hopes for speedy recovery and narrowing of the gap in economic welfare between East and West should be fading quickly.

The closeness to developed market economies in western Europe will undoubtedly be in many ways beneficial to the Eastern economies. However, the propensity to emigrate from these countries to the West will remain strong if these economies continue to lag behind western Europe for years to come, well into the next century. The fears of massive immigration from the East have been very real and strongly felt in Western Europe since the breakdown in the centrally planned economies began. These fears have most probably spurred Western governments' readiness to provide various forms of assistance to Eastern economies. On the other hand, as is generally acknowledged, the loss of skilled labor through migration in particular would be damaging to Eastern economies. The reasonable level of education of their citizens is an important economic resource of these economies because it should facilitate the introduction and diffusion of the advanced western technologies and techniques necessary for better economic performance and higher growth in Eastern economies. Emigration could weaken this resource base and hence the growth potential of these economies.

The rundown real capital stock and the risk of losing the most productive and mobile human capital by emigration point to the need to get on quickly with the transition of Eastern economies to some form of functioning market economy. The ongoing economic decline is a strong warning signal.

The sufficient accumulation of productive capacity through investment must be one of the primary objectives of the reform process. But equally important is the mobilization of sufficient saving to ensure the realization of required investment. It has been emphasized that institutional changes will be necessary to mobilize domestic and foreign saving and ensure a better allocation of saving (see, for example, Borensztein and Montiel 1991). However, it is highly uncertain what contribution institutional reforms can make toward raising enough public and private saving. Even if the effect on saving would prove to be positive in the medium term, it is beyond doubt that foreign saving will be required to complement domestic saving. It has even been argued that all of the capital accumulation in the medium term will have to be financed by foreign saving. A Centre for Economic Policy Research (CEPR) study from 1990 made this assumption and estimated that to double the GDP per capita in Eastern Europe by the year 2000, without the Soviet Union, would require annual investments amounting to 5 to 10 percent of the total annual investment of the OECD countries. The experience up to now does not suggest that the investment flow from West to East would be that significant.

The prospects of eventually achieving high and sustained growth in the Eastern economies are inextricably bound with the unresolved issue of saving: Will the necessary saving be forthcoming?

2   Western Europe after the War

At the end of the Second World War most countries in Western Europe were faced with an array of problems that bear a resemblance to the problems facing Eastern economies today. In the immediate postwar period, Western Europe consisted of highly regulated economies that were facing great problems of reconstruction and restructuring. Furthermore, the threat of inflation and balance of payments constraints hampered the attempts by governments to find effective solutions to the range of serious problems faced by the more or less war-damaged economies. A major concern for policymakers was also that the postwar expectations of the populations in the European countries might rise faster than the capacity to satisfy them, thereby increasing the risk of social unrest and political insta- bility. These policy preoccupations encouraged the governments to main- tain their wartime controls after the war although there was no general consensus for retaining controls indefinitely. The consensus was rather for a return in the course of time to a decentralized market economy. However, there was a change of attitudes toward government policy. Growth and development became important objectives of active economic policies. Mixed economies as a new form of market economies emerged.

Although some of the problems in Western Europe after the war—for example, the poor state of the productive system, severe shortages of consumer goods, and inflation—are similar to those now facing the Eastern economies, there are also important differences. (These differences are well formulated in *Economic Survey of Europe* 1990, pp. 13–14.) A fundamental difference is that the Western European countries did not have to construct market economies from first principles. The free workings of the market mechanism were overridden or suspended in many countries for part or most of the war, but it was generally quite clear that this was a temporary state of affairs based on pragmatic considerations about how to focus activity on achieving a number of limited objectives. A clear system of property rights remained. It should also be noted that the basic incentive structure was constrained but not eliminated by wartime planning.

The Marshall Aid program may have at least provided the necessary margin for Western Europe to move toward a strong postwar recovery. In Western Europe the economic institutions then had the capacity to make efficient use of financial aid from abroad. On the other hand, it has been pointed out that the entire structure of institutions in Eastern economies is radically different from that prevailing in postwar Western Europe and their capacity to absorb new capital and technology from the West is also limited.

3 Recovery in Finland after the Second World War

Postwar reconstruction and recovery of the Finnish economy followed the same general pattern transformation from a highly regulated system to a decentralized, market-oriented, mixed-economy system as in the rest of Western Europe. The special political and economic circumstances in Finland after the war made, however, the road from war to peace long and arduous. There is a popular Finnish saying that the big Soviet Union won the war, but small Finland came in a good second. In Finland the human and material losses from the war were considerable. But compared to other countries that participated in the war, the Finnish losses were less heavy. This was due above all to the fact that Finland was not occupied by foreign troops and the main military actions, including bombings of civilian targets, inflicted limited damage in the main economic regions of the country. However, the battles in 1944—1945 during which the German forces were driven out of Lapland destroyed much of the northern part of Finland. A very heavy burden was inflicted on the economy as Finland had to surrender about 12 percent of its territory to the Soviet Union immediately after the signing of the Armistice Treaty in the autumn of 1944. For example, about 25 percent of the pulp industry and of power production was located in the ceded area.

The Finnish economy was not turned immediately into a peacetime economy after the war was over. Besides the fighting against the German forces, Finland was faced with several big challenges such as the payment of war reparations, compensations to war veterans, and the resettlement of over 400,000 Carelians (more than 10 percent of the population) from the ceded areas later and the reconstruction of Lapland.

The war economy system was maintained to deal with the difficult situation confronting the country in 1944. Finland had to find the means to pay for peace and independence, while the general economic situation was extremely precarious during the winter of 1944—1945. Substantial economic aid from Sweden helped Finland through the first year after the war. In 1945 Sweden was the only source of foreign borrowing. This is worth mentioning because later on during the reconstruction period Finland did not rely to any significant extent on foreign economic assistance. It did not accept Marshall Aid, which was so important for the economic recovery in the rest of Western Europe. The policies of the Finnish government were by necessity very much focused on a small number of objectives that were of primary importance for the survival of the country in circumstances of considerable political pressure from the Soviet Union.

The basic agreement about the Finnish war reparations to the Soviet Union was signed before the end of 1944. According to this agreement, Finland was to deliver to the Soviet Union within six years war reparation products with a total value of $300 million. The deliveries were valued at world market prices of 1938. Later the delivery period was extended to eight years and the nominal value of the reparations was reduced to $226 million. In addition to the war reparation obligations, Finland had to surrender property to the Soviet Union, and the German claims on Finland were taken over by the Soviet Union. The agreement contained a detailed breakdown of commodities to be delivered. Metal industry products accounted for about two-thirds of the program. This meant that the Finnish engineering industry and shipyards, which had been producing mostly for the home market, had to expand and adapt in order to make large export deliveries. Fortunately, the timing of the deliveries allowed the required expansion of industrial capacity to take place.

Investments in the metal industry were given high priority, and thus at the end of the 1940s the volume of production in this industry had nearly doubled from its prewar level. War reparations opened the Soviet markets to Finnish industry and later exports also expanded to the Western market. In hindsight one may conclude that, for the metal industry at least, reparations were an important impetus changing the structure of Finnish industry and exports away from the one-sided dominance of the wood and paper industry.

The burden of the war reparations was felt immediately after the armistice because the deliveries were to begin without delay. In 1945 to 1947 the share of war reparations was about 5 to 6 percent of the net national product. Besides the war reparations, the resettlement of the displaced Carelian population (and war veterans) and reconstruction of Lapland received high priority. The necessary legislation for the acquisition of land for the purpose of resettlement was approved by the Finnish parliament in the spring of 1945 and the program was for the most part completed by 1948. In this program new farms were set up, land was cleared for cultivation, and buildings for housing and other purposes were constructed. The total cost of the program was probably not much less than that of the war reparations (Pihkala 1954).

Political consensus was a necessary condition for carrying out the two huge programs of war reparations and settlements. After the parliamentary elections in 1945 a center-left coalition government (including a few Communists) was formed. This and the following coalition governments had sufficient majorities in parliament to be able to receive enough political backing for the difficult policies that strained the Finnish economy to the extreme. There were three governments during the latter half of the forties. The Communist party was left in opposition in 1948.

The resettlement program was envisaged as a means to avoid social and political unrest after the war when Finland was still a genuine "shortage economy." This program also helped to generate enough social consensus so that the Finnish people accepted the general social strain in the immediate postwar circumstances and the economic sacrifices that were required for the reconstruction of the country. There was clearly enough political and social consensus in the country to carry the country through the long and burdensome transition period from war to peace.

The general energy shortage after the war held back the reconstruction and expansion of the industrial capacity in the country. With the help of a special program new power plants were constructed, and in 1948 the rationing of electricity ceased. Since traditional wood and paper industries are very dependent on the supply of energy, the recovery and expansion of these industries began only toward the end of forties, when their output had not quite reached the prewar level. The paper industry expanded very rapidly thereafter, and the volume of output doubled in the fifties. When the needs of housing construction for the resettlement program eased, there was scope for expanding housing construction in urban areas. A social housing program was set up in 1949. In the following decade the government financed as much as two-thirds of all new housing in the country. Investment needs in the country remained quite high in the forties and fifties.

Fixed investments as a share of GNP were on the increase until the early fifties and remained high throughout that decade (table 6.1). It took three years after the war for the share of investment to recover to its prewar level. While the share of public consumption was on average a few percentage points above its prewar level, the share of private consumption had to

Table 6.1
Ratios of aggregate demand and aggregate supply to GDP at market prices, 1938 and
1945–1960

Year	Imports of goods	Exports of goods	Private consump.	Public consump.	Gross fixed capital form.	Increase of stocks
1938	22.4	21.7	67.1	10.5	18.3	4.8
1945	4.7	3.6	60.2	14.2	12.3	14.4
1946	11.1	10.5	62.5	10.3	16.7	11.1
1947	15.8	15.2	62.4	9.4	17.8	10.9
1948	16.2	13.8	66.3	9.9	21.6	6.2
1949	17.7	21.4	64.3	10.6	22.2	−0.9
1950	18.7	19.8	64.9	11.5	22.3	0.2
1951	22.3	28.6	60.5	10.1	22.8	0.3
1952	24.8	23.8	64.1	10.9	26.0	−0.1
1953	17.5	19.2	64.7	12.1	27.0	−5.5
1954	18.7	20.4	62.0	11.0	26.0	−0.8
1955	19.9	21.6	60.7	11.4	25.3	0.9
1956	20.5	19.5	62.4	12.2	25.8	0.6
1957	21.2	21.2	62.1	12.4	24.0	1.5
1958	20.0	22.2	60.0	12.6	24.4	0.9
1959	21.5	22.2	60.4	13.1	25.3	0.5
1960	24.0	23.3	59.0	12.5	27.1	2.2

Source: Riitta Hjerppe, *The Finnish Economy 1860–1985, Growth and Structural Change*
(Table 3B1).

Table 6.2
Rate of saving (%), 1938 and 1948–1958

	Total	General government	Private sector	Households
1938	17	18	17	14
1948	20	53	10	7
1949	19	49	10	7
1950	20	50	10	7
1951	27	57	17	14
1952	21	57	8	5
1953	22	53	10	8
1954	24	51	15	12
1955	24	46	17	15
1956	23	43	16	13
1957	22	48	12	9
1958	23	45	15	13

Source: O. E. Niitamo, *Säästämisestä ja sen mittaamisesta Kansantaloudellinen aikakauskirja*
1959.

give way to the other uses of national output. The share of private consumption was considerably lower than before the war. In 1946 its share was about 60 percent compared with 67 percent in 1938.

The structure of the financing of capital formation reveals the important role played by the public sector in the reconstruction of the Finnish economy. The total of domestic saving (the share of net saving of net national income) had to increase from the prewar level (table 6.2) in order to make room for expanding capital accumulation. The important thing to note is that government saving, in absolute and relative terms, rose very sharply. Compared with the share of government saving of 15 percent of total domestic saving in 1938, it varied between 45 percent and 75 percent during the period 1948 to 1959. Private sector saving fell correspondingly from 85 percent to perhaps half of total domestic saving. One aspect of this decline was that the household saving rate was on average clearly lower than before the war. The high government saving rate guaranteed the financing of the required capital formation from domestic sources. The role of foreign saving remained rather marginal in the mobilization of saving.

Some net foreign borrowing took place in the first few years after the war. The current account deficits from 1945 to 1949 totaled not more than 7 billion Finnmarks (Fmk) compared with the annual value of exports of goods and services of Fmk 74 billion in 1949 alone (see Bärlund 1951). In the decade from 1950 to 1959 the current accounts were on average in surplus. The net surplus totaled Fmk 65 billion in that period. It is evident that the large capital accumulation required in the reconstruction period was essentially financed by domestic saving.

The central government mobilized the major part of the increased share of public saving. Central government gross saving increased in real terms by more than three times from 1938 to the first half of the fifties (Viita 1956). Consequently, it also generated most of public sector saving formation. It is not surprising therefore that the central government had an important impact, directly and indirectly, on the size and direction of the investments in the economy. It is to be noted, however, that the real fixed investment by the central government itself increased only moderately from the late thirties (Valvanne 1954). On the other hand, the government lending to the private sector expanded strongly. The emphasis in government investment policy was primarily on the immediate investment needs related to the war reparations, the resettlements, the reconstruction of Lapland, and the energy program. Later the emphasis shifted to other priority areas such as housing and transportation. In the early fifties, when the war reparations were over, the central government financed less than 5 percent of gross investment in manufacturing industry, whereas in transportation the government financed more than one-third of the investments. Investments in state-owned companies did not grow significantly from the prewar years except when the war reparations required expansion in the state-owned metal industry in 1946–1948.

For a few years after the war the Finnish economy was a highly regulated economy. The war reparations were supervised by a special body comprised of representatives from government and industry. This body had very extensive authority to plan and supervise the production and delivery of reparation goods and to negotiate with domestic suppliers about the prices of these goods that were paid from government funds. Although industry was represented in this body, it meant in practice that the key industries functioned under very tight government control. Government control was of course not limited to activities related to the war reparations. Thus the construction sector was kept under strict control for several years after the war for various priority reasons and because of shortages of labor and raw materials.

Once general economic conditions began to ease, controls directly affecting the allocation of resources were loosened. The return from a controlled economy to a market economy system was in several ways in clear evidence by the late forties. An important feature was that most consumer goods were released from rationing; a clear exception was the control of external trade that was in force for a number of years after the war. Following tendencies in the international economy with a lag, definite steps toward more liberal foreign trade were taken only in the mid-fifties and later. The real turning point was the big devaluation in 1957; soon after the Finnmark became convertible for current account transactions. The intention was to make a liberalization of trade possible.

The heavy war reparations gave a strong impetus to the process of rapid structural change of the Finnish economy, which later continued through the postwar period. By the early fifties the growth objective found a central place not only in the policy discussions but also in the actual policies carried out. Industrial policy, in particular, became an important element in the growth-oriented policies adopted. The important role of the government in the industrialization process was clearly envisaged. It was even stated by one leading politician in the fifties that funds were to be collected ruthlessly from the public by means of taxation to be allocated for industrialization purposes. Consequently, the central government remained an important source of lending to the economy. Out of total lending, the share of the central government in 1960 was still about a quarter.

A wrong picture of the postwar situation in Finland would be given if it were not stressed that social and political tension was a permanent state of affairs, leading finally in 1956 to a general strike that the trade unions had threatened for a long time. Policy-making was much of the time a difficult tightrope act under internal and external pressures. At the political level pressures for socialization had already dwindled a few years after the war (Paavonen 1987).

The internal tensions manifested themselves in inflationary pressures that burst through wage and price controls. In the first postwar year, prices doubled and wages trebled. Afterwards inflation slowed, but the inflationary bias in the economy remained strong. The worst was over, however, at the end of the decade when controls and rationing eased. In order to calm the dissatisfaction among the population, the lower income groups were favored in wage policy settlements in the late forties. As a consequence the distribution of income became more even than before the war and has remained so since then.

It is interesting to note that the state budget was not the primary source of inflation finance (Valvanne 1954) because of the traditional adherence to a balanced budget philosophy. Instead the Bank of Finland carried out an accommodating monetary policy and thus made possible a rapid expansion of bank credit (Tudeer 1951). While the money supply increased strongly, the income velocity was also very much on the rise during the first postwar decade—more so than in other countries (Larna 1959). Thus enough scope was created for the inflationary pressures to remain persistent. Some tightening in the monetary policy regime was in evidence already before the big devaluation in 1957. However, the genuine activation of monetary policy took place later at the end of the decade (Tarkka 1988).

The high quality of life in Sweden, which had not suffered from the war, served as a model and great attraction to the people in the postwar Finland. The close geographical location, historical and economic ties between the countries, as well as the personal ties between Swedes and Finns kept the Finnish people very much aware of the relative poverty of their own country. However, in spite of the great difference in the standard of living, emigration from Finland to Sweden was not very significant during the first two decades after the war. The opening of the joint Nordic labor market in 1954 did not make very much difference to the modest emigration flows to Sweden.

The great burst of emigration took place only in the latter half of sixties. It was a period when Swedish industry suffered from labor shortage and the rate of unemployment in Finland increased to a higher level than at any time after the war (to 3–4 percent). The gap in wages, or more broadly in the standard of living, did not in itself trigger important emigration, although wages in manufacturing in Finland were clearly lower than in

Table 6.3
Hourly wages (Finnmarks per hour) in the Finnish and Swedish manufacturing industries

Year	Finland	Sweden	Net immigration from Sweden to Finland
1981	22.80	37.13	5565
1982	25.18	35.25	6729
1983	27.58	35.33	5639
1984	30.42	39.38	3370
1985	32.86	42.40	2279

Source: The Finnish Employers Association.

Sweden. At times Finnish wages were about 60 percent of Swedish wages. A diverging labor market development was needed to widen the gap in wages and to really set in motion the flow of emigration. In the peak year of emigration in 1969 (net emigration of 32,000), hourly wages in Finnish manufacturing had fallen to 46 percent of the corresponding wages in Sweden. After 1970 the emigration flow to Sweden slowed. It eventually turned into net immigration during the eighties while the wage gap in favor of Swedish wages still existed, although the gap had narrowed from what it had been earlier after the war (table 6.3).

4   Concluding Remarks

The postwar reconstruction of the Finnish economy was—in macro-economic terms—quite satisfactory. GNP per capita increased from 1945 to 1959 by two-thirds. It surpassed the prewar level already in 1948. However, a strong inflationary bias prevailed for most of the one and a half decades after the war, and external balance was achieved only by means of tight controls.

The major challenges facing the Finnish economy at the end of the war compelled the government to continue the tight wartime economic controls. As soon as economic conditions permitted, the controls were eased. The movement back toward a decentralized market system was largely completed toward the end of fifties. The Finnish transformation process of that period contains elements and features that can be found also in the current developments of the Eastern economies.

The Finnish experience suggests that the Eastern economies should accept a long transition period after fundamental changes in the economic system have been made. It will be necessary that the policy capabilities of the governments are preserved and improved. The systems of public finance should be clearly structured with the aim to provide governments with policy tools for short- and long-term economic policies. During the transition period the governments should adhere to strong structural and macroeconomic policy positions and have the capability to influence the actual development process. It will be extremely important that the governments act on the basis of clearly defined objectives as regards capital accumulation and general welfare of the population.

The war reparations and other reconstruction tasks represented a challenge to the Finnish people of the magnitude that Eastern economies are confronted with today. The Finnish success depended on broad political and social consensus achieved among the population. In postwar Finland the basic principles of the market-dominated mixed economy system were never under serious threat. The partial suspension of the market system after the war was considered a temporary state of affairs. There existed a majority-based market economy consensus. Analogously, the success of what will inevitably be a long transition in the Eastern economies requires that the general aims regarding the nature of the emerging economic system are well understood and endorsed by the people. The same holds also for the targets concerning social and economic developments in these countries.

The role of the government in the Finnish reconstruction process was very much in evidence in the mobilization of sufficient domestic saving, without foreign borrowing, to finance the great investment needs of the country. The presumption for Eastern economies would likewise be to rely first and foremost on domestic saving and, if necessary, on considerable public saving because there is hardly enough foreign saving available to support the much needed increase in investment.

The potential for considerable emigration from Finland to Sweden existed after the war as a consequence of the big difference in the standard of living in favor of Sweden. However, it never really happened, except for a period of very few years. Again the Finnish experience could be a useful lesson for the Eastern economies. The threat of mass emigration from Eastern countries may be held back if the internal political and social conditions are considered satisfactory by the people in these countries even though the standard of living, defined in narrow economic terms, may be considerably higher in the neighboring Western countries.

References

Ahvenainen, J., Pihkala, E., Rasila, V. (1982) Suomen taloushistoria 2. Helsinki.

Auer, J. (1956) Suomen sotakorvaustoimitukset Neuvostoliitolle. Helsinki.

Auer, J.(1963) Finland's War Reparation Deliveries to the Soviet Union. *Finnish Foreign Policy.*

Borensztein, E., Montiel, P. J. (1991) Saving, Investment and Growth in Eastern Europe. *IMF Working Paper. June 1991.*

Bärlund, R. (1951) Suomen maksutase jälleenrakennuskauden aikana. *Suomen Pankin taloudellisia selvityksiä, Sarja A:12.* Helsinki.

Bärlund, R. (1957) Suomen maksutase vuosina 1950–1956. *Suomen Pankin taloudellisia selvityksiä, Sarja A:18.* Helsinki.

Centre for Economic Policy Research (1990) The Impact of Eastern Europe.

Commission of the European Communities. *European Economy, No. 43, March 1990.*

ECE (1990) *Economic Survey of Europe in 1989–1990.* New York.

ECE (1991) *Economic Survey in Europe in 1990–1991.* New York.

Hjerppe, R. (1989) The Finnish Economy 1860–1985. Helsinki.

IMF (1990) The Economy of the USSR. Washington.

International Institute for Applied Systems Analysis (1991) The Soviet Economic Crisis: Steps to Avert Collapse.

Kaukiainen, Y., Pihkala, E., Hoffman, K., Harmo, M. (1988) Sotakorvauksista vapaakauppaan. Helsinki.

Kindleberger, C. P. (1987) Suomen sotakorvaukset. *Kansantaloudellinen Aikakauskirja 2.*

Lagus, K. (1949) Palkat ja hinnat vuonna 1948. *Suomen Pankin taloudellisia selvityksiä, Sarja A:8.* Helsinki.

Larna, K. (1959) The Money Supply, Money Flows and Domestic Product in Finland 1910–1956. Helsinki.

Lehto-Sinisalo, P. (1991) Valuutan säännöstelyn vuosikymmenet. *Suomen Pankin keskustelualoitteita 14/91.*

Niitamo, O. E., Paunio, J. J. (1956) Säästämisen käsitteestä sekä säästämisen muodostumisesta Suomen kansantaloudessa. *Kansantaloudellinen Aikakauskirja, Nide 1.*

Niitamo, O. E. (1959) Säästämisestä ja sen mittaamisesta. *Kansantaloudellinen Aikakauskirja, Nide 3.*

Oksanen, H., Pihkala, E. (1975) Suomen ulkomaankauppa 1917–1949. Helsinki.

Paavonen, T. (1987) Talouspolitiikka ja työmarkkinakehitys Suomessa toisen maailmansodan jälkeisellä jälleenrakennuskaudella vuosina 1944–1950. *Turun yliopiston julkaisuja. Sarja C 64.*

Pihkala, K. V. (1954) Arviointia asutusohjelmamme taloudellisista vaikutuksista. *Kansantaloudellinen Aikakauskirja.*

Portes, R. (1991) The Path of Reform in Central and Eastern Europe. *CEPR Discussion Paper Series No. 559, May 1991.*

Rossi, R. (1947) Suomen korkotaso ja korkopolitiikka vuosina 1918–1947. *Suomen Pankki A:7*.

Saarinen, V. (1986) Liikepankkien keskuspankkirahoituksen ehdot 1950–1984. *Suomen Pankki A:63*.

Suviranta, Br. (1952) The Completion of Finland's War Indemnity. *Unitas*.

Tarkka, J. (1988) Kahlitun rahan aika—Suomen rahoitusmarkkinoiden säännöstelyn vuosikymmenet. *Raha, inflaatio ja talouspolitiikka. Helsingin yliopiston kansantaloustieteen laitos*.

Tudeer, A. E. (1948) Rahamarkkinat. *Suomen Pankin selvityksiä, Sarja A:8*. Helsinki.

Törnqvist, E. (1946) Palkka—ja hintapolitiikka. *Suomen Pankin taloudellisia selvityksiä, Sarja A:6*. Helsinki.

Törnqvist, E. (1947) Vakauttamispolitiikka. *Suomen Pankin taloudellisia selvityksiä, Sarja A:7*. Helsinki.

United Nations (1991) *World Economy Survey 1991*. New York.

Vartia, P. (1991) Experiences from Growth and Transformation in the Post-War Period—The Country Study for Finland. *ETLA Discussion Papers No. 353*. Helsinki.

Valvanne, H. (1954) Valtiontalous vuosina 1938–1951. *Suomen Pankin taloudellsia selvityksiä, Sarja A:15*. Helsinki.

Viita, P. (1956) Valtiontalouden kautta rahoitettu pääomanmuodostus vuosina 1937, 1938 ja 1951–1954. *Suomen Pankin taloudellisia selvityksiä, Sarja A:17*. Helsinki.

Wiman, R. (1975) Työvoiman kansainvälisen muuttoliikkeen mekanismi. *ETLA B9*. Helsinki.

7 The Reconstruction and Stabilization of the Postwar Japanese Economy: Possible Lessons for Eastern Europe?

Koichi Hamada and
Munehisa Kasuya

In August 1945, when Japan surrendered to the Allied Forces, the country was in a state of complete destruction. The situation reminded us of lines from a famous poem by Tu Fu in the Tang dynasty, "The country laid to ruins, mountains and rivers remain..."[1] Japan was deprived of colonial territories, her productive capacities were dwarfed to about two-thirds of the prewar peak, and her GNP was about 60 percent of the average of 1934–36. General Douglas MacArthur, the Supreme Commander of Allied Powers (SCAP), commented that the I.Q. of the Japanese was like that of a twelve-year-old. The path to economic recovery was plagued with many difficulties—near starvation, severe inflation, and the balance of payments crisis were just a few of the problems challenging the government. It was a path of continuing struggles for policymakers as well as for the Japanese public. We doubt if anybody, Japanese or not, imagined at the time of the defeat that Japan would recover in the next several years and start to grow remarkably during the sixties.

In this chapter we trace the process of recovery and reconstruction in postwar Japan. Since there have already been many studies on the real aspect of postwar Japanese development, we emphasize the process of monetary stabilization that contained the severe inflationary pressure that existed in the early stage of reconstruction.[2] Then we consider how the Japanese experience could be a beacon for Eastern Europe and the Soviet Union half a century hence.

The Japanese postwar experience presents many intriguing questions, among which are the following: Should monetary stabilization take the form of a gradual, stop-gap approach or the "once and for all" single-stroke approach? Is the combination of macroeconomic stabilization policy and free market principle preferable to government intervention in specific sectors through industrial policy and financial control? Was the existence of supernational authority as represented by the allied occupation force helpful or even essential for the successful implementation of difficult and drastic measures?

It is difficult to answer these questions because history provides us only a single sample in time series, and we cannot exercise, except conceptually, counterfactual experiments. Only a particular combination of market mechanism and government intervention was actually tried in this historical development, and we do not know what would have happened with a different combination of economic policies. We hope, however, that the following discussion will at least give some clues as to what can be recommended and, in particular, what can be avoided.

Before proceeding to our main discussion, we would like to point out that Japan had not experienced the intense hyperinflation after the First World War as did Germany and the Eastern European countries. Japan did not participate in active war actions in the First World War and was rather an economic free rider that enjoyed the spillover of increased, worldwide effective demand. Table 7.1 illustrates the contrast between the boom after World War I and the galloping inflation after World War II. The Japanese people were overwhelmed by their first experience with severe price increases, but they did not have the traumatic memory of hyperinflation—except that some knew about the hyperinflation that the Japanese army caused by the issue of military bills in East Asia. Whether the absence of the memory worked as a positive or negative impact on the attitude of the Japanese after World War II is not clear, but we must keep in mind that the Japanese people had a different perspective on inflation from that of Europeans.

In section 1, we review briefly the factors that enabled the Japanese economy to recover from the destruction of the war rather quickly. In section 2, our main descriptive section, we cover in more detail the process

Table 7.1
Postwar movements of Japan: 1918–1922 and 1945–1949

	World War I			World War II		
	1918	1920 (1914 = 1)	1922	1945	1947 (1937 = 1)	1948
WPI	2.02	2.72	2.05	2.79	55.89*	116.93*
CPI	1.63	2.24	2.05	11.85	99.45*	172.29*

Note: Annual average. The sign * indicates effective rates reflecting black market prices.
Sources: *Hundred-Year Statistics of the Japanese Economy*, the Bank of Japan, 1966. *One Hundred Year History of the Bank of Japan*, the Bank of Japan, 1985, (in Japanese).

of monetary stabilization during the half decade 1945 to 1950. In section 3, we follow the effect of monetary stabilization on economic development during the fifties—a process that prepared Japan for remarkable growth during the sixties. In section 4, we address our central question: What kinds of lessons could the Japanese postwar experiences provide for the reconstruction and growth of Eastern Europe?

1   Postwar Reforms and Real Factors behind the Reconstruction

The main theme of this chapter is to illustrate how harmful inflation is for economic recovery and how monetary stability can promote that recovery. Nevertheless, economic recovery by itself is a real phenomenon, so that it cannot be brought about only by monetary stability unless real economic factors are ready. In postwar Japan, the Supreme Commander of Allied Powers (SCAP) or the General Headquarters (GHQ)—these terms were used interchangeably—exercised supernational authority to realize various social, educational, and economic reforms. (Even though SCAP was representing thirteen countries, including the United Kingdom and the Soviet Union, the occupation policies actually adopted were mostly planned and implemented by the United States.) The first objective was to demilitarize and democratize Japan. General MacArthur (SCAP) was not requested to promote the economic recovery of Japan. The deepening of the cold war and the emergence of the bamboo curtain in Asia had already begun in 1947 and changed the American occupation policy to one of promoting economic reconstruction and building an industrial power in the Pacific.

Actually SCAP utilized the Japanese political system quite cleverly to implement its reform policies. It preserved, though as a symbol without any concrete political power, the Emperor system to which people were still attached and delegated the implementation of occupation policies to the Japanese government. This indirect governance in Japan can be compared with the direct one in Okinawa where many conflicts took place between residents and the occupying military force (Takemae 1983). One of the reasons that the Japanese accepted these reforms rather calmly was, as Yutaka Kosai points out, that the Japanese had sympathy and support for the idealism that was "pressed forward by the missionary fervor."[3]

Three important economic reforms implemented by the occupation were land reform, the dissolution of *zaibatsu* (family financial combines), and labor reform. Social and educational reforms by themselves were not necessarily economic, but, along with other social measures to firmly establish democracy, they were important factors in molding the excellence in human capital that was an essential ingredient for the rapid development of the Japanese economy.

1.1   Land Reform

A modest reform was proposed initially from the Japanese side, but the actual reform enacted in October 1946 was very radical and reflected SCAP's policy. The maximum amount of land held by noncultivating residents was limited to 1 cho (= 2.45 acres or a little less than 1 hectare) and that of landed tenants was limited to 3 cho. Land in excess of the limit held by any landowners was sold to their tenant farmers at extremely cheap prices. In fact, this procedure was tantamount to confiscation in many cases.[4] Thus, the ownership of about 81 percent of all the tenant land was transferred to the former tenants.[5] Fragmented land ownership has not essentially been changed until the present time and is regarded as a substantial constraint to the development of a large-scale farm. At the time of implementation, however, the positive impact of the reform was enormous. New farmers with land obtained more incentives to work, to improve the land, and to modernize agricultural technology. This positive aspect led to a remarkable increase in agricultural productivity. According to Tatsuro Uchino, "among the many nations that implemented land reform programs after World War II, Japan's land reform was an unparalleled success."[6]

1.2   Dissolution of Zaibatsu

GHQ regarded *zaibatsu*, family-based, large industrial and financial combines, as an important source of Japan's military power and an obstacle to the development of a democratic business society. Stock-holding companies representing zaibatsu were liquidated and deprived of their stock holdings. Two typical trading companies, Mitsui Bussan and Mitsubishi Shoji, were dissolved. In 1947 the Antitrust Law was enacted and the Fair Trade Commission was established. The breakup of a large concentration of business power gave industries more flexibility and enabled new enterprises to compete freely regardless of whether or not they belonged to a zaibatsu group. At the same time, GHQ expelled—it was called a "purge" —business leaders who were believed to have cooperated with the military government, that is, virtually all the established leaders. Young people were promoted to the top of many companies and "new management" conducted business activities with intensity, youthful vigor, and flexibility.

After the San Francisco Peace Treaty was effected in April 1952, the

Antitrust Law was revised to relax the restrictions on monopolies. The Fair Trade Commission's power was countervailed by caretaking activities of ministries such as the Ministry of International Trade and Industry (MITI), and the commission never had the same degree of influence as it did in the United States. In the meantime, zaibatsu firms and others were reorganized as *keiretsu* (networks of firms). The effect of the postwar dissolution of zaibatsu should not be undervalued because it helped to create a competitive, kin-free business atmosphere. Moreover, business relations in keiretsu are much less hierarchic, more democratic, and more functional than those in zaibatsu used to be.[7] Incidentally, those young business leaders remained in control until quite recently.[8]

1.3   Labor Reforms

Soon after the occupation, GHQ announced the intention to establish the basic rights of workers. The Trade Union Law (1945) established the right of workers to organize trade unions; the Labor Standards Law (1947) stipulated the minimum requirements for working conditions that had sometimes been inhumanly harsh, particularly for women and minors; and the Labor Relations Adjustment Law (1947) established the way in which labor disputes were to be settled by negotiations, agreements, and possibly by strikes. Encouraged by legislation, the number of unions increased at a tremendous speed. Compared to about five hundred unions that existed in 1945, the number of unions exceeded twenty-three thousand in 1947 and thirty-three thousand in 1948. In 1947 more than half of the workers were unionized.[9] Disputes and strikes took place quite frequently, and productive processes were disrupted seriously in many firms. Confusion was reinforced by the inexperience of both labor and management.

As mentioned earlier, due to the deepening of the cold war, the American occupation policy was changing in 1947. A general strike was planned for February 1 of that year. To the surprise and disappointment of Japanese labor leaders, GHQ ordered the strike to stop. The occupation policy turned out to be less liberal than it appeared just after the war. Civil servants were deprived of the right to strike and the "red purge" ousted communist-oriented union leaders.

The reversal of the occupation policy might have appeared to be inconsistent to liberal intellectuals in Japan, but it seemed that the American idea was to foster trade unions as long as their activities did not interfere with the democratic market economy. Also, Americans probably had in mind the development of American-style craft or industrywide trade unions. At first union workers were quite militant, and Japanese industrial relations traced a thorny path. However, with skillful tactics, and by giving carrots to some employees and sticks to others, the management in private sectors succeeded in taming trade unions after many serious strikes.[10] Eventually, Japanese unions also turned out to be enterprise-based unions. This process was certainly helped by the reversal of the GHQ's attitude toward Japanese labor movements and by the recession after the Dodge Line (the contractionary policy advised by Joseph Dodge in 1949). Compared to the private sector, where profits affect the future well-being of workers, industrial disputes in the public sector remained serious for more than two decades.[11]

1.4   Social and Educational Reforms

The new constitution was drafted by the GHQ and "imposed" upon the Japanese in 1947. Under the new constitution, which was based upon an idealized type of pacifism and democracy, Japan renounced war and vowed to maintain the basic human rights of her people. Educational reforms introduced a core curriculum and a single educational track: six years of elementary school, three years in junior high, three years in senior high, and four years in college. This system replaced the multitrack system that screened students into elites, technicians, and nonelites at a very young age. After the occupation forces left, there were reactions toward more traditional education, and the left-wing teachers' union ironically transformed the education system, which was based originally on American pragmatism, into a style of extremely unindividualistic uniformity.

On the whole, however, educational reforms succeeded in producing homogeneous workers who possessed high verbal and quantitative skills as well as a positive attitude for cooperation and discipline in the workplace. It also instilled a competitive meritsystem that turned Japan into a highly mobile society with respect to social status. Moreover, pacifism enabled the Japanese economy to dispense with large military expenditures. The decision of Japan, after the peace treaty, to be under the umbrella of U.S. nuclear power was important in keeping Japan's pacifist posture. Of course, the element of luck in the course of events in the Pacific should not be overlooked. Nevertheless, we should remind ourselves that the economic success of Japan in the past four and a half decades was partly a dividend of her pacifism.[12]

In addition to the reforms that were conducted under the supranational political authority of the occupation, we must pay attention to the legacy

of wartime goods-mobilization and price-control policies that affected substantially the economic policies of the immediate postwar period. According to Takafusa Nakamura, the spread of lifetime employment and the
seniority wage system was facilitated by the wage and price freeze during
the war.[13] The Material Mobilization Plan of 1937 seemed to have triggered the idea of the *Priority Production System*, which meant in Japanese,
literally, the "sloping or inclining production plan." Since coal was essential
for the production of producers' goods, coal production should be increased. Import of petroleum, another energy source, was severely limited.
But the shortage of rolled steel limited coal production; on the other hand,
the shortage of coal hurt steel production. The priority production system
channels products and scarce resources reciprocally among the more important sectors first. For example, surplus steel is channeled toward coal
production and the resulting production of coal toward steel production.
Only when the targets for the most important products were fulfilled
would the surplus be put into the next priority sectors. It is interesting to
note that the priority production system was based on an idea similar to
Leontief's input-output analysis.[14] This autonomous Japanese reconstruction plan barely worked. The difficult situation could only be alleviated by
using as input to these sectors the crude oil that the occupation authorities
allowed the Japanese to import.[15]

In order to finance the loops of production, the Reconstruction Finance
Bank was established in January 1947. It channeled to such priority industries as coal, electric power, fertilizer, iron, and machinery the funds it
raised from issuing bonds. Since more than two-thirds of the bonds were
accepted by the Bank of Japan, investments in these sectors were in fact
financed by printing money. At this stage of recovery, financial decisions
through the bank were capable of affecting real investments at the firm
level. Savings were directed to investment projects. In March 1949, the
Reconstruction Finance Bank owned about one-third of the total nation-
wide loans to industries.[16] John Zysman claims that the industrial policy of
Japan has been implemented through the allocation of financial resources.[17]
His view was certainly right at the time when the Reconstruction Finance
Bank was at work. At present, the legacy of this system remains, though
weakly, as the Fiscal Investment Loan Program (FILP) that channels the
funds from postal savings to public and public-related sectors. However,
private market force has become so dominant that FILP cannot be regarded
as the primary instrument to implement industry policies.

The immediate effect of the Priority Production System was inflationary,
but production began to increase in early 1948 accompanied by a reduced

rate of inflation.[18] There is some controversy as to whether or not the strong, single-stroke deflationary policy was in fact needed for reconstruction. Some authors point out that the priority production system alone would have increased production and curbed inflation. For example, Uchino says, "While the Dodge Line had certainly brought inflation to an end, it had achieved this at the cost of almost undermining the policy of priority production, which had enabled the country to take the first step toward economic recovery."[19] In order to explore this controversy further, we have to review more closely the way in which monetary policies were implemented during the reconstruction period.

2   The Process of Monetary Stabilization

At the end of the war, there was a wide gap between the limited availability of goods and the massive level of accumulated nominal wealth. Prices

Table 7.2
Japan's government debts

		100 mill yen	% of GNP
CY	1940	310	78.7
	1941	417	92.9
	1942	571	104.7
	1943	851	133.4
	1944	1520	204.0
	1945	1994	n.a.
	1946	2653	56.0
FY	1947	3606	27.6
	1948	5244	19.7
	1949	6373	18.9
	1950	5540	14.0
	1951	6454	11.9
	1952	8267	13.5
	1953	8511	12.0
	1954	9327	12.5
	1955	10572	12.8
	1956	10002	10.7
	1957	9703	9.6
	1958	10755	10.3
	1959	12530	10.0
	1960	13403	9.1

Source: *Hundred-year Statistics of the Japanese Economy*, the Bank of Japan, 1966.

Table 7.3
Production, prices, and interest rates of postwar Japan

CY	Industrial production index 1935 = 100	Industrial production growth rate (%)	Wholesale price index 1934–36 = 1	Wholesale price inflation (%)	Consumer price index 1934–36 = 1	Consumer price inflation (%)	Interest rates loans on bills (%)
1943	157.8	1.3	2.05	7.0	3.21	17.6	4.49
44	160.4	1.7	2.32	13.3	4.01	24.9	4.64
45	69.3	−56.8	3.50	51.1	13.00	224.3	4.53
46	28.1	−59.5	16.27	364.5	50.60	289.2	5.84
47	35.0	24.7	48.15	195.9	109.10	115.6	7.12
48	46.2	32.1	127.90	165.6	189.00	73.2	9.27
49	60.1	30.0	208.80	63.3	236.90	25.3	10.00
50	73.6	22.5	246.80	18.2	219.90	−7.1	9.23
51	101.7	38.1	342.50	38.8	255.50	16.2	9.09
52	108.9	7.1	349.20	2.0	266.10	4.1	9.13
53	133.0	22.1	351.60	0.7	286.29	7.6	8.76
54	144.2	8.4	349.20	−0.7	301.80	5.5	8.76
55	155.1	7.6	343.00	−1.8	297.40	−1.5	8.54
56	189.8	22.3	358.00	4.4	300.20	0.9	8.14
57	224.1	18.1	368.80	3.0	308.90	2.9	8.14
58	220.1	−1.8	344.80	−6.5	312.10	1.0	8.40
59	264.4	20.1	348.30	1.0	316.20	1.3	7.96
60	330.0	24.8	352.10	1.1	328.00	3.7	8.25

Source: *Hundred-Year Statistics of the Japanese Economy*, The Bank of Japan, 1966.

Koichi Hamada and Munehisa Kasuya

were controlled by the government at lower levels so that purchasing power based on accumulated nominal wealth created intense excess demand in almost all sectors.

The reduction of production capacity due to World War II was devastating. According to a report of the Economic Stabilization Board, the war destroyed about one-quarter of the nation's wealth. On the other hand, the extent of the accumulation of individuals' financial assets, which at the same time were government liabilities, was enormous. In 1945, government debts exceed 200 percent of GNP (table 7.2). It was estimated that national bonds, wartime indemnity obligations, other government liabili-

Table 7.4
Growth rate of GNP deflator and money in Japan (Annual growth rate, %)

		Nominal GNP	Real GNP	GNP deflator	High-powered money	M1	M2
CY	1940	19.0	−5.9	26.0	28.4	n.a.	n.a.
	1941	14.0	1.4	12.2	27.1	n.a.	n.a.
	1942	21.2	1.4	19.8	20.0	n.a.	n.a.
	1943	17.3	0.0	17.7	43.0	57.6	53.3
	1944	16.8	−3.7	20.7	73.2	93.5	71.7
	1945	n.a.	n.a.	n.a.	145.9	267.7	184.4
FY	1946	(152.2)*	(−43.7)*	(236.6)*	73.9	−36.4	−36.7
	1947	176.1	8.6	154.5	128.6	94.4	82.8
	1948	103.7	12.7	80.2	56.9	56.4	59.6
	1949	26.6	2.1	23.9	−3.9	30.2	44.5
	1950	16.9	11.0	5.4	18.7	14.5	22.9
	1951	37.9	13.0	22.0	19.5	30.3	39.3
	1952	12.4	11.0	1.1	18.1	29.7	39.9
	1953	15.8	7.4	8.2	14.0	15.9	24.1
	1954	5.4	3.7	1.6	−0.8	8.0	14.2
	1955	10.3	11.1	−0.8	5.4	12.6	19.2
	1956	12.8	6.4	6.0	19.5	24.4	24.6
	1957	9.2	6.8	2.2	11.4	13.9	17.8
	1958	2.4	3.9	−1.5	0.5	10.9	17.3
	1959	21.0	16.6	3.9	18.7	9.8	16.7
	1960	16.7	12.8	3.3	10.5	19.3	20.8

Notes: * indicates annual growth rate between 1944 and 1946. M1 and M2 are average outstandings.
Sources: *Hundred-Year Statistics of the Japanese Economy*, the Bank of Japan, 1966. Asakura, Kokichi and Nishiyama, Chiaki, *The Monetary Analysis of the Japanese Economy*," (in Japanese), 1974.

Table 7.5
GNP, GNP deflator, and money in Japan

	Nominal GNP (bil Yen)	Real GNP (bil Yen, 1934–36 base prices)	GNP deflator	High-powered money (bil Yen)	High-powered money (ratio of GNP, %)	M1 (bil Yen)	M1 (ratio of GNP, %)	M2 (bil Yen)	M2 (ratio of GNP, %)
CY 1940	39.4	20.8	1.9	6.6	16.8	n.a.	n.a.	n.a.	n.a.
1941	44.9	21.2	2.1	8.3	18.5	n.a.	n.a.	n.a.	n.a.
1942	54.4	21.4	2.5	10.0	18.4	32.1	59.0	58.7	107.9
1943	63.8	21.4	3.0	14.3	22.4	50.6	79.3	90.0	141.1
1944	74.5	20.6	3.6	24.7	33.1	97.9	131.4	154.5	207.4
1945	n.a.	n.a.	n.a.	60.8	n.a.	360.0	n.a.	439.4	n.a.
FY 1946	474.0	11.6	40.9	105.8	22.3	228.9	48.3	278.0	58.6
1947	1308.7	12.6	104.1	241.8	18.4	444.9	34.0	508.3	38.8
1948	2666.1	14.2	187.6	379.4	14.2	695.8	26.1	811.4	30.4
1949	3375.2	14.5	232.4	364.6	10.8	906.0	26.8	1172.8	34.7
1950	3946.7	16.1	244.9	432.6	11.0	1037.3	26.3	1441.2	36.5
1951	5444.2	18.2	298.9	517.2	9.5	1351.9	24.8	2007.0	36.9
1952	6118.0	20.2	302.3	610.9	10.0	1753.2	28.7	2808.5	45.9
1953	7084.8	21.7	327.2	696.4	9.8	2032.7	28.7	3485.5	49.2
1954	7465.7	22.5	332.5	691.1	9.3	2194.7	29.4	3981.5	53.3
1955	8235.5	25.0	329.9	728.7	8.8	2470.5	30.0	4744.6	57.6
1956	9292.9	26.6	349.7	871.1	9.4	3073.2	33.1	5912.8	63.6
1957	10149.8	28.4	357.5	970.4	9.6	3500.4	34.5	6966.2	68.6
1958	10394.7	29.5	352.3	975.4	9.4	3882.5	37.4	8173.6	78.6
1959	12577.8	34.4	365.9	1157.5	9.2	4264.9	33.9	9541.0	75.9
1960	14678.9	38.8	378.1	1278.9	8.7	5088.5	34.7	11524.9	78.5

Note: M1 and M2 are average outstandings.
Sources: *Hundred-Year Statistics of the Japanese Economy*, the Bank of Japan, 1966. Asakura, Kokichi and Chiaki Nishiyama, *The Monetary Analysis of the Japanese Economy*, (in Japanese), 1974.

Table 7.6
Gross saving of Japan I (billion yen)

	Provisions for capital consumption	Undistributed corporate surplus	Personal saving	Government current surplus	(less) Surplus on current account	Discrepancy	Total
CY 1941	3.2	1.8	10.1	−7.0	−0.9	2.9	11.7
1942	3.7	2.2	11.4	−8.4	−0.9	4.9	14.6
1943	4.3	2.5	14.1	−11.4	−0.6	5.8	15.9
1944	5.3	3.0	20.1	−15.5	0.4	8.1	20.7
1945	NA	NA	NA	NA	NA	NA	NA
FY 1946	24.4	−1.0	8.3	−22.6	−5.5	90.8	105.4
1947	56.6	−4.4	−39.8	148.0	7.0	191.8	345.2
1948	107.7	2.3	−7.9	317.4	21.2	353.9	752.2
1949	157.8	37.6	−43.0	551.5	74.6	201.3	830.6
1950	207.0	192.0	409.8	351.3	171.4	18.6	1007.3
1951	280.0	214.9	717.7	452.2	157.4	156.5	1663.8
1952	359.4	196.4	688.9	338.8	3.3	97.8	1678.0
1953	473.3	297.2	523.0	394.3	−94.7	195.5	1978.0
1954	558.8	232.9	558.9	304.1	56.0	150.8	1749.5
1955	650.5	273.8	833.7	318.9	91.9	101.6	2086.6
1956	794.4	531.6	979.2	515.0	−137.5	−2.5	2955.2
1957	932.4	434.0	1092.4	684.2	−101.4	−34.2	3210.2
1958	1035.2	331.0	1172.0	617.4	113.7	−210.2	2831.7
1959	1261.3	754.9	1561.3	828.3	85.8	84.7	4404.7
1960	1537.7	1058.8	2042.2	1236.4	−1.0	−262.4	5613.7

Source: *Hundred-Year Statistics of Japanese Economy*, the Bank of Japan, 1966.

Table 7.7
Gross saving of Japan II (ratio of GNP, %)

	Provisions for capital consumption	Undistributed corporate surplus	Personal saving	Government current surplus	(less) Surplus on current account	Discrepancy	Total
CY 1941	7.1	4.0	22.5	-15.6	-2.0	6.5	26.1
1942	6.8	4.0	21.0	-15.4	-1.7	9.0	26.8
1943	6.7	3.9	22.1	-17.9	-0.9	9.1	24.9
1944	7.1	4.0	27.0	-20.8	0.5	10.9	27.8
1945	NA	NA	NA	NA	NA	NA	NA
FY 1946	5.1	-0.2	1.8	-4.8	-1.2	19.2	22.2
1947	4.3	-0.3	-3.0	11.3	0.5	14.7	26.4
1948	4.0	0.1	-0.3	11.9	0.8	13.3	28.2
1949	4.7	1.1	-1.3	16.3	2.2	6.0	24.6
1950	5.2	4.9	10.4	8.9	4.3	0.5	25.5
1951	5.1	3.9	13.2	8.3	2.9	2.9	30.6
1952	5.9	3.2	11.3	5.5	0.1	1.6	27.4
1953	6.7	4.2	7.4	5.6	-1.3	2.8	27.9
1954	7.5	3.1	7.5	4.1	0.8	2.0	23.4
1955	7.9	3.3	10.1	3.9	1.1	1.2	25.3
1956	8.5	5.7	10.5	5.5	-1.5	-0.0	31.8
1957	9.2	4.3	10.8	6.7	-1.0	-0.3	31.6
1958	10.0	3.2	11.3	5.9	1.1	-2.0	27.2
1959	10.0	6.0	12.4	6.6	0.7	0.7	35.0
1960	10.5	7.2	13.9	8.4	-0.0	-1.8	38.2

Source: *Hundred-Year Statistics of Japanese Economy*, the Bank of Japan, 1966.

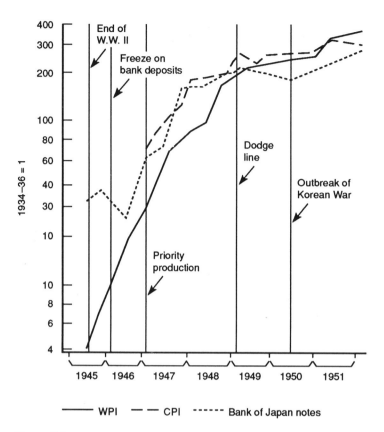

Figure 7.1
Prices and money in the immediate postwar period

ties, cash, bank notes, and other monetary assets in the hand of the public amounted to about ¥500 billion. Within this amount, approximately ¥200 billion were liquid liabilities such as national debt, public bonds, corporate bonds, and stocks (Kosai 1986, p. 39). These excess monetary assets in the face of confronting limited real wealth and dwarfed productive capacity naturally threatened the Japanese economy with inflation (table 7.3). Thus the postwar Japanese economy faced a typical case of monetary overhang and inflation (table 7.4). Table 7.5 vividly illustrates the process in which the Marshallian k, ratio of GNP, of the high-powered money was reduced by stabilization policy. Similarly, those of M1 and M2 decreased. In other words, the velocity of money increased. In order to maintain the subsistence level of families, households were compelled to sell their kimonos,

Table 7.8
Official and black market prices: Japan 1945–51

	Free market WPI 1946/Aug = 100	Free-official price ratio (end of period)		Free market CPI Tokyo 1945/Sept = 100	Free-official price ratio (end of period)
			Dec/45	128	29.7
46/Sept–Dec	115.9	7.2	46	192	8.3
47	304.3	5.3	47	412	5.1
48	479.2	2.9	48	711	2.9
49	444.1	1.7	49	758	1.8
50	371.3	1.2	50	543	1.3
51/Jan–Apr	549.0	1.1	51	642	1.1

Sources: *Hundred-Year Statistics of the Japanese Economy*, the Bank of Japan, 1966. *Report of Household Survey: 1946–1962*, the Prime Minister's Office, 1964.

utensils, furniture, and valuables in exchange for food. Actually Japan's personal saving rates showed minus signs during this period (tables 7.6, 7.7). Their lives were given the label of "bamboo shoot life" because in oriental cooking the bamboo shoot is stripped of its multilayered skins so many times (Uchino 1978, 28). At one time even the use of dollar military scrip was proposed by the GHQ. This was not realized because of the strong resistance from the Japanese government and the Bank of Japan.[20]

Inflation began just after the war. Figure 7.1 illustrates the movement of official prices with other indicators. The government continued, even after the war, ongoing price control, production subsidies, and rationing to some key sectors. Because of the severe shortage of food and basic necessities after the war, black-market prices became extremely high as compared with official prices. At the end of 1945, the average black-market price of consumer goods was about 30 times higher than the official price (table 7.8). Uchino illustrates interesting numbers from the National Policy Agency Report: (Uchino 1978, 26, figure 1). At the end of October 1945—that is, two and a half months after the defeat—sugar and soap were traded in the black market with the price more than 200 *times*—not percent—as high as in the official market; rice about 140 times as high; and cotton stockings, eggs, and turnips about 80 times as high. In order to lessen the gap, official prices needed to be increased gradually, and the gap did not disappear until the early fifties.

In order to understand the mechanism of inflation, we have to examine the complex structure of subsidies that in fact funneled the money supply further into the system.

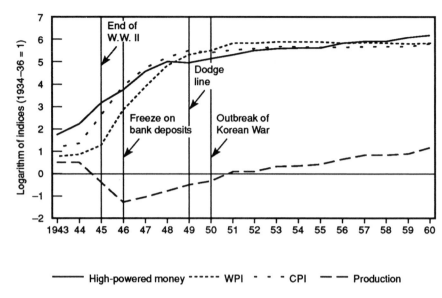

Figure 7.2
Production, prices and money in Japan

First, price-differential subsidies were set up in such a way that the difference between the producers' cost and the officially fixed (consumers') price would be disbursed from the general account of the government budget. These price-differential subsidies were a part of the priority production system, and the alleged purposes were to stimulate production without inflating prices. The amounts disbursed came to ¥12.1 billion in 1946 (11 percent of the general account), ¥45 billion in 1947 (21 percent), and ¥114.1 billion in 1948 (24 percent) (Kosai 1986, 47). These complex subsidies also became factors in the acceleration of inflation. Even if price-differential subsidies might have been useful in bringing down certain individual consumer prices, their macroeconomic consequence was expansion of fiscal expenditures. Because they were mainly financed by the Bank of Japan, they implied the expansion of money supply.

Second, subsidies were hidden in the operation of the government to buy export goods from, and to sell import goods to, the public. The yen prices of exports were determined officially, and exports were purchased by the national government budget (Trade Financial Special Account). When these goods were sold abroad at international prices, proceeds were received by the Foreign Currency Accounts that were managed by GHQ. On the other hand, imports were bought by the government at interna-

Table 7.9
Japan's balance of payments ($ mil)

	Exports	Imports	Trade balance	Freight & insurance	Government (military procurements)	Transfer	Current balance
1946	65	303	−238	−36	0	195	−78
47	181	449	−267	−88	0	405	46
48	262	547	−284	−120	19	462	75
49	533	728	−194	−164	49	514	207
50	920	886	34	−90	63	429	476
51	1354	1645	−291	−226	624	171	329
52	1289	1701	−413	−162	788	34	225
53	1257	2050	−791	−183	803	21	−205
54	1611	2041	−429	−178	602	29	−51
55	2006	2061	−54	−157	511	21	227
56	2482	2613	−131	−316	505	25	−34
57	2855	3256	−401	−353	472	−30	−620
58	2871	2501	368	−15	411	−195	264
59	3414	3052	362	−35	373	−23	361
60	3979	3711	268	−90	406	−25	143

Source: *Hundred-Year Statistics of the Japanese Economy*, the Bank of Japan, 1966.

tional prices and paid for from the Foreign Currency Accounts. The imports were sold in Japan at the official prices that were determined to be very low, and proceeds were received by the Trade Financial Special Account. Accordingly, the ratio of the yen price and the foreign currency price of each traded commodity could only be calculated *ex post*. Thus, Japan neither had a single unified exchange rate nor systematic multiple exchange rates.

During this period Japan's trade balance in terms of U.S. dollars showed deficits (table 7.9). However, the Trade Financial Special Account showed yen deficits. Through the Trade Financial Special Account the government sold imports for domestic official prices that were much lower than international prices and purchased exports for official prices that were higher than international prices. These large yen deficits were financed by borrowing from the Bank of Japan. This borrowing was equivalent to increasing the high-powered money. The accumulative deficits of the Trade Fund Special Account amounted to ¥26 billion at the end of March 1949, and ¥25 billion of that amount was financed by borrowing from the Bank of Japan (the Bank of Japan 1985). In normal situations under the fixed exchange rate, yen deficits in such an account would have corresponded to surpluses in the dollar trade account because the account paid more for the exports than it received from selling the imports. During the occupation period, these yen deficits coexisted with the deficits in the dollar trade account. Here again the complex subsidy system created excess money supply that stimulated the inflated purchasing power. On the external side, the Foreign Currency Accounts showed a deficit and were financed by the Government Account for Relief in Occupied Areas (GARIOA). GARIOA in fact functioned as the channel of income transfers from abroad that mitigated the current account deficit of Japan.

In any case, the government was compelled to cope with inflation—both explicit and implicit in the form of black market prices. On February 17, 1946, the Emergency Monetary Measures Ordinance and the Bank of Japan Note Deposit Ordinance were announced by GHQ for the purpose of implementing monetary reforms as well as assessing the value of assets for new property taxes. They froze all the deposits in financial institutions and required people to exchange the old yen currency for the new yen. The purpose of the freeze on bank deposits was naturally to contain inflation by reducing the money supply that had stimulated the excess purchasing power for goods. It was stipulated that all old yen notes would cease to be legal tender on March 2, 1946, and that they should be deposited in the frozen accounts by March 7. During the intervening period no more than ¥300 for a household head and ¥100 for each additional family member could be withdrawn in new yen notes. Also, withdrawals by families without monthly incomes were limited to the same level. Wage and salary earners could be paid up to ¥500 monthly in new yen, but the remainder was to be paid into the frozen accounts. Under such galloping inflation as existed in 1946, the freeze in deposits was tantamount to confiscation.[21]

Although these measures sounded, and actually were, really drastic, their effects turned out to be only temporary. In fact, the balance of new bank notes increased 68 percent during 1946 (in the total money supply, see table 7.4). There are several possible explanations for this phenomenon (the Bank of Japan 1985).

First, financing of government deficits by the Bank of Japan credit continued until 1949 when the Dodge Line policy was implemented.

Second, there were several loopholes in these measures. For example, while the payment of taxes using the blocked deposit was possible, government expenditures to private sectors were made by issuing new notes or unblocked deposits. Also companies were allowed to withdraw new yen by checks to pay for operating expenditures.

Certainly, some credit should be given to the Emergency Financial Measures for moderating money supply and inflation. As a whole, however, the experiment seems to have demonstrated that attempts to contain inflation, without coherent measures for restraining the government budget and for linking the current account deficit to the reduction of money supply, would not achieve stabilization to the full extent.

In the meantime, there were economists and politicians who believed, often under the influence of J. M. Keynes, that stimulating production was a more urgent issue than curbing inflation. In a budget speech of July 1946, citing explicitly *The General Theory*, Fiscal Minister Ishibashi made an earnest appeal to the people for support for his conviction (Kosai 1986), "In order to achieve the goal of resuming production there is no harm if government deficits occur. Since both capital stock and labor force were clearly underemployed, the problem was simply that bottleneck factors such as the lack of raw materials from overseas stood in the way" (Kosai 1986, 43). Thus Ishibashi spoke of the need to increase coal production and of the priority production system that was partly responsible for solving the problem. The means of providing financial support for the system were the transfer of savings through the Reconstruction Finance Bank and the use of price-differential subsidies.

Both of them were mainly financed by the Bank of Japan through the printing of money that was itself a cause of inflation. Actually the period of priority production overlapped the period when inflation that had been checked once by Emergency Financial Measures became resurgent.

For mobilizing unused resources, some expansionary macro policy might have been useful. To start and sustain growth, however, people should be motivated to work harder and to save more. The stabilization of prices makes people engage in productive activities rather than in speculative ones that take advantage of inflation and makes it easier to plan for the future. Thus, in order to prepare the path for the remarkable growth in the sixties, the Japanese economy needed to pass through a painful period of recession during which not only excess demand but also inflationary expectations were calmed down.

In May 1948, Ralph Young of the Federal Reserve System visited Japan and made the following recommendations regarding the exchange rate system (the Bank of Japan 1985; and Fukao, Oumi, and Etoh 1991):

1. Establish a unified exchange rate. The lack of a unified exchange rate was a serious cause of inflation in Japan. A unified exchange rate would promote export that is a prerequisite for the economic independence of Japan.

2. Adopt a strong anti-inflationary policy and, subsequently, a cut in fiscal expenditures. These measures combined with an increase in tax revenues through a tax reform would help to maintain a single exchange rate.

3. Discontinue the borrowing by the Trade Financial Special Account from the Bank of Japan. This practice was an inflationary factor.

4. Set the exchange rate of the yen at a level that can maintain the current amount of exports and possibly promote more exports in the future. This would urge industries with high costs to become more efficient and protect them from a possible surge of inflation. He also recommended a single yen-dollar exchange rate of 300 yen per dollar, plus or minus 10 yen.

In 1946, the fiscal department of the U.S. military government in occupied Germany was headed by Joseph Dodge, a bank president from Detroit. A report prepared by Gerhard Colm, Joseph Dodge, and Raymond Goldsmith drew the blueprint for the 1948 currency reform in the Western-occupied areas of Germany that had achieved unanticipated success in paving the way for unprecedented German economic growth. At the end of 1948, the U.S. government, which was trying to hasten the economic recovery of Japan under the tightening East-West military tension in Asia, reappointed Dodge to advise on the Japanese economy. He compared the performance of the Japanese economy to a person walking on bamboo stilts, one of which is U.S. aid and the other one hidden subsidies like the Reconstruction Finance Bank. He suggested that the stilts had to be removed because they were dangerously high (Uchino 1978, 49).

On December 18, 1948, GHQ issued a nine-point directive on economic stabilization. The first four points contained anti-inflationary provisions that became the nucleus of the Dodge Plan and were as follows: (1) to balance the general budget; (2) to tighten up on tax collection; (3) to restrict credit; and (4) to stabilize wages. The next five points contained considerations for further control and were as follows: (5) to strengthen and expand the price controls; (6) to improve and reinforce the trade and foreign exchange controls; (7) to upgrade the materials rationing system; (8) to increase domestic production of raw materials and manufactured goods; and (9) to improve food cargo collection.

The implementation of the stabilization plan was enforced by Dodge, who was sent by President Truman to Japan with the rank of minister. Dodge did not follow up control policies, as stated in the latter half of the program's nine points, but advocated the adoption of a single exchange rate and stressed the sound principle of public finance as well as the merit of price mechanism.

In 1949 Dodge advised the Japanese government to achieve a genuine balance in the general budget—this advisory was commonly known as the *Dodge Line*. The 1947 Public Finance Law had prohibited the issue of national bonds, and a formal balance was achieved even then in the general account. However, hidden public bonds issued through special accounts such as the Trade Special Account and the Reconstruction Finance Bank had reached an enormous level. Those issues had been directly linked with the creation of excess money supply. Under the Dodge Line, postal rates as well as fares on the national railways were greatly increased. The new lending by the Reconstruction Finance Bank to firms was suspended. The proceeds from the sale of American aid commodities were set aside as a Counterpart Fund Special Account. A fixed exchange rate for the yen, 360 yen per U.S. dollar, was established on April 23, 1949, and was to continue until 1971, exactly one hundred years after the creation of the yen.

In order to reduce American assistance, Dodge recommended that the government budget be balanced by tightening tax collections and cutting down expenditures. To motivate the self-reliance of business firms, he recommended that price-differential subsidies be discontinued and that households pay much higher taxes. He encouraged saving at the same time. As a result of the Dodge Line, the volume of Bank of Japan notes declined, black market prices fell steeply, the abolition of commodity and price controls progressed, and increases in productivity were remarkable. The household saving rate showed a remarkable upsurge (tables 7.6, 7.7).

The process to recover full working of the price mechanism was a gradual one, even though establishment of a fixed exchange rate and recovery of surplus budget were realized rather quickly. Price controls still continued for some time. In the meantime, black market prices as well as free market prices calmed down by the surplus budget policies, and official prices were increased. Gradually it was possible for the government to lift price control on most goods. Price rises shown in the statistics of 1949 reflect the increases in official prices and not price increases due to abolition of price control.

In any case, this cold-turkey policy had a substantial cooling impact on economic activities. Mining and manufacturing production faltered after having increased until the middle of 1949. Under the fixed exchange rate, exports expanded greatly during the first half of 1949 and had virtually doubled by the end of that year (table 7.9), but the future of exports was threatened by the devaluation of the pound sterling in October. Inventories piled up due to the financial stringency and the sluggishness of demand.

Table 7.10
Macroeconomic indicators just before and after Korean War

Fiscal year	BOP transfer balance (% of GNP)	Special military procurement (% of GNP)	Central government deficit (% of GNP)
1946	3.12	0.00	13.9
47	5.29	0.00	7.3
48	4.99	0.21	6.1
49	5.48	0.52	3.3
50	3.91	0.57	−2.1
51	1.13	4.13	1.7
52	0.20	4.64	3.0
53	0.11	4.08	0.3
54	0.14	2.90	1.1
55	0.10	2.21	1.5

Source: *Hundred-Year Statistics of the Japanese Economy*, the Bank of Japan, 1966. *Japan's Experience in the Immediate Postwar Period*, Fukao, Oumi, and Etoh 1991.

Coincidentally, on June 25, 1950, the North Korean army invaded South Korea, and the United States came to the assistance of South Korea, with its navy, air force, and army. The Korean War produced a sudden change in Japan's economic situation. As orders were concentrated in special procurement and munitions, exports grew rapidly along with the worldwide demand accompanying military expansion (table 7.10). Markets boomed, inventory backlogs were wiped out, and mining and manufacturing production also started to increase at a fast tempo that eventually reached an increase of about 40 percent during the following year. The balance of payments improved, sources of funds became plentiful, and profits rose as well (the Bank of Japan 1985, and Kosai 1986).

In any event, a drastic stabilization policy was needed to bring the postwar economy to a stable growth path with price stability, business confidence, and capital accumulation. It seems that the timing of the Dodge Line was most fortunate, because labor pains due to the stabilization policy were cut short by the increased demand stimulated by the war procurement. Had the Dodge Line been implemented one or two years earlier, the Japanese economy might have been on the brink of total collapse. On the other hand, had it been postponed for a year or two, the Korean War might have led to a very inflationary situation in the absence of an extremely cautious macroeconomic policy.[22]

3   Transition to the Era of High-Speed Growth: A Brief Sketch of the 1950s

The drastic stabilization policy of the Dodge Line that followed the Korean War procurement boom let the Japanese economy complete its reconstruction stage. It was headed for the preparation stage of the golden era of high-speed growth in the 1960s. The GNP exceeded the prewar level (table 7.5). The 1956 Economic White Paper of the Economic Stabilization Board stated, "We are no longer in the postwar reconstruction period." We consider that the most relevant part of the economic history of Japan to Eastern Europe was from the late 1940s through 1951 when the San Francisco Peace Treaty between Japan and Western countries was signed. Thus we sketch briefly the development of the Japanese economy during the 1950s.

The direct effect of the war procurement demand peaked in 1951, but its indirect effect supported a consumption boom in 1952 and an investment boom in 1953 when the Korean War ended. After these years, macro-economic management traced a path of "stop and go" policy in order to maintain the fixed exchange parity. Excessive expansion of the domestic economy generated a balance-of-payments deficit, which necessitated the anti-inflationary monetary policy. Thus the Japanese economy experienced the succession of booms and recessionary balance-of-payments adjustment periods. In 1955 Japan enjoyed a growth rate above 10 percent with price stability and balance-of-payments surplus (table 7.9)—this was called "boom in volume" (instead of price). The prosperity was interrupted in 1956 by a balance-of-payments deficit, but soon after, the next prosperity started. The economic white paper named the successive booms by referring to Japan's mythology in reverse order—the Jimmu Boom (1956–57, the greatest since Emperor Jimmu who was assumed to be the first emperor in Japan), and the Iwato Boom (1959–61, the greatest since Iwato, the stone cave behind which the Sun Goddess hid herself out of rage).[23]

Through the alternation of prosperities and balance-of-payments adjustment, the prerequisites for the remarkably high growth era of the 1960s were gradually established (Kosai, 1986).

The Japanese labor force incorporated high-quality human capital with the potential capacity to be cooperative in a well-disciplined atmosphere. During the fifties there was an abundant supply of labor from rural areas in the Lewis fashion. Trade unions were organized on the enterprise basis, and industrial relations improved. In 1955 a new system of wage bargaining collect *Shunto* (spring offensives) started. In this new system, management and trade unions bargained once a year, in the spring, throughout the country. In the negotiation of shunto, relevant economic data such as productivity increases and producer as well as consumer price indices were taken into consideration for calculating the rates of wage increases. One may interpret this as the Japanese form of incomes policy. In this period, most of the private enterprise unions more or less cooperated with management, and serious labor confrontations in large companies in the private sector ended with the Miike coal mine strike in 1960. Trade unions in public or semipublic sectors such as the Japan Teachers' Union and the National Railway Union, remained quite militant for many years.

The savings rate and the investment rate remained low during the forties (table 7.6) but increased, however, in the fifties. Both the household savings rate and the rate of private plant and equipment investment exceeded 10 percent, although their levels would exceed more than 20 percent during the next high-growth decade.

Abundant supply of well-educated labor and plentiful savings for capital accumulation were basic ingredients for the high rate of growth. Technological improvement in both agriculture and manufacturing industry was also proceeding, resources were transferred from less productive to more productive sectors, and the pace of progress quickened through import of foreign technology (Goto 1991). Abundant factors of production were combined under new technology. Thus the resulting high productivity in the manufacturing sector enabled Japan to export goods in such a way that the balance of payments created no difficulty in maintaining the fixed exchange rate of 360 yen per dollar, and no substantial import of capital was needed to finance ever-increasing investment demand.

In the domestic political scene, the largest conservative party after the war, the Liberal Democratic Party (LDP), was created in 1955 by a merger of the Japan Liberal Party and the Japan Democratic Party. LDP kept the majority vote in most of the elections and continues to be in power. This political stability contributed to the consistency of economic policies and the public's confidence in the market economy.

On the international scene, the peace treaty with the Allied forces (excluding China and the Soviet Union) was signed in San Francisco in September 1951 and went into effect in April 1952. Japan was admitted to the International Monetary Fund (IMF) in 1952 and to the General Agreement on Tariffs and Trade (GATT) in 1955.

In 1960, the question of whether or not to renew the U.S.-Japan Security Treaty that had been initially signed with the peace treaty sharply divided the Japanese into two groups, those who advocated the continuation of military alliance and those who did not. The city of Tokyo echoed with demonstrations by students and workers. Prime Minister Kishi, who was a hard-liner against the protest, had to cancel the visit of President Eisenhower and, subsequently, he resigned. Labor relations were also heated by the Miike coal mine strike. Prime Minister Ikeda, who succeeded Kishi, took a more flexible political attitude and tried to direct people's attention to economic growth. The famous Income Doubling Plan by Ikeda—which was nothing more than an indicative plan without any enforceability in a market economy like Japan—opened the way to the era of high-speed growth during the sixties (Kosai 1986).

4 Concluding Remarks

What can we learn from the postwar Japanese experience in order to help the economic resurgence of Eastern Europe and the Soviet Union? As we mentioned at the outset, it is hard to derive definitive policy prescriptions from a single historical observation. We hope, however, that the following discussions on certain aspects of the recovery process will be at least suggestive. We will consider macroeconomic, microeconomic, international, and political-economy aspects.

The most controversial question of the Japanese reconstruction process seems to be how to evaluate the relative *macroeconomic* significance of the Ishibashi Keynesian policy and the Dodge Line one-stroke stabilization policy.

In any case, in order to wipe out monetary overhang, excess money supply should be eliminated either by increased production, an increase in price levels, a decrease in money supply, or more indirectly by changes in the velocity of circulation of money (Dornbusch 1990). The Ishibashi expansionary policy stressed the increase in production through priority production, but it was linked to a substantial increase in money supply because his version of Keynesianism was to finance the government budget deficits and the lending of the Reconstruction Finance Bank by borrowing from the Bank of Japan, that is, by increasing the high-powered money. Before his expansionary policy, the Emergency Finance Measures had tried to freeze the money supply and to slow down the velocity of circulation, but there could only be temporary relief because the money supply was not under control and people did not expect the recovery of price stability in the near future. Moreover, the expansionary Ishibashi policy undermined still further the credibility of future price stability.

The Dodge Line policy was successful because it was combined with the surplus budget policy that was consistent with stable money supply. Also, the commitment to the fixed exchange rate of 360 yen per dollar prevented the monetary authorities from expanding money supply excessively. After the Dodge Line policies, prices became stable and household savings showed a remarkable surge. The recession after this cold-turkey policy was severe, but most fortunately short, because of the procurement demand brought by the Korean War.

Still, some (like Uchino, cited in section 2) may argue that the Dodge Line was too drastic and gave the Japanese an excessive burden of succeeding recession. We could agree with them to the extent that if the Dodge Line had come much earlier, it might have collapsed the whole economy. The postwar economy was too devastated to let the invisible hand of price mechanism work not only with respect to productive capacity but also with respect to social overhead capital. However, at some time a single-stroke stabilization had to be implemented to prepare the Japanese economy for taking off toward the high-growth path.

It is certainly relevant to the situation that we are considering to appeal to the theoretical apparatus of macroeconomic disequilibrium analysis, even though the apparatus may seem too rigid to analyze market economies of industrialized economies. For the case of monetary overhang, an excess demand in the goods market exists because the price level is too low. At the same time, an excess supply in the labor market exists presumably because the real wage is too high. Thus, monetary overhang can be identified as a typical case of classical unemployment in which "individuals would not find jobs, others could not buy all the goods they want" (Malinvaud 1977, 65).

In the case of Keynesian unemployment, the goods market as well as the labor market is under an excess supply (Barro and Grossman 1976, and Malinvaud 1977). Here an increase in public expenditures can be an effective remedy, whereas in the case of classical unemployment an increase in the price level without increasing the money balance is effective. "To cure Keynesian unemployment, one would lower prices or raise wages. To cure classical unemployment, one should do precisely the reverse" (Malinvaud 1977, 71). From this standpoint, Ishibashi might have mistaken classical unemployment for the Keynesian type when he advocated the expansion of government expenditures financed by the Bank of Japan lending.[24]

Furthermore, the expansionary policy under Minister Ishibashi does not seem to be a good recommendation for Eastern European countries or the Soviet Union because people in these countries are not at the same subsistence level as were the Japanese immediately after the war. What is needed in those countries is a combination of macroeconomic policies that would recover incentives of economic agents to respond to price signals. One-stroke stabilization policy with uncontrolled prices seems to be what should be advised for them.

On the *microeconomic* level, we have to assess the effectiveness of the priority production system. The system is organized to encourage producer goods through quantity signals while keeping prices of producer goods relatively cheaper than consumer goods. (See tables 7.1 and 7.3 for the relative move of WPI and CPI). This system has its intrinsic difficulty because price signals do not encourage production of key products very much. The full reliance on price mechanism after the Dodge Line allowed Japan to prepare for remarkable growth. Table 7.3 again shows that WPI growth is relatively higher than CPI growth only after 1949. Thus, the combination of price incentives with stable macroeconomic policy is what we would recommend to Eastern Europe and the Soviet Union.

Of course, many occupational reforms such as land reform, labor reform, dissolution of zaibatsu, and educational reforms also helped microeconomic incentive structures and a competitive environment. It should be stressed at the same time that the Japanese already possessed capacities to absorb favorable aspects of these reforms. Those capacities had been cultivated through the long history of the importation of foreign culture and technology from China as well as Western countries and by the advanced level of education. In Eastern Europe and the Soviet Union, we do not see the lack of well-educated human capital. What is missing—even though there are exceptions like Hungary—seems to be the capability to respond to price signals because of the absence of experience, and more basically because of continued government regulation.

In the *international* aspects, we have seen that the return to a fixed exchange rate and the commitment to the rate for a prolonged period were important for macroeconomic stabilization as well as for the efficient functioning of price mechanisms (Fukao, Oumi, Etoh 1991). Stabilizing macroeconomic policies had to be accomplished in order to keep a fixed exchange rate. The establishment of a single exchange rate recovered the price specie-flow mechanism as a safety valve against inflation. The yen rate was fixed at a level that the Japanese could successfully maintain in spite of the hardship due to the devaluation of the pound sterling. This enabled the government to keep its promise of the fixed exchange rate for a long period without devaluation. Moreover, a unified exchange rate meant the elimination of complex subsidies for export as well as import goods.

One may wonder whether Japan's emphasis on exports that is now often under criticism had its origin during the reconstruction period. Since both exports and imports were under the control of GHQ, there were hardly any options left to Japan on the trade policy during the immediate reconstruction period. The Japanese generally are nervous about the national lack of energy resources and natural resources. This sentiment was probably reinforced by the experience of stop-go policies during the fifties, and remained as inertia even after Japan started accumulating trade surplus in the late sixties.

If we make some comparison here with Eastern Europe, Japan found it could sell most of its exports in the late forties and early fifties; the problem was to produce them. Hungary, Poland, and Czechoslovakia have a recession from the collapse of trade with the Soviet Union. Their manufacturers lack the quality to sell in the West. Each has substantial exportable surpluses of agricultural products, steel ingot, and textiles but encounter everywhere trade barriers for these products.

We also have to pay substantial attention to several functions in the *political economy* aspect of the reconstruction period. First, the existence of supernational authority was instrumental in implementing several important reforms that were difficult in many countries. Often Germany, Italy, and Japan are referred to as countries whose defeat in war might have helped their growth. Usually the faster pace of modernization due to wartime destruction is given as one reason for success. In our opinion, the feasibility of radical reforms that promote incentive mechanisms can be another important reason.

Second, there seems to be a good reason to recommend a fixed exchange rate to a country facing inflationary pressure because of the monetary overhang. Milton Friedman emphasizes the merit of flexible exchange rates that allow autonomous monetary policy for the reason that one can trust one's own government in determining its price level. When a government faces so many political difficulties against implementing a genuine stabilization policy, then the same logic will work as a case for linking its currency by a fixed exchange rate to a currency of a country that enjoys price stability.

Third, the adoption of the Dodge Line and gradual transition to market principle from a prior production system that emphasizes more government interventions coincides with the establishment of the second Yoshida cabinets from the short-lived socialist and coalition cabinets. Prime Minister Yoshida did not favor government interventions that were common in policies of the Ministry of International Trade and Industry (MITI). After the second Yoshida government, the conservative parties—after 1955 the Liberal Democratic Party (LDP)—have stayed in power. Continuation of the same type of government has merit in keeping some time consistency (or the belief of it) in its policies emphasizing price mechanism.

In general, Japan had a fairly efficient government bureaucracy. In Eastern Europe and particularly the Soviet Union, there is certainly a large government bureaucracy, but it is inefficient and corrupt. Also the Japanese government enjoyed obedience and at least some degree of popular support. This does not appear to be the case in the Soviet Union. Japan has had no ethnic strife nor fights between levels of government. In contrast, the new legislatures in Eastern Europe are busy raising pensions and other Soviet expenditures. These differences make the implementation of a recovery plan harder in Eastern Europe and the Soviet Union.

Fourth, the transformation of military labor unions during the initial postwar period to more or less cooperative enterprise-based unions and the adoption of a kind of income policy through Shunto were essential factors in stabilizing prices and wages in Japan. Japanese management was, even though the change in GHQ's attitude and recession helped, skillful enough to subdue the power of trade unions.

In Eastern Europe, enterprise managers often are selected on the basis of party loyalty. Employees are not used to working hard. Thus, although Eastern Europe and the Soviet Union have a work force with considerable human capital as measured by years of school, they seem to have started the reform process with a labor force that is probably less trained than that in postwar Japan.

The final point on the political-economy aspect is the role of pacifism. Yoshida's basic attitude that Japan keep only the minimum level of defense and that she be under the nuclear umbrella of the United States dispensed with much of her military expenditures and transferred resources for modernization and productivity increases.

To close this chapter, it would be fair for us to mention several factors of luck in the process of Japan's recovery. Occupation powers changed their policy from the demilitarization of Japan to reconstruction of her economy soon after the war. Also occupation policies imposed by supernational force helped the incentive mechanism. Reparation payments were reduced to a nominal level. Instead of the procurement demand of the Korean War came the best timing of the recession after the cold-turkey

Dodge Line policy. Pacifism worked because the international situation allowed Japan to keep out of direct military conflicts.

At the same time, it was also true that Japan had inherited from the prewar years well-educated human capital and economic institutions in which market mechanism could work. It was ingenuity as well as much hard work on the part of the nation that enabled its economy to take advantage of the opportunities that were available to postwar Japan.

Appendix

A Chronology of Immediate Postwar Economic Events in Japan

1945	Aug	End of World War II
1946	Feb	Introduction of "Emergency Economic Crisis Policy" (including freeze of bank deposits)
	Aug	Establishment of the Economic Stabilization Board
	Dec	Introduction of Priority Production System
1947	Jan	Establishment of the Reconstruction Finance Bank
1948	July	Publication of Japan's first economic white paper "A Report on Actual Conditions in the Economy"
	May	Ralph Young's visit to Japan
1949	Feb	Joseph Dodge's visit to Japan
	May	Declaration of framework for Dodge's economic policy for Japan, the "Dodge Line (Plan)"
	Apr	Establishment of a single 360 yen/dollar exchange rate
	Dec	Enactment of the Foreign Exchange and Trade Control Act Liberalization of private sector exports
1950	Jan	Introduction of the Foreign Exchange Budget Liberalization of private sector imports
	June	Outbreak of Korean War
1951	Sep	San Francisco Peace Treaty
1952	Jan	Liquidation of Reconstruction Finance Bank
	May	Admission of Japan to IMF and World Bank
1953	July	End of Korean War
1955	Sep	Admission of Japan to the GATT
1956	Dec	Admission of Japan to the U.N.

Notes

This is a revised version of the paper presented at the Hamburg Conference on Post-War Reconstruction, September 5–7, 1991.

We are indebted to Michisato Ishikawa, who edited Bank of Japan (1985), Charlie Kindleberger, M. Joe Peck, Rudi Dornbusch and Yasukichi Yasuba for their valuable comments. We also thank Ryoko Okazaki for her research assistance and Carolyn M. Beaudin for her advice to improve our English. Errors and opinions expressed are strictly ours and by no means reflect the view of the Bank of Japan.

1. Uchino (1978) p. 15. But Uchino continues, "In Japan in 1945, even the mountains and rivers are laid to ruin."

2. The account of the reconstruction is a kind of sentimental journey for those who lived through the hope and despair during the postwar period. For example, Kosai (1986) and Uchino (1978) contain vivid and often personal memories of the period. Nakamura (1981) provides a concise account of the postwar Japanese economy. Bank of Japan (1985) gives valuable and detailed documentation of the stabilization policy during the reconstruction period, Takemae (1983) provides useful analysis on the occupation policy, and Fukao, Oumi, and Etoh (1991) would serve as a good complement to this essay because it focuses on the international aspects of the stabilization policy after World War II.

3. Kosai (1986) p. 17.

4. Kosai (1986) p. 20, Cohen (1949) p. 444.

5. Uchino (1978) p. 20.

6. Ibid.

7. Hadley (1970).

8. Kosai (1986) p. 25, Uchino (1978) p. 23.

9. Kosai (1986) pp. 27–28.

10. We owe this point to James Gibbons, Yale student.

11. Gordon (1986), Cole (1971), Moore (1983).

12. The Japanese are now in a position to be proud of the achievement of their pacifism, even though there are elements of luck in it. Instead of apologizing at the criticism of free-ridership on the Gulf war, they may positively develop their philosophy of a merchant nation.

13. Nakamura (1981) chapter 1.

14. The text of Leontief (1941) was brought into Japan before the war and studied by people at the Planning Agency; see Hamada (1986).

15. Nakamura (1981) pp. 32–33, Kosai (1986) pp. 41–43.

16. Kosai (1986) p. 45.

17. Zysman (1983) chap. 5.

18. Nakamura (1981) p. 33, Kosai (1986) p. 42.

19. Uchino (1978) p. 53.

20. One of the authors still remembers vividly that his parents regretted that they had not bought a piano for their children before the freeze.

21. The Bank of Japan found the intention of the GHQ first, and immediately the Finance Minister protested against the use of military bills. This protection of the seigniorage right was quite crucial.

22. Of course, if the Japanese could have fully anticipated the outbreak of the Korean War, they could have instituted even better stabilization policies. The fact is that nobody can be so omniscient.

23. Nakamura, 1981, pp. 50–54. This naming continues finally to the Izanagi Boom during the high-growth period (1967–69, the best since Goddess Izanagi who gave birth to the Japan Islands).

24. See also Portes (1991) for the related issue of real and nominal anchors.

References

Asakura, Kokichi and Chiaki Nishiyama, 1974, *The Monetary Analysis of Japanese Economy*, Sobunsya, (in Japanese).

Bank of Japan, 1985, *Nihon Ginko Hyakunen Shi* (One Hundred Year History of the Bank of Japan), Vol. 5, (in Japanese).

Bank of Japan, 1966, *Hundred-Year Statistics of Japanese Economy*.

Barro, R. J. and H. I. Grossman, 1976, *Money, Employment and Inflation*, Cambridge University Press.

Cohen, J. B., 1949, *Japan's Economy in War and Reconstruction*. Minneapolis, University of Minnesota Press.

Cole, Robert E., 1971, *Japanese Blue Collar, The Changing Tradition*, Berkeley, University of California Press.

Dornbusch, Rudiger, 1990, "Monetary Overhang and Reforms in the 1940s," Research Department, International Monetary Fund.

Fukao, Mitsuhiro, Masao Oumi, and Kimihiro Etoh, 1991, "Japan's Experience in the Immediate Postwar Period: Process toward a Single Exchange Rate and De-nationalization of Trade," International Department, the Bank of Japan.

Gordon, Andrew, 1985, *The Evolution of Labor Relations in Japan: Heavy Industry, 1853–1955*. Cambridge, Mass. Council on East Asian Studies, Harvard University.

Goto, Akira, 1991, "Technology Importation: Japan's Postwar Experience," Department of Economics, Yale University.

Hadley, Eleanor M., 1970, *Antitrust in Japan*, Princeton University Press.

Hamada, Koichi, 1986, "The Impact of the General Theory in Japan," *Eastern Economic Journal*, Vol. XII, No. 4.

Kosai, Yutaka, 1986, *The Era of High-Speed Growth*. Tokyo, University of Tokyo Press.

Leontief, Wasily, 1941, *The Structure of the American Economy*.

Malinvaud, Edmond, 1977, *The Theory of Unemployment Reconsidered*, John Wiley & Sons, New York.

Moore, Joe, 1983, *Japanese Workers and the Struggle for Power*. Madison, University of Wisconsin Press.

Nakamura, Takafusa, 1981, *The Postwar Japanese Economy*. Tokyo, University of Tokyo Press.

Portes, Richard, 1991, "The Path of Reform in central and Eastern Europe: An Introduction," CEPR Discussion Paper No. 559.

Takemae, Eiji, 1983, *GHO*, Iwanami Syoten, (in Japanese).

Uchino, Tatsuro, 1978, *Japan's Postwar Economy*. Tokyo, Kodanshasha International.

Zysman, John, 1983. *Governments, Markets, and Growth*. Ithaca, Cornell University Press.

8

The Marshall Plan: History's Most Successful Structural Adjustment Program

J. Bradford De Long and Barry Eichengreen

[T]he world of suffering people looks to us for leadership. Their thoughts, however, are not concentrated alone on this problem. They have more immediate and terribly pressing concerns where the mouthful of food will come from, where they will find shelter tonight, and where they will find warmth. Along with the great problem of maintaining the peace we must solve the problem of the pittance of food, of clothing and coal and homes. Neither of these problems can be solved alone.
—George C. Marshall, November 1945

Can you imagine [the plan's] chances of passage in an election year in a Republican congress if it is named for Truman and not Marshall?
—Harry S. Truman, October 1947

1 Introduction

The post–World War II reconstruction of the economies and polities of Western Europe was an extraordinary success. Growth was fast, distributional conflicts in large part finessed, world trade booming. The stability of representative democracies in Western Europe made its political institutions the envy of much of the world. The politicians who in the post–World War II years laid the foundations of the postwar order had good warrant to be proud. They were, as Truman's Secretary of State Dean Acheson put it in the title of his memoirs, *Present at the Creation* of an extraordinarily successful set of political and economic institutions.

Perhaps the greatest success of the post–World War II period was the establishment of representative institutions and "mixed economies" in that half of Europe not occupied by the Red Army. A similar opportunity is open today in Eastern Europe, with the possibility of replacing Stalinist systems with market-oriented industrial democracies. The future will judge politicians today as extraordinarily farsighted if they are only half as successful as Acheson and his peers.

Many argue that the West should seize this opportunity by extending aid to the nations of Eastern Europe in exchange for a commitment to reform. Advocates evoke as a precedent the Marshall Plan—the program that transferred $13 billion in aid from the United States to Western Europe in the years from 1948 to 1951. They argue that we should emulate the steps taken by the founders of the postwar order half a century ago by extending aid to Eastern Europe.

Any such argument by analogy hinges on two links. First, that the Marshall Plan in fact played a key role in inaugurating the postwar era of prosperity and political stability in Western Europe. Second, that the lessons of the postwar era translate to present-day Eastern Europe. In this chapter we examine both propositions. The bulk of this chapter evaluates the Marshall Plan. The conclusion steps back and weighs the extent to which the lessons of the post–World War II period can be applied to Eastern Europe including the regions of the Soviet Union today.

Summary of Conclusions

Our central conclusion is that the Marshall Plan did matter. But it did not matter in the way that the folk wisdom of international relations assumes. Milward (1984) is correct in arguing that Marshall Plan aid was simply not large enough to significantly stimulate Western European growth by accelerating the replacement and expansion of its capital stock. Nor did the Marshall Plan matter by financing the reconstruction of devastated infrastructure, for as we show, reconstruction was largely complete before the program came on stream.[1]

The Marshall Plan did play a role in alleviating resource shortages. But this channel was not strong enough to justify the regard in which the program is held. By 1948 and the beginning of Marshall Plan aid, bottlenecks were scarce, and markets were good at alleviating their impact.

Rather, the Marshall Plan significantly sped Western European growth by altering the environment in which economic policy was made. In the immediate aftermath of World War II, politicians who recalled the disasters of the Great Depression were ill-disposed to "trust the market," and eager to embrace regulation and government control. Had European political economy taken a different turn, post–World War II European recovery might have been hobbled by clumsy allocative bureaucracies that rationed scarce foreign exchange and placed ceiling prices on exportables to protect the consumption of urban working classes.

Yet in fact the Marshall Plan era saw a rapid dismantling of controls over product and factor markets in Western Europe. It saw the restoration of price and exchange rate stability. To some degree this came about because underlying political-economic conditions were favorable (and no one in Europe wanted a repeat of interwar experience). To some degree it came about because the governments in power believed that the "mixed economies" they were building should have a strong promarket orientation. Marshall Plan aid gave them room to maneuver in order to carry out their intentions: without such aid, they would have soon faced a harsh choice between contraction to balance their international payments and severe controls on admissible imports. To some degree it came about because Marshall Plan administrators pressured European governments to decontrol and liberalize even when they wished to otherwise.

In post–World War II Western Europe the conditions imposed, formally and informally, for the receipt of U.S. aid encouraged the reductions in spending needed for financial stability, the relaxation of controls that prevented markets from allocating resources, and the opening of economies to trade. Marshall Plan "conditionality" pushed governments toward versions of the mixed economy that had more market orientation and less directive planning in the mix. While post–World War II European welfare states and governments are among the most extensive in proportion to economic life in history, they are built on top of, and do not supplant or bypass, the market allocation of goods and factors of production. The Marshall Plan should thus be thought of as a large and highly successful structural adjustment program.[2]

The experience of the Marshall Plan therefore suggests lessons for the role the West can play today. It suggests that the yield of a Marshall Plan for Eastern Europe and the Soviet Union could be high, but the benefits are not direct increases in productive capacity made possible by aid. Aid to Eastern Europe will accelerate growth in the manner of the Marshall Plan if it leads to policies that accelerate the move toward market organization, free trade, and financial stability. Aid can help as an incentive and as a cushion to make reform possible. But aid cannot substitute for reform. The key remains the successful execution of structural adjustment.

Organization of the Chapter

After this introduction, section 2 of the chapter develops the "folk image" and contrasts it with the reality of the Marshall Plan. It is followed by a series of sections that consider in turn alternative channels through which the Marshall Plan could have accelerated economic recovery. First, Marshall Plan aid might have quickened the pace of private investment. Second, it might have supported public investment in infrastructure. Third, it might have eliminated bottlenecks. Fourth, it might have facilitated the negotiation of a progrowth "social contract" that provided the political stability and climate necessary to support the postwar boom. We argue that the first two were of negligible importance, that the third had some but not overwhelming significance during the years of the Marshall Plan, and that the fourth was vital but is difficult to quantify.

Throughout the chapter we use two sets of comparisons to structure and discipline the argument. The first comparison is with Europe after World War I. In contrast to the post–World War II era, after World War I European reconstruction had been a failure. Alternating inflation and deflation retarded recovery. Growth had been slow, distributional conflicts had been bitter, and the network of trade fragile and stagnant. Representative government had been tried and rejected by all save a handful of European nations.[3] The critical question from our perspective is to what degree the Marshall Plan was responsible for the different outcomes of the two postwar periods. The comparison addresses this issue and highlights features of the international environment besides the Marshall Plan that must figure in an adequate analysis.

The second comparison is with the experience of Argentina. Before the war, Argentina had been as rich as Continental Europe. In 1913 Buenos Aires was among the top twenty cities of the world in telephones per capita. In 1929 Argentina had been perhaps fourth in density of motor vehicles per capita, with approximately the same number of vehicles per person as France or Germany. Argentina from 1870–1950 was a country in the same class as Canada or Australia.

Yet after World War II, Argentina grew very much more slowly than France or Germany, rapidly falling from the ranks of the First World to the Third (see figure 8.1). Features of the international economic environment affecting Argentina as well as Europe—the rapid growth of world trade under the Bretton Woods system, for example—are not sufficient therefore to explain the latter's singular stability and rapid growth. Again the comparison points to factors aside from the direct effects of foreign aid that mattered, and factors in conjunction with which foreign aid must work in order to unleash a period of rapid growth.

The concluding section of the chapter summarizes our argument and applies our analysis of the Marshall Plan to options for dealing with Eastern Europe.

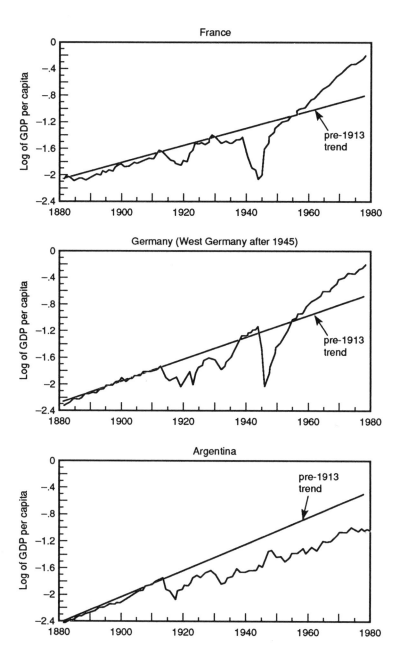

Figure 8.1
Very long run economic growth, 1880–1980
Sources: Angus Maddison, *Phases of Capitalist Development*; Robert Summers and Alan
Heston, *Penn World Table V*; Carlos Diaz Alejandro, *Essays on the Economic History of the
Argentine Republic*

2 The Marshall Plan: Image and Reality

The Folk Image

Western Europe's recovery from World War II had ground to a halt by the end of 1947.[4] The first phase of postwar expansion and recovery had come to an end. Reserves of foreign assets had been depleted. Export earnings were insufficient to finance purchases of raw materials and equipment from the only remaining functioning industrial economy, the United States. Bankers in the United States recalled the dismal returns on investments in Europe after World War I. Observing Communist electoral strength, they were unwilling to loan capital to Europe on any terms.[5] Incomes were too low to provide savings needed to finance reconstruction. Taxes were inadequate to balance government budgets. Inflation and financial chaos eroded Western Europe's ability to reconstruct and reorganize its economy. Internal U.S. State Department memoranda spoke of an approaching breakdown of the division of labor between town and country, and between resource extraction, manufacturing, and distribution sectors. Many feared an economic collapse in Europe as soon as U.S. humanitarian aid ceased to prop it up.

Such is the picture of Western Europe on the eve of the Marshall Plan painted by biographers of statesmen and by historians of international relations.[6] The Marshall Plan, they allege, solved these problems at a stroke. It provided funds to finance investment and public expenditure. It allowed countries to import from the United States. It eliminated bottlenecks that had obstructed economic growth. It set the stage for prosperity. European growth was very rapid after 1948 and the beginning of Marshall Plan aid, as figure 8.2 charts.

At the time, it was not even clear that post–World War II Western Europe would utilize market mechanisms to coordinate economic activity. Belief in the ability of the market to coordinate economic activity and support economic growth had been severely shaken by the Great Depression. Wartime controls and plans, while implemented as extraordinary measures for extraordinary times, had created a governmental habit of control and regulation. Seduced by the very high economic growth rates reported by Stalin's Soviet Union and awed by its war effort, many expected centrally planned economies to reconstruct faster and grow more rapidly than market economies. Memory of the Great Depression was fresh, and countries relying on the market were seen as likely to lapse into a period of underemployment and stagnation. Communists predicted that post–World War

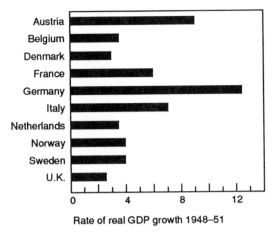

Figure 8.2
Economic growth in European nations during the Marshall Plan years

II reconstruction would dramatically reveal the superiority of central planning. Europe's East would pull ahead of whatever regions in the West remained attached to market organization and private property.[7]

Moreover, it seemed at least an even bet that the United States would withdraw from Western Europe. The U.S. government had done so after World War I, when the cycles of U.S. politics had led to the erosion of the internationalist Wilson administration and the rise to dominance of a Republican isolationist Congress. The same pattern appeared likely after World War II: Republican Congressional leader Robert Taft, the dominant figure in the Senate after the election of 1946, was extremely isolationist in temperament.

By all indications, the American commitment to relief and reconstruction was limited. The end of hostilities against Japan had led to the immediate cessation of lend-lease to Britain. Humanitarian aid under the auspices of the United Nations was seen as limited and transitional. The Truman administration was viewed as internationalist, but weak. Congressional critics called for balanced budgets. The 1946 congressional elections were a disaster for the Democratic party.

Considerable economic aid had been extended to Europe from the United States after World War I, first by the Herbert Hoover-led relief and reconstruction effort and then by private capital speculating on a restoration of monetary stability and pre–World War I exchange rates. The very magnitude of U.S. private capital flows after World War I militated against their repetition. Post–World War I reconstruction loans had been sold as sound private investments. They did not turn out to be so. Seymour Harris (1948) calculated that in present value terms nearly half of American private investments in Europe between the wars had been lost. Once burned, twice shy.[8] With strong Communist parties in Italy and France, a nationalization-minded Labour government in Britain, and a Germany once again pressed for reparations transfers, capital flows from American investors gambling on European recovery and political stability seemed unlikely.

Nevertheless, within two years after the end of the war it became U.S. government policy to build up Western Europe politically, economically, and militarily. The first milestone was the Truman Doctrine: President Truman asked Congress to provide aid to Greece to fill the gap left by the retreating British. The Truman Doctrine inaugurated the policy of containment. Included in the doctrine was a declaration that containment required steps to quickly regenerate economic prosperity in Western Europe. This policy extended beyond Greece and Turkey to the rest of Western Europe as well. As columnist Richard Strout summarized the informal conversations, leaks, and trial balloons emanating from the government in early 1947, "State Department strategists have now come around—to the point a good many 'visionaries' have been urging all along—that one way of combating Communism is to give western Europe a full dinner pail."[9]

Employing Secretary of State George C. Marshall's reputation as the architect of military victory of World War II, conservative fears of the further extension of Stalin's empire, and a political alliance with influential Republican Senator Arthur Vandenberg, Truman and his administration outflanked isolationist and antispending opposition and maneuvered the Marshall Plan through Congress. In the first two post–World War II years, the United States contributed about $4 billion a year to relief and reconstruction through United Nations Relief and Recovery Administration (UNRRA) and other programs.[10] The Marshall Plan continued these flows at comparable rates. But a significant difference was that UNRRA aid could be, and was expected to be, cut off at any time. Each additional quarter it was continued was a windfall. Its continuation was not something upon which Europe could count.

By contrast, the Marshall Plan was a multiyear commitment. From 1948 to 1951, the United States contributed $13.2 billion to European recovery: $3.2 billion went to the United Kingdom, $2.7 billion to France, $1.5 billion to Italy, and $1.4 billion to the Western-occupied zones of Germany that would become the post–World War II *Bundesrepublik*.

In its first year, half of all Marshall aid was devoted to food. Overall, 60 percent was spent on primary products and intermediate inputs: food, feed, fertilizers, industrial materials, and semifinished products, divided evenly between agricultural goods and industrial inputs. One-sixth was for fuel. One-sixth was spent on machinery, vehicles, and other commodities.[11]

The received image of the Marshall Plan sees it as the catalyst for Western European recovery. Before Marshall aid began to arrive, all was stagnation and fear of collapse. After, all was growth and optimism. Charles Mee's (1984) narrative is one of the most enthusiastic: "The ink was not dry before the first ships set sail—[with] 19,000 tons of wheat—followed by the SS *Godrun Maersk* with tractors, synthetic resin, and cellulose acetate; the SS *Gibbes Lykes* with 3,500 tons of sulfur; the SS *Rhondda* with farm machines, chemicals, and oil; the SS *Geirulo*, and SS *Delmundo*, and the SS *Lapland* with cotton. When shipments of carbon black began to reach Birmingham—Europe's largest tire plant was put back into production and 10,000 workers returned to their jobs."

The Reality: The European Economy following the Two Wars

Such is the folk image of the Marshall Plan. We now seek to contrast that image with historical reality. In this section we reassess the state of Europe's economy, turning in subsequent sections to our reassessment of the Marshall Plan. This section brings out four points. (1) World War II was more destructive than World War I. (2) Economic recovery was significantly faster after World War II. (3) There is no necessary relationship between the two preceding points. Rapid growth after World War II was not mainly a "rubber band effect" (the reversal of wartime output losses); rather, it was a sustained acceleration. (4) Nor did rapid postwar growth simply reflect a favorable international economic environment. Not all countries experienced comparable accelerations despite all being exposed to the same favorable international economic climate.

1. World War II was more destructive. When World War II ended, more than 40 million people in Europe were dead by violence or starvation. More than half of the dead were inhabitants of the Soviet Union. Even west of the post–World War II Soviet border, perhaps one in twenty were killed—close to one in twelve in Central Europe. In World War I the

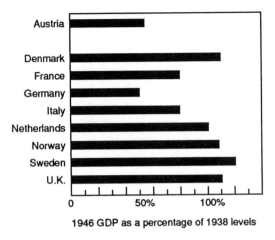

Figure 8.3
Production immediately after World War II

overwhelming proportion of those killed had been soldiers. During World War II fewer than half of those killed were in the military.[12]

Material damage in World War II was spread over a wider area than in World War I. Destruction in the First World War was by and large confined to a narrow belt around a static trenchline. Although material destruction along the trenchline was overwhelming, it extended over only a small proportion of the European continent. World War II's battle sites were scattered more widely. Weapons were a generation more advanced and more destructive. World War II also saw the first large-scale strategic bombing campaigns.[13] Figure 8.3 plots relative levels of national product in the year immediately after World War II, relative to a prewar 1938 base.

Thus the aftermath of World War II saw many of Western Europe's people dead, its capital stock damaged, and the web of market relationships torn. Relief alone called for much more substantial government expenditures than reduced tax bases could finance. The post–World War I cycle of hyperinflation and depression seemed poised to repeat itself. Prices rose in Italy to thirty-five times their prewar level. France knocked four zeroes off the franc.

Industrial production recovered somewhat more rapidly than agricultural output after 1945. But two years after the end of the war, coal production in Western Europe was still below levels reached before or during the war. German coal production in 1947 proceeded at little more than half of the pre—World War II pace. Dutch and Belgian production was 20 percent below, and British 10 percent below, pre—World War II 1938 levels.[14] Demands for coal for heating reduced the continent's capacity to produce energy for industry. During the cold winter of 1946—47 coal earmarked for industrial uses had to be diverted to heating. Coal shortages led to the shutdown of perhaps a fifth of Britain's coal-burning and electricity-using industry in February 1947. Western European industrial production in 1946 was only 60 percent, and in 1947 only 70 percent, of the pre—World War II norm.[15]

Problems of agriculture were, if anything, more serious. Denmark's 1945—46 crops were 93 percent of prewar averages, but those in France, Belgium, Germany, and Italy were barely half. The harvest of 1947 was a disaster. Fertilizer and machinery remained in short supply. A fierce winter and a dry spring froze and withered trees and crops. Financial chaos meant that a large part of the harvest was not marketed. Farmers hoarded crops for barter and home consumption. Western Europe in 1946—47 had four-fifths its 1938 supply of foods. Its population had increased by twenty million—more than a tenth—even after accounting for military and civilian deaths.

Europe's ability to draw resources and import commodities from the rest of the world was heavily compromised by World War II. Traditionally, Western Europe had exported industrial goods and imported agricultural goods from Eastern Europe, the Far East, and the Americas. Now there was little prospect of rapidly restoring this international division of labor. Eastern European nations adopted Russian-style central planning and looked to the Soviet Union for economic links. Industry in the United States and Latin American had expanded during the war to fill the void created by the cessation of Europe's exports. Imports of food and consumer goods for relief diverted hard currency from purchases of capital goods needed for long-term reconstruction.

Changes in net overseas asset positions reduced Western Europe's annual earnings from net investments abroad. Britain had liquidated almost its entire overseas portfolio in order to finance imports during the war. The reduction in invisible earnings reduced Western Europe's capacity to import by approximately 30 percent of 1938 imports. The movement of the terms of trade against Western Europe gave it in 1947—48 32 percent fewer imports for export volumes themselves running 10 percent below pre—World War II levels; higher export volumes might worsen the terms of trade further. The net effect of the inward shift in demand for exports

Table 8.1
European balance of payments position, 1946–47 and 1919–20 (billions of 1946–47 dollars at annual rates)

	1946–47	1919–20
European imports	11.2	11.8
European exports	5.2	4.6
Trade account	−6.0	−7.2
Net income from investments	0.4	1.1
Other current account	−1.1	1.3
Total current account	−6.7	−4.8
Reduction in European assets	−1.8	−2.0
Total loans and grants from U.S.	4.9	2.8

Source: Authors' calculations based on United Nations (1948) and United Nations (various years).

and the collapse of the net investment positions was to give Europe in 1947–48 only 40 percent of the capacity to import that it had possessed in 1938.

By contrast, after World War I Europe's external position had appeared more favorable. Europe emerged from the Great War with its overseas investments still large.[16] European shipping still generated substantial net revenues. Invisible receipts financed more than 20 percent of European imports in the years immediately after World War I. The shift in terms of trade against Europe was smaller after World War I than after World War II.

More important, virtually every European nation quickly regained access to the international capital markets after World War I. This was true even of reparations-burdened Germany until the spring of 1921, when the stage for hyperinflation was set.[17] American private investors were eager after World War I to make loans for European recovery. In the decade after World War I, they loaned more than $1 billion a year overseas, primarily to European nations. Government restrictions on foreign loans were rare and by and large limited to cases in which countries had unsettled war debts owing to the United States.[18]

Table 8.1 summarizes Europe's balance-of-payments position after the two wars. Even though United States-provided UNRRA and other government-provided assistance in the pre–Marshall Plan years was much larger in real terms than all sources of financing—public and private loans and public and private grants—had been in the equivalent period after World War I,

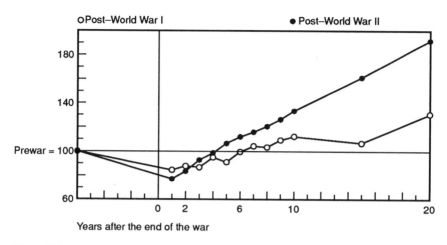

Figure 8.4
Post–World War I and Post–World War II recoveries of GDP per capita, average of
Britain, France, and Germany*
Sources: Angus Maddison, *Phases of Capitalist Development*; Robert Summers and Alan
Heston, *Penn World Table V*

the higher volume of financing did not allow Europe to import more from
the rest of the world. Real imports were in fact a shade higher after World
War I than after World War II because of the substantial deterioration in
Europe's invisible balance in the latter instance.

Thus Europe after World War II was in at least as bad economic shape
as it had been after World War I. Rapid reconstruction and a return to
prosperity did not seen inevitable. Another episode of financial and political chaos like that which had plagued the Continent following World War
I appeared likely. U.S. State Department officials wondered whether Europe
might be dying—like a wounded soldier who bleeds to death after the
fighting. State Department memoranda in 1946–47 presented an apocalyp-
tic vision of a complete breakdown in Europe of the division of labor—
between city and country, industry and agriculture, and between different
industries themselves.[19] In the aftermath a Communist triumph was seen as
a distinct possibility.

2. Recovery from World War II was faster. In 1946, the year after the end
of World War II, national product per capita in the three largest Western
European economies had fallen at least 25 percent below its 1938 level.
This was half again as much as production per capita in 1919 had fallen

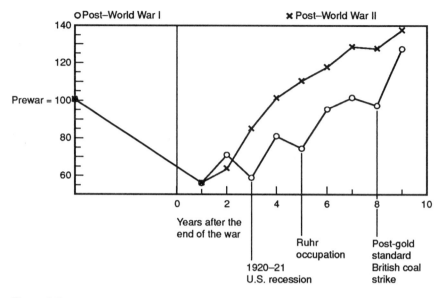

Figure 8.5

Post–World War I and Post–World War II recoveries of Western European steel production*

Sources: B. R. Mitchell, *European Historical Statistics*; U.N. Economic Commission for Europe, *Economic Survey of Europe since the War*; Ingmar Svennilson, *Growth and Stagnation in the European Economy*

below its prewar (1913) level. Yet the pace of post–World War II recovery soon surpassed that which followed World War I. As figure 8.4 shows, by 1949 national income per capita in Britain, France, and Germany had recovered to within a hair of prewar levels.

Recovery at that date was some two years ahead of its post–World War I pace. By 1951, six years after the war and at the effective end of the Marshall Plan, national incomes per capita were more than 10 percent above prewar levels. Measured by the yardstick of the admittedly imperfect national product estimates, the three major economies of Western Europe had achieved a degree of recovery that post–World War I Europe had not reached in the eleven years separating World War I from the Great Depression. Post–World War II Europe accomplished in six years what took post–World War I Europe sixteen.

Post–World War II recovery dominated post–World War I recovery by other economic indicators as well. Figures 8.5 though 8.7 plot the comparative pace of post–World War I and post–World War II recoveries of

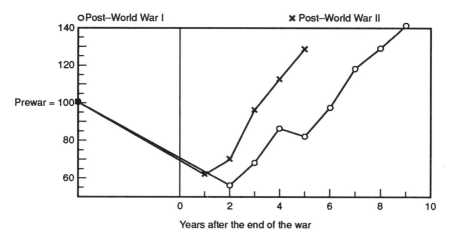

Figure 8.6
Post–World War I and Post–World War II recoveries of Western European cement
production*
Sources: B. R. Mitchell, *European Historical Statistics*; U.N. Economic Commission for
Europe, *Economic Survey of Europe since the War*; Ingmar Svennilson, *Growth and Stagnation
in the European Economy*

Western European steel, cement, and coal production. Since all three are
measured in physical units, these indices are not vulnerable to the potential
sources of error afflicting national income and product accounts. Figure 8.5
shows that by 1950—five years after the end of the Second World War—
Western European steel production had surpassed its prewar level. After
World War I, in contrast, steel production did not exceed its 1913 level
until nine years after the fighting ended. Figure 8.6 shows that the relative
recovery of cement production after World War II ran three years ahead of
its post–World War I pace.

The recovery of coal production after World War II also outran its
post–World War I pace by a substantial margin, as figure 8.7 shows, even
though coal was seen as in notoriously short supply in the post–World
War II years. By contrast, the recovery of coal production after World War
I was erratic. Coal production declined from 1920 to 1921—falling from
83 percent of pre–World War I levels in 1920 to 72 percent in 1921—as
a result of the deflation imposed on the European economy by central
banks that sought the restoration of pre–World War I gold standard
parities, accepted the burden of deflation, and allowed the 1921 recession
in the United States to be transmitted to their own countries. After World

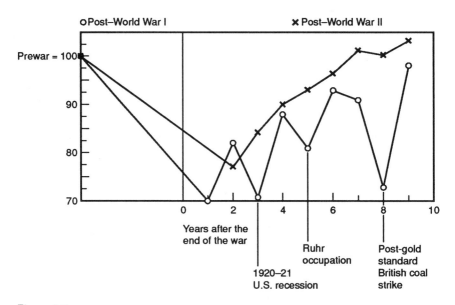

Figure 8.7
Post–World War I and Post–World War II recoveries of Western European coal
production*
Sources: B. R. Mitchell, *European Historical Statistics*; U.N. Economic Commission for
Europe, *Economic Survey of Europe since the War*; Ingmar Svennilson, *Growth and Stagnation
in the European Economy*

War II, no central bank or government pursued monetary orthodoxy so
aggressively in order to roll back price and wage increases and preserve the
real wealth of rentiers.

Coal production fell again in 1922–23. The breakdown of negotiations
over German reparations led the French to occupy the Ruhr. Their occupation did not lead to significantly increased transfers from Germany to
France. But it did begin the German hyperinflation.

Coal production fell for yet a third time in 1926. Attempts to reduce
wages in the aftermath of Britain's deflationary return to gold triggered a
walkout by British coal miners, accompanied by a short-lived general strike.
The twenties in Britain saw stubborn attachment by successive governments to a policy of a high real exchange rate and deflation, and an extraordinary degree of downward nominal wage inflexibility as well.

The course of coal production shows that to a large extent the slow
post–World War I recovery was inflicted by Europeans on themselves.

The major factors hindering a rapid post–World War I recovery were not strictly economic but social and political. One interpretation is that post–World War I Europe saw the recovery of output repeatedly interrupted by political and economic "wars of attrition," in the language of Alesina and Drazen (1991), that produced instability in European finance, politics, and labor relations.

In the aftermath of World War I, the distribution of wealth both within and between nations, the question of who would bear the burden of post-war adjustment, and the degree to which government would act to secure the property of the rentier were all unresolved issues. Social classes, political factions, and nation-states saw that they had much to lose if they did not aggressively promote their claims for favorable redistribution. Much of the social and economic history of interwar Europe can be seen in terms of such "wars of attrition," in which fiscal, financial, monetary, and labor relations instability—and concomitant slow economic growth—are trials of strength over who would succeed in obtaining a favorable redistribution of wealth.

After World War II such "wars of attrition" were less virulent. Memories of the disastrous consequences of the aggressive pursuit of redistributional goals during the interwar period made moderation appear more attractive to all. The availability of Marshall Plan aid to nations that had accomplished stabilization provided a very strong incentive to compromise such distributional conflicts early and gave European countries a pool of resources that could be used to cushion the wealth losses sustained in restructuring.[20]

3. *This was "supergrowth" and not simply a "rubber band effect."* Moreover, post–World War II reconstruction did more than return Western Europe to its previous growth path. As figure 8.1 showed, French and West German growth during the post–World War II boom raised national product per capita at rates that far exceeded pre–World War II, pre-1929, or even pre-1913 trends.

This was not merely a process of making up ground lost during the war. In fact, there is no strong connection between the fall in levels of production across the wartime period and the pace of the subsequent recovery, contrary to what would be expected if fast post–World War II growth was primarily a process of catch-up to prewar trends. The bivariate relationship is statistically significant at standard confidence levels (see Dumke 1990), but when one controls for other characteristics of countries like openness and the investment rate, the significance of the relationship evaporates and even its sign becomes uncertain (see Eichengreen and Uzan 1991).

The reconstruction of Western Europe in the aftermath of World War II appears to have created economies capable of dynamic economic growth an order magnitude stronger than had previously been seen in Europe. Postwar Europe's "supergrowth," as Charles Kindleberger has termed it, was much more than catch-up and reattainment of a prewar neoclassical growth path.

4. "Supergrowth" reflected more than a favorable environment. Yet such rapid growth and recovery as Western Europe saw after World War II was not inevitable. It was not a natural consequence of a favorable international regime. The post–World War II expansion of world trade under Bretton Woods was a great aid to European recovery, but Western European growth reflected more than a rising tide of international trade lifting all boats.

As figure 8.1 showed, a Latin American country like Argentina, as rich in the years before and immediately after World War II as industrial Western Europe, grew slowly even under the post–World War II expansionary Bretton Woods regime. Fast post–World War II growth and catch-up to American standards of productivity were to a large degree specific to Western Europe, and thus to the countries that received Marshall Plan aid.

3   The Marshall Plan and Private Investment

Investment is an obvious channel through which the Marshall Plan might have accelerated economic growth in post–World War II Western Europe. Postwar Europe was poor and capital scarce. Maintaining living standards at levels the citizenry regarded as minimally tolerable consumed a large share of total product, leaving little for the replacement of railroads, buildings, and machines damaged by war. The Marshall Plan could have relaxed this constraint.

It is difficult to ascribe large effects to this channel. Viewed relative to total investment in the recipient countries, the Marshall Plan was not large. Marshall Plan grants were provided at a pace that was not much greater in flow terms than previous UNRRA aid and amounted to less than 3 percent of the combined national incomes of the recipient countries between 1948 and 1951. They equalled less than a fifth of gross investment in recipient countries. Only 17 percent of Marshall Plan dollars were spent on "machinery and vehicles" and "miscellaneous." The rest were devoted to imports of industrial materials, semi-finished products, and agricultural commodities. The commodities bought directly with Marshall Plan dollars were not additions to the fixed capital stock of Western Europe that would have boosted output permanently.

Marshall Plan dollars did significantly affect the level of investment: countries that received large amounts of Marshall Plan aid invested more. Eichengreen and Uzan (1991) calculate that out of each dollar of Marshall Plan aid some 65 cents went to increased production and 35 cents to increased investment. The returns to new investment were high. Eichengreen and Uzan's analysis suggests that social returns may have been as high as 50 percent a year: an extra dollar of investment raised national product by 50 cents in the subsequent year.

Even with such strong links between the Marshall Plan and investment and between investment and growth, the investment effects of Marshall Plan aid were simply too small to trigger an economic miracle. U.S. aid in the amount of 3 percent of West European output per year raised the share of private investment in national income by one percentage point. An increase of one percentage point in the ratio of investment to national income would increase economic growth by one-half of one percentage point.

Over the four years of the Marshall Plan, this increase in growth cumulates to 2 percent of national product. Eichengreen and Uzan's estimates of the strength of this investment channel suggest thus that it led to Western European national income levels after 1951 that were some 2 percent higher than would have been the case otherwise. While this was a valuable addition, it is hardly the sort of dramatic change trumpeted by champions of the Marshall Plan. It was too little to make the difference between prosperity and stagnation. It was not enough to make the Marshall Plan a decisive factor in the long boom of the post–World War II period.

4 The Marshall Plan and Public Investment

A second channel through which the Marshall Plan could have stimulated growth was by financing public spending on infrastructure. Western European roads, bridges, railroads, ports, and other infrastructure had been severely damaged by the war. They were prime targets of the Allied strategic bombing campaign. Their destruction had been the first priority of retreating Nazis. The social rate of return to their repair and reconstruction was very high. This task was one of the principal objectives of postwar governments. Those same governments had limited resources out of which to finance infrastructure repair. National tax systems were in disarray. The tax base had been eroded by the war. Social programs competed for scarce

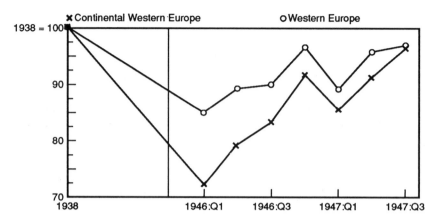

Figure 8.8
Post–World War II recovery of Western European rail traffic*
Source: U.N. Economic Commission for Europe, *Economic Survey of Europe 1948*

public revenues. Inflationary finance was at odds with the imperative of financial stabilization.

The question is how tightly the fiscal constraint limited public spending on infrastructure repair. In fact, the damage to European infrastructure was not that thorough or that long lasting. Although Allied generals had learned during World War II that strategic bombing could destroy bridges, paralyze rail yards, and disrupt the movement of goods and troops, they had also learned that bridges could be quickly rebuilt and tracks quickly relaid.

Europe's transportation infrastructure was in fact quickly repaired. As figure 8.8 shows, by the last quarter of 1946 almost as much freight was loaded onto railways in Western Europe as had been transported in 1938. Including British railways, total goods loaded and shipped in the last quarter of 1946 amounted to 97 percent of prewar traffic. Weighted by the distance traveled—measured in units not of tons carried but multiplying each ton carried by the number of kilometers traveled—1947 railroad traffic was a quarter higher than pre–World War II traffic. European recovery was not significantly delayed by the lack of track and rolling stock.[21]

5   Bottlenecks and Foreign Exchange Constraints

Another channel through which the Marshall Plan might have stimulated growth was by relaxing foreign exchange constraints. Marshall Plan funds were hard currency in a dollar-scarce world. They might have allowed Europe to obtain imports that would relieve bottlenecks. After the war, coal, cotton, petroleum, and other materials were in short supply. The Marshall Plan allowed them to be purchased at a higher rate than would have been possible otherwise. Marshall Plan dollars added to Europe's international liquidity and played a role in restoring intra-European trade. To the extent that the breakdown of the intra-European division of labor was reducing production, added liquidity may have relieved bottlenecks in foreign exchange.

In a well-functioning market economy, it is difficult to argue that such bottlenecks had more than a transient impact on the level of production. The European economy was not without possibilities for substitution. Market economies are very good at finding and utilizing such possibilities. However, assume for argument's sake that little active substitution of cheap goods for scarce imports was possible on the production side. It is still the case that Europe would not have seen lower production without Marshall Plan aid if governments had made sustaining production a priority when allocating foreign exchange. Absent the Marshall Plan, according to this scenario, imports of consumption goods would have been reduced as foreign exchange was diverted to purchase industrial raw materials, but output would not have been noticeably affected.

Had substitution possibilities been lacking in both production and use of foreign exchange, materials shortages might then have reduced production. But consider the following back-of-the-envelope calculation for the most severe bottleneck: coal. In 1938 Western Europe consumed 460 million tons of hard coal. It produced only 400 million tons in 1948. Over the life span of the Marshall Plan, Western Europe imported about 7 percent of its coal consumption from the United States. Assuming that coal was the most important bottleneck, that half of national product was produced in coal-burning sectors, and that these coal-burning sectors used fixed coefficients in production, then elimination of coal imports would have reduced Western European total product over the duration of the Marshall Plan by no more than 3 percent.

This back-of-the-envelope calculation neglects indirect effects and general equilibrium repercussions. One can imagine that, for example, a small decline in coal consumption might have produced a large decline in steel output, which in turn provoked an even larger fall in output in sectors for which steel was an essential input.

Input-output analysis is the classic way of analyzing such a situation. Consider Italy, for which Marshall Plan administrators prepared a 1950 input-output table.[22] Italy imported $72 million—L 13 billion—worth of coal during the Marshall Plan. Assume that all uses of coal would have been proportionately reduced in the absence of Marshall Plan imports, that all industry production functions were Leontief, and that slack resources would have remained idle.[23] Then input-output analysis reveals that industrial production would have fallen by 6.8 percent and transportation by 7.3 percent of a year's production.[24] The coal bottleneck would have produced secondary bottlenecks in steel production, refining, and transport. But agriculture and services would have been unaffected. Since industry and transport account for less than half of national product, the latter would have fallen by 3.2 percent of a year's production.[25]

This, of course, is an overestimate of the likely effects in 1950 of a coal bottleneck. The economy did possess substitution possibilities in production and foreign-exchange allocation. If the market was functioning and so uncovering substitution possibilities, it is plausible that losses due to all bottlenecks together would have been less than this calculation for coal. And even 3 percent is small relative to the speed of the remarkable European recovery. In individual periods—such as the winter of 1947—bottlenecks, primarily in coal, were present. Earlier in recovery, bottlenecks and resource scarcities may well have been very important. But the elimination of bottlenecks more than three years after the end of the war as a result of Marshall aid is unlikely to have been a significant factor driving the rapid Western European recovery, at least if the counterfactual is one in which the market is doing its job of adjustment and reallocation.

6   The Political Economy of European Reconstruction

But would the market economy have been allowed to do its job? The thirties had seen not chronic bottlenecks but chronic deficiencies of aggregate demand. Production had fallen far below normal for the entire decade; market forces had failed to restore demand to normal levels. Circumstances during the Great Depression had been exceptional, but circumstances in the aftermath of World War II were exceptional as well. Many feared the return of the Depression.[26]

Thus a live possibility in the absence of the Marshall Plan was that governments would not stand aside and allow the market system to do its job. In the wake of the Great Depression, many still recalled the disastrous outcome of the laissez-faire policies then in effect. Politicians were predisposed toward intervention and regulation: no matter how damaging "government failure" might be to the economy, it had to be better than the "market failure" of the Depression.

Had European political economy taken a different turn, post–World War II European recovery might have been stagnant. Governments might have been slow to dismantle wartime allocation controls and thereby severely constrain the market mechanism. In fact the Marshall Plan era saw a rapid dismantling of controls over product and factor markets in Western Europe and the restoration of price and exchange rate stability. An alternative scenario would have been the maintenance and expansion of wartime controls in order to guard against substantial shifts in income distribution. The late forties and early fifties might have seen the creation in Western Europe of allocative bureaucracies to ration scarce foreign exchange and the imposition of price controls on exportables in order to protect the living standards of urban working classes.

Europe in the Argentine Mirror

The consequences of such policies can be seen in the Argentine mirror. In response to the social and economic upheavals of the Depression, Argentina adopted demand stimulation and income redistribution. These policies were coupled with a distrust of foreign trade and capital and an attraction to the use of controls instead of prices as allocative mechanisms. Argentina's growth performance in the post–World War II period was very poor. Figure 8.9 displays the post–World War II growth of Argentine GDP per capita along with that of the four largest European economies. Even in the fifties, and even relative to Britain, Argentine growth was slow.

Díaz-Alejandro (1970) provides a standard analysis of Argentina's post–World War II economic stagnation. According to his interpretation, the collapse of world trade in the Great Depression was a disaster of the first magnitude for an Argentina tightly integrated into the world division of labor. While Argentina continued to service its foreign debt, its trade partners took unilateral steps to shut it out of markets. The experience of the Depression justifiably undermined the nation's commitment to free trade.[27]

In this environment Juan Perón gained mass political support. Taxes were increased, agricultural marketing boards created, unions supported, urban real wages boosted, international trade regulated. Perón sought to generate rapid growth and to twist terms of trade against rural agriculture and redistribute wealth to urban workers who did not receive their fair share. The redistribution to urban workers and to firms that had to pay their newly increased wages required a redistribution away from exporters, agricultural oligarchs, foreigners, and entrepreneurs.

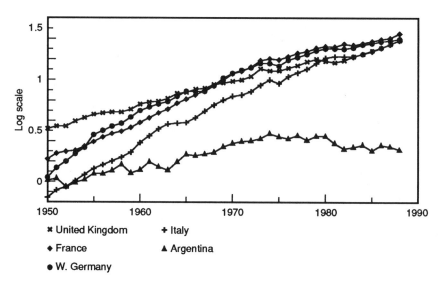

Figure 8.9
Post–World War II GDP per capita growth in Argentina, Britain, France, West Germany, and Italy
Source: Robert Summers and Alan Heston, *Penn World Table V.*

The Perónist program was not prima facie unreasonable given the memory of the Great Depression, and it produced almost half a decade of very rapid growth. The exports fell sharply as a result of the international business cycle as the consequences of the enforced reduction in real prices of rural exportables made themselves felt. Agricultural production fell because of low prices offered by government marketing agencies. Domestic consumption rose. The rural sector found itself short of fertilizer and tractors. Squeezed between declining production and rising domestic consumption, Argentinian exports fell. By the first half of the fifties the real value of Argentine exports was only 60 percent of the depressed levels of the late thirties, and only 40 percent of twenties levels. Due to the twisting of terms of trade against agriculture and exportables, when the network of world trade was put back together, Argentina was by and large excluded.

The consequent foreign exchange shortage presented Perón with unattractive options. First, he could attempt to balance foreign payments by devaluing to bring imports and exports back into balance in the long run and in the short run by borrowing from abroad.[28] But effective devaluation would have entailed raising the real price of imported goods and therefore cutting living standards of the urban workers who made up his political base. Foreign borrowing would have meant a betrayal of his strong nationalist position. Second, he could contract the economy, raising unemployment and reducing consumption, and expand incentives to produce for export by decontrolling agricultural prices.[29] But once again this would have required a reversal of the distributional shifts that had been the central aim of his administration.

The remaining option was one of controlling and rationing imports. Not surprisingly, Perón and his advisors chose the second alternative, believing that a dash for growth and a reduction in dependence on the world economy was good for Argentina. Díaz-Alejandro writes: "First priority was given to raw materials and intermediate goods imports needed to maintain existing capacity in operation. Machinery and equipment for new capacity could neither be imported nor produced domestically. A sharp decrease in the rate of real capital formation in new machinery and equipment followed. Hostility toward foreign capital, which could have provided a way out of this difficulty, aggravated the crisis..." Subsequent governments did not fully reverse these policies, for the political forces that Perón had mobilized still had to be appeased. Thus post–World War II Argentina saw foreign exchange allocated by the central government in order to, first, keep existing factories running and, second, keep home consumption high. The third and last priority under the controlled exchange regime went to imports of capital goods for investment and capacity expansion.

As a result, the early fifties saw a huge rise in the price of capital goods. Each percentage point of total product saved led to less than half a percentage point's worth of investment. Díaz-Alejandro found "[r]emarkably, the capital ... in electricity and communications increased by a larger percentage during the depression years 1929–39 than ... 1945–55," although the 1945–55 government boasted of encouraging industrialization. Given low and fixed agriculture prices, hence low exports, it was very expensive to sacrifice materials imports needed to keep industry running in order to import capital goods. Unable to invest, the Argentine economy stagnated.

In 1929 Argentina had appeared as rich as any large country in continental Europe. It was still as rich in 1950, when Western Europe had for the most part reattained pre–World War II levels of national product. But by 1960 Argentina was poorer than Italy and had less than two-thirds of the GDP per capita of France or West Germany. One way to think about post–World War II Argentina is that its mixed economy was poorly oriented: the government allocated goods, especially imports, among alternative uses; the controlled market redistributed income. Thus neither the private nor the public sector was used to its comparative advantage: in Western

Europe market forces allocated resources—even, to a large extent, for nationalized industries—the government redistributed income, and the outcome was much more favorable.

The European Analogy

In the absence of the Marshall Plan, might have Western Europe followed a similar trajectory? In Díaz-Alejandro's estimation, four factors set the stage for Argentina's relative decline: a politically-active and militant urban industrial working class, economic nationalism, sharp divisions between traditional elites and poorer strata, and a government used to exercising control over goods allocation that viewed the price system as a tool for redistributing wealth rather than for determining the pattern of economic activity.

From the perspective of 1947, the political economy of Western Europe would lead one to think that it was at least as vulnerable as Argentina to economic stagnation induced by populist overregulation. The war had given Europe more experience than Argentina with economic planning and rationing. Militant urban working classes calling for wealth redistribution voted in such numbers as to make Communists plausibly part of a permanent ruling political coalition in France and Italy.[30] Economic nationalism had been nurtured by a decade and a half of Depression, autarky, and war. European political parties had been divided substantially along economic class lines for a generation.

Yet Europe avoided this trap. After World War II Western Europe's mixed economies built substantial redistributional systems, but they were built on top of and not as replacements for market allocations of goods and factors. Just as post–World War II Western Europe saw the avoidance of the political-economic "wars of attrition" that had put a brake on post–World War I European recovery, so post–World War II Western Europe avoided the tight web of controls that kept post–World War II Argentina from being able to adjust and grow.

7   The Role of the Marshall Plan

Did the Marshall Plan play a role in Western Europe's successful avoidance of these traps? In answering this question, it is important to distinguish three effects of the American Marshall Plan program: its immediate contribution to the restoration of financial stability, its role in restoring the free play of market forces, and its part in the negotiation of the social contract upon which the subsequent generation of supergrowth was based.

The Restoration of Financial Stability

Financial instability was pervasive in post–World War II Europe. Relief expenditure sent budgets deep into deficit. Governments responded to inflation by retaining controls, prompting the growth of black markets and discouraging transactions at official prices. Farmers refused to market produce as long as prices were restricted to low levels. With receipts vulnerable to inflation or taxation, they were better off hoarding inventories. The post–World War II food shortage reflected not merely bad weather in 1947 but also the reluctance of farmers to deliver food to cities. Moreover, manufactured goods farmers might have purchased remained in short supply. Manufacturing enterprises had the same incentive to hoard inventories. As long as food shortages persisted, workers had little ability—or incentive—to devote their full effort to market work. Few were willing to sell goods for money when inflation threatened to accelerate at any time.[31]

The liberal, market-oriented solution to the crisis was straightforward. Prices had to be decontrolled to coax producers to bring their goods to market. Inflation had to be halted for the price mechanism to operate smoothly and to encourage saving and initiative. Budgets had to be balanced to remove inflationary pressure. With financial stability restored and market forces given free reign, individuals could direct their attention to market work. Without financial stability, the allocative mechanisms of the market could not be relied on—and government controls over the process of goods allocation would appear the more attractive option.

For budgets to be balanced and inflation to be halted, however, political compromise was required. Consumers had to accept higher posted prices for foodstuffs and necessities. Workers had to moderate their demands for higher wages. Owners had to moderate demands for profits. Taxpayers had to shoulder additional liabilities. Recipients of social services had to accept limits on safety nets. Rentiers had to accept that the war had destroyed their wealth. There had to be broad agreement on a "fair" distribution of income, or at least on a distribution of the burdens that was not so unfair as to be intolerable. Only then could pressure on central banks to continually monetize budget deficits and cause either explicit or repressed inflation be removed.

Here the Marshall Plan may have played a critical role. It did not obviate the need for sacrifice. But it increased the size of the pie available for division among interest groups. Marshall Plan aid as a share of recipient GDP was 2.5 percent—not an overwhelmingly large change in the size of the pie. But if the sum of national demands exceeded aggregate supply by

5 or 7.5 percent, Marshall Plan transfers could reduce the sacrifices required of competing distributional interests by a third or as much as a half. The presence of Marshall Plan aid could thus have significantly reduced the costs of compromise relative to the benefits.[32]

Dangerous instability arises if the failure to compromise leads to a "war of attrition." Suppose that the difference between the total sum of claims to output and output itself shows up as a deficit in the government's budget. Then even small conflicts over "fair shares" can easily lead to aggregate demand that exceeds supply by some 7 or 8 percent. To meet such a shortfall of revenues relative to demands for services and transfers through money creation, the government has to increase the high-powered money supply by 8 percent of GDP each year. The consequences of such a rate of increase in high-powered money are likely to be disastrous.

Marshall Plan aid of 2.5 percent of national product goes a substantial way toward closing this excess demand gap. Moreover, its potential availability if the government's stabilization plan meets the criteria required by Plan administrators provides a powerful incentive for governments to impose financial discipline. With Marshall Plan aid available, the benefits for quick resolution of "wars of attrition" were greater, and so the Plan in all likelihood advanced the date of financial stabilization. While internal price stabilization after World War II took four years, the German hyperinflation took place in the sixth year after the end of World War I, and France's post–World War I inflation lasted for eight years. Some large part of the credit for this early stabilization goes to the Marshall Plan and to earlier aid programs.[33]

Along with the carrot of Marshall Plan grants, the United States also wielded a stick. For every dollar of Marshall Plan aid received, the recipient country was required to place a matching amount of domestic currency in a counterpart fund to be used only for purposes approved by the United States government. Each dollar of Marshall Plan aid thus gave the United States government control over two dollars' worth of real resources. Marshall Plan aid could be spent on external goods only with the approval of the U.S. government. And the counterpart funds could be spent internally only with the approval of the Marshall Plan administration as well.

In some instances the United States insisted that the funds be used to buttress financial stability. Britain used the bulk of its counterpart funds to retire public debt. Vincent Auriol claims that the United States refused to release French counterpart funds in 1948 until the new government affirmed its willingness to continue policies leading to a balanced budget.[34]

French officials were outraged: nevertheless, they took steps to obtain release and raised taxes. This was policy: nations undergoing inflation could not draw on counterpart funds until the Marshall Plan administration was satisfied that they had achieved a workable stabilization program (Price 1955).

Marshall Plan administrators believed that their veto power over the use of counterpart funds considerably increased U.S. leverage over Western European economic policies. Moreover, counterpart funds were only one of several available levers. Plan administrators believed that if governments could afford to divert funds from reconstruction to social services, Marshall aid could be eliminated proportionately. Britain lost its Marshall Plan timber line item as a result of the government's entry into the construction of public housing. West Germany found the release of counterpart funds delayed until the nationalized railway had reduced expenditures to match revenues (Arkes 1972). Marshall Plan administrators and Lucius Clay, military governor of the American zone of Germany, viewed with alarm British schemes for unifying and nationalizing the coal industries of the Ruhr, then part of the British zone of occupation, and successfully lobbied against them. The United States was not interested in having Marshall Plan aid support policies of nationalization. The United States even put pressure on Britain's Labour government to delay and shrink its own nationalization programs.

The Free Play of Market Forces

Renewed growth required, in addition to financial stability, the free play of market forces. Though there was support for the restoration of a market economy in Western Europe, it was far from universal. Wartime controls were viewed as exceptional policies for exceptional times, but it was not clear what was to replace them. Communist and some Socialist ministers opposed a return to the market. It was not clear when, or even if, the transition would take place.

On this issue the Marshall Plan—specifically, the conditions attached to U.S. aid—left Western Europeans with no choice. Each recipient had to sign a bilateral pact with the United States. Countries had to agree to balance government budgets, restore internal financial stability, and stabilize exchange rates at realistic levels. Europe was still committed to the mixed economy. But the United States insisted that market forces be represented more liberally in the mix. This was the price that the United States charged for its aid.

The demand that European governments trust the market came from the highest levels of the Marshall Plan administration. Dean Acheson describes the head administrator, Economic Cooperation Administration Chief Paul Hoffman, as an "economic Savonarola." Acheson describes watching Hoffman "preach ... his doctrine of salvation by exports" to British Foreign Secretary Ernest Bevin. "I have heard it said," wrote Acheson, "that Paul Hoffman ... missed his calling: that he should have been an evangelist. Both parts of the statement miss the mark. He did not miss his calling, and he was and is an evangelist."[35]

European economic integration was pursued intensely by the Plan administration. Even where domestic markets were highly concentrated, they believed competition could be injected via intra-European and international trade. Government intervention and other efforts to interfere with the operation of market forces would be disciplined by foreign competition. As a condition for receiving Marshall Plan aid, each country was required to develop a program for removing quotas and other trade controls. In 1950, discussions culminated in the European Payments Union, a system of credits to promote multilateral trade among European countries.[36]

It was not inevitable that Western Europe would have accepted the bargain. Marshall aid was ostensibly offered to Eastern Europe and even to the U.S.S.R. Moscow's rejection can be seen in part as unwillingness to allow the United States to sidetrack its satellites' progress toward central planning. It is critical to acknowledge that the price charged for the aid was a price Western Europe might have paid for its own sake in any event. Support for the market was widespread, although just how widespread was uncertain. The Marshall Plan at most tipped the balance.

Post–World War II Europe was far from laissez-faire. Government ownership of utilities and heavy industry was substantial. Government redistributions of income were large. The magnitude of the "safety nets" and social insurance programs provided by the post–World War II welfare states were far beyond anything that had been thought possible before World War I. But these large welfare states were accompanied by financial stability and by substantial reliance on market processes for allocation and exchange.

The Social Contract and Long-Term Growth

The restoration of financial stability and the free play of market forces launched the European economy onto a two-decade-long path of unprecedented rapid growth. European economic growth between 1953 and 1973 was twice as fast as for any comparable period before or since. The growth rate of GDP was 2 percent per annum between 1870 and 1913 and 2.5 percent per annum between 1922 and 1937. In contrast, growth accelerated to an astonishing 4.8 percent per year between 1953 and 1973 before slowing to half that rate from 1973 to 1979.[37]

Because the roots of postwar Europe's supergrowth are not adequately understood, it is difficult to isolate the contribution of the Marshall Plan. We will nonetheless hazard some speculations about the role that U.S. aid might have played.[38]

Europe's rapid growth in the fifties and sixties was associated with exceptionally high investment rates.[39] The investment share of GNP was nearly twice as high as it had been in the last decade before World War II or it was again to be after 1972. Accompanying high rates of investment was rapid growth of productivity. Even in Britain, the laggard, productivity growth rose sharply between 1924 to 1937 and 1951 to 1973, from 1 to 2.4 percent per annum.[40] This high investment share did not, however, reflect unusual investment behavior during expansion phases of the business cycle. Rather, it reflected the tendency of investment to collapse during cyclical contractions and the absence of significant cyclical downturns between 1950 and 1971.

It would be tempting to ascribe Europe's cyclical stability to the advent of Keynesian stabilization policy but for the fact that Keynesian policy was not forgotten when increasingly volatile cyclical fluctuations recurred after 1972. A possible reconciliation is that Keynesian policy was effective only so long as labor markets were accomodating. So long as increased pressure of demand applied by governments in response to slowdowns produced additional output and employment rather than higher wages and hence higher prices, the macroeconomy was stable. Investment was maintained at high levels, and rapid growth persisted.

The key to Europe's rapid growth, from this perspective, was its relatively inflation-resistant labor markets.[41] So long as they accommodated demand pressure by supplying more labor input rather than demanding higher wages, the other pieces of the puzzle fell into place. What then accounted for the accommodating nature of postwar labor markets?

The conventional explanation, following Kindleberger (1967), is elastic supplies of underemployed labor from rural sectors within the advanced countries and from Europe's southern and eastern fringe. Elastic supplies of labor disciplined potentially militant labor unions. A problem with this argument is that the competition of underemployed Italians or Greeks or Eastern European refugees was hardly felt in the United Kingdom, yet labor market behavior was transformed in the United Kingdom as in other countries after World War II.[42]

Another explanation is history. Memory of high unemployment and strife between the wars served to moderate labor-market conflict. Conservatives could recall that attempts to roll back interwar welfare states had led to polarization, destabilizing representative institutions and setting the stage for fascism. Left-wingers could recall the other side of the same story. Both could reflect on the stagnation of the interwar period and blame it on political deadlock.

Yet another potential explanation is the Bretton Woods system. Bretton Woods linked the dollar to gold at $35 an ounce and other currencies to the dollar. So long as American policymakers' commitment to the Bretton Woods parity remained firm, limits were placed on the extent of inflationary policies. So long as European policymakers were loath to devalue against the dollar, limits were placed on their policies as well. Price expectations were stabilized. Inflation, where it surfaced, was more likely to be regarded as transitory. Consequently, increased pressure of demand was less likely to translate into higher prices instead of higher output, higher employment, and greater macroeconomic stability.

A final potential explanation is the Marshall Plan. Putting the point in this way serves to underscore that the Marshall Plan was but one of several factors contributing to observed outcomes. In principle, the Marshall Plan could have mattered directly. Marshall Planners sought a labor movement interested in raising productivity rather than in redistributing income from rich to poor. With labor peace a potential precondition for substantial Marshall Plan aid, labor organizations agreed to push for productivity improvements first and defer redistributions to later. Moreover, money was channeled to non-Communist labor organizations. European labor movements split over the question of whether Marshall aid should be welcomed —which left the Communists on the wrong side, opposed to economic recovery (Maier 1987).

In practice, we believe, the Marshall Plan's indirect effects were important. One way to think about the post–World War II settlement, and the contrast with the interwar period, is as a coordination problem. Labor, management, and government in Europe could, in effect, choose to try to maximize their current share of national income—as after World War I. Inflation, strikes, financial disarray, cyclical instability, and productivity problems can all be seen as corollaries of this equilibrium. Alternatively, the parties could trade current compensation for faster long-term growth and higher living standards, even in present-value terms. Workers would moderate their wage demands, management its demands for profits. Government agreed to use demand management to maintain employment in return for wage restraint on the part of unions. Higher investment and faster productivity growth could ensue, eventually rendering everyone better off.

Such a social contract is advantageous only if it is generally accepted. If workers continued to aggressively press for higher wages, management had little incentive to plow back profits in return for the promise of higher future profits. If management failed to plow back profits, workers had little incentive to moderate current wage demands in return for higher future productivity and compensation. If labor relations were conflictual rather than harmonious, productivity would be the casualty. The Marshall Plan could have shifted Europe onto this social contract equilibrium path, for once workers and management began coordinating on the superior equilibrium they had no obvious reason to stop.[43]

The Marshall Plan provided immediate incentives for wage moderation in the late forties. U.S. policy encouraged European governments to pursue investment-friendly policies. Productivity soared in the wake of financial stabilization and the advent of the Marshall Plan. The advantages of the cooperative equilibrium were suddenly clear.

It is intriguing that, within the group of reconstructing nations, those where the United States had most leverage had the fastest-growing economies. U.S. influence was strongest in Germany, weaker in France and Italy, and weakest in Britain. In the post–World War II period the German economy was the most successful, the British economy least. Japan, where MacArthur was proconsul, might be seen as an even more extreme case of this process at work.

8   Implications for Eastern Europe

Do conditions like those that made the Marshall Plan a success after World War II exist in Eastern Europe and the Soviet Union today? There are important parallels. Just as in Western Europe in 1947–48, enterprises hold back inventories in anticipation of higher prices once controls are relaxed. Excess liquidity and government budget deficits create the specter of rampant inflation. Belief that reform must occur soon, but uncertainty about its nature, provides a powerful incentive to delay investment and rationalization until the situation is clarified.

A paradox of reform in Eastern Europe is that the workers in heavy industry who initiated the rebellion against Communist domination were, from an economic standpoint, relatively unproductive at world prices and thus "privileged" under the ancien régime. Their wages were relatively high. The industries in which they worked were massively subsidized. Their real wages will be among the first to fall, and must fall the farthest. Their jobs are most likely to disappear during transition. Ironically, those in the vanguard of rebellion against the ancien régime may be the first to withdraw their support for reform. Even with substantial aid to cushion the fall in consumption during adjustment, it is not clear that adjustment can be successfully completed.

As in Europe after World War I, political struggles over economic structure could lead to damaging "wars of attrition." Conflict over distribution could produce inflation, price controls, and foreign-exchange rationing. Alternatively, market prices could be controlled in the interest of stabilizing income distributions. The government's fiscal and investment stance would be used to allocate resources. This would result in stagnation, for the market should handle the allocation of resources and the government's welfare state structure should moderate the distribution of income, not the other way around. If post–World War II Argentina is any guide, such a controlled, semiplanned economy could persist for a generation before being discredited.

To avoid both the post–World War I "distributional conflict" trap and the Argentinian "populist overregulation" trap, Eastern Europe will have to be lucky. A substantial aid program might help them to make their own luck. Supporting Eastern European living standards could limit public opposition to economic reform when output initially falls during the transition to a market economy. Hard currency would allow higher imports of much-needed commodities from the West. Reserves would make monetary stabilization and currency convertibility possible.

Important differences weaken the case for a Marshall Plan, especially for the regions of the Soviet Union. In post–World War II Western Europe there already existed widespread support for and experience with the market. The Marshall Plan only tipped the balance. It is not clear that comparable support exists in the Soviet Union today, or in much of Eastern Europe. Powerful elements still oppose economic liberalization. And many advocates have no clear idea of what liberalization entails.

In post–World War II Western Europe, Marshall Plan aid was effective at least in part because Europe had experience with markets. It possessed the institutions needed for their operation. Property rights, bankruptcy codes, court systems to enforce market contracts—not to mention entrepreneurial skills—all were in place. None of this holds in Eastern Europe

today. For fifty years potential entrepreneurs have been labeled as "speculators" and attacked as public enemies. One principle of a market economy
is that entrepreneurial profits tell not how much the entrepreneur is an
exploiter but how wasteful of resources the situation would have been in
his absence. This principle is not yet established, and so political leaders
will be tempted to try to earn populist applause by renewed crackdowns
on speculators.

In post–World War II Western Europe, U.S. aid and U.S. conditionality
encouraged the reductions in government spending needed for financial
stability. It encouraged the elimination of controls and the liberalization
of trade. It is far from certain that aid today will have the same effect.
Transfers to the central government may delay rather than accelerate the
process of privatizing industry and creating a market economy. It is critical
that whatever programs are adopted, aid should be provided on the basis
of actions taken rather than need.

These observations all point toward caution on the part of those con-
templating the extension of Western aid to the East. They are reminders
that aid for Eastern European reform is a gamble. But the stakes are high,
the downside risk limited, and the potential gain enormous.

The original Marshall Plan was a gamble as well. The Marshall Plan's
Senate floor leader, Arthur Vandenberg, did not promise success. In his
final speech before the Senate vote he warned that "... there are no blue-
prints to guarantee results. We are entirely surrounded by calculated risks.
I profoundly believe that the pending program is the best of these risks..."

Notes

Prepared for the Centre for Economic Performance and Landeszentralbank Ham-
burg conference on Post–World War II European Reconstruction, Hamburg, Sep-
tember 5–7, 1991. We thank Marco Becht for research assistance, and Marc Uzan,
Lawrence Summers, Steven Schran, Richard Layard, Charles Kindleberger, Rüdiger
Dornbusch, Alessandra Casella, and Geoffrey Carliner for helpful comments. Barry
Eichengreen's research was supported by the Center for German and European
Studies of the University of California at Berkeley. Bradford De Long's was sup-
ported by the NBER and by the National Science and Olin Foundations.

1. Wartime relief, post–World War II UNRRA aid, and pre–Marshall Plan interim
aid may well have significantly speeded up the reconstruction process. Although
we do not address the question of the role of pre–Marshall Plan aid in this chapter,
we hope to examine its effects in future work.

2. Without the Marshall Plan, the pattern of the post–World War II European
political economy might well have resembled the overregulation and relative eco-

nomic stagnation of post–World War II Argentina, a nation that has dropped from First to Third World status in two generations. Or post–World War II Europe might have replicated the financial instability—alternate episodes of inflation and deflation—experienced by much of Europe in the twenties as interest groups and social classes bitterly struggled over the distribution of wealth and in the process stalled economic growth. This is not to say that post–World War II Western Europe was a laissez-faire economy.

3. Among others, Italy, Turkey, Portugal, Spain, Bulgaria, Greece, Rumania, Yugoslavia, Hungary, Albania, Poland, Estonia, Latvia, Lithuania, Austria, Germany— not to speak of Japan, China, and many Central and South American countries —tried and then abandoned representative governments in the interwar period. See John Lukacs (1991).

4. See for example Hogan (1987), van der Wee (1986), Mee (1984), Price (1955), and Tinbergen (1954).

5. See Block (1977) for a discussion of reasons U.S. private investors were unwilling to loan money to Europe after World War II. Eichengreen and Portes (1989) describe the very different post–World War I experience when U.S. private investment bankers were relatively eager to channel capital for European reconstruction.

6. For example, see Wexler (1983), Mee (1984), Mayne (1973), Gimbel (1976), and Arkes (1972). At variance with the folk image conveyed by these accounts is Milward (1984), one of the few who pays close attention to the quantitative dimensions of the American aid program. Milward's revisionist downplaying of the importance of the Marshall Plan and his conclusion that the pace of European recovery would not been very different in its absence have recently colored discussions of policy toward Eastern Europe. See for example *The Economist* (15 June 1991), or Collins and Rodrik (1991). As shall become apparent, we believe that Milward's revisionism is overstated.

7. See Sweezy (1943) for an extreme but surprisingly widely held contemporary view. See Maier (1987) for a historian's account of attitudes toward the market. In the immediate aftermath of World War II, the remaining pillar of market economics was the United States, but its performance during the Great Depression had been far from inspiring. Maier (1987) quotes British historian A. J. P. Taylor as speaking in late 1945 to how "nobody in Europe believes in the American way of life—that is, in private enterprise; or rather those who believe in it are a defeated party—a party which seems to have no more future."

8. One of us has suggested previously that Harris's estimate of realized returns is overly pessimistic. See Eichengreen and Portes (1989). But Harris could not anticipate the settlement negotiations between U.S. creditors and debtor governments that would occupy the first postwar decade and return to American investors at least a portion of their principal. If Harris could not anticipate this outcome, neither were contemporary investors likely to do so. Thus, from the perspective of 1947, the returns on post–World War I loans to Europe appeared disappointing.

9. TRB, *The New Republic*, May 5, 1947.

10. Costs of the German occupation, however, were largely borne by Germany.

11. The remaining 7 percent was spent employing the U.S. merchant marine rather than lower cost competitors.

12. On the consequences of World War II and the situation at its end, see Milward (1984), Calvocoressi and Wint (1972), and Halle (1967).

13. We do not pass judgment here on the economic implications of strategic bombing. See U.S. Strategic Bombing Survey (1976) for a contemporary assessment. Also see Milward (1965, 1984), and Ellis (1990).

14. Although 1938 was a recession year in the United States, its use as a baseline for post–World War II comparisons should not be misleading for Europe. The European slowdown in economic activity in 1938 was relatively minor.

15. Italian industrial production had fallen to one-third of its pre–World War II level. In the three Western-occupied zones of Germany (including the Saar), industrial production had fallen to one-fifth of that of 1938.

16. The existence of war debt liabilities to the United States complicates the picture. But typically service of these obligations did not begin until the second half of the twenties, facilitating immediate post–World War I adjustment.

17. Holtfrerich (1986) analyzes the massive flow of short-term capital from the United States to Germany in 1919–21.

18. A strict loan embargo was imposed against the Soviet Union, the absence of a war-debt funding agreement led to the disapproval of a Romanian loan in 1922, and refunding issues for France were delayed. But Eichengreen (1989a) concludes that U.S. government restrictions were more bark than bite, and that "in almost all cases where the government entered an objection, [they] could be gotten round." Eichengreen (1989a), quoting Feis (1950).

19. William Clayton, Undersecretary of State for Economic Affairs, was the strongest voice. See Mayne (1973). The influential Harriman Report (1947), *European Recovery and American Aid*, a key piece of the administration's lobbying effort, took the same perspective. On U.S. State Department thinking before the Marshall Plan, see Acheson (1966), Bohlen (1973), and Pogue (1990).

20. Olson (1982) argues that World War II destroyed distributional coalitions and delayed the development of new ones, thus limiting the extent to which post–World War II European political economy could follow the post–World War I pattern of intensive redistributional strife. Below we suggest, however, that there was no absence of distributional coalitions after World War II; the difference lay rather in their behavior—and in the selective incentives to which they responded.

21. Similarly, the rapid repair of other forms of publicly provided infrastructure prevented them from constraining recovery. Water systems were quickly restored. The electrical grid was put back into operation (although there was not always coal to fuel the power plants). In fact, public spending did not rise in countries receiving large amounts of Marshall Plan aid. Countries that were major aid recipients saw

the government spending share of national income fall relative to other nations (see Eichengreen and Uzan 1991). The Marshall Plan did not accelerate growth by releasing resource constraints that prevented governments from rebuilding infrastructure. Earlier pre–Marshall Plan post–World War II aid may, however, have helped in the speedy reconstruction of Europe's infrastructure.

22. 1950 is almost precisely the midpoint of the Marshall Plan. The MSA mission, led by Hollis Chenery, in fact provided several such tables. We use the 16-sector input-output table provided by U.S. Mutual Security Agency (1953), pp. 132–133.

23. Of course, these assumptions are patently false, a point whose implications we explore below.

24. We derive these estimates by reducing each element of the vector of final demands by the same proportion until the coal constraint is just binding.

25. Compare the back-of-the-envelope calculation in the preceding paragraph, which came to 3 percent.

26. In fact, aside from the possibility that fear of a renewed Great Depression would act as a self-fulfilling prophecy, the return of the Great Depression was not likely in the forties. The memory of the Depression, and the greater strength and incorporation of social democratic political movements in government, kept right-wing governments from adopting policies of out-and-out national deflation. The availability of the large U.S. market to European exports—especially with the coming of the Korean War Boom and NATO in the early fifties—prevented any large world-aggregate demand shortfall as in the Great Depression. With the American locomotive under full steam, Western European economies were unlikely to suffer from prolonged Keynesian demand-shortfall depressions.

27. Moreover, conservative dictatorships in the thirties had sharpened lines of political cleavage. Landowner and exporter elites had always appropriated the lion's share of the benefits of free trade. They had in the thirties shown a willingness to sacrifice political democracy in order to stunt the growth of the welfare state.

28. Foreign borrowing would have appeared even less attractive to Argentines who recalled the extraordinarily high, real-effective interest rates that their foreign debt had carried during the deflation of the thirties. See Díaz-Alejandro (1970).

29. The experience of the previous generation, however, suggested ex ante that Argentina did not need to further specialize in the international division of labor. Demand for its export products had been depressed for twenty years.

30. For details, see Casella and Eichengreen (1991).

31. Wallich (1955) describes how German industries that made consumer goods would pay their workers in the factory's output so that its workers would have something with which to barter, while industries that made producer goods paid their workers some of their wages in coal, which managers had diverted from power generation.

32. This is the argument developed for Italy and France in Casella and Eichengreen (1991).

33. Banca Italiana Governor Menichella attributed Italian stabilization to the pre–Marshall Plan interim aid program. In his belief, "stabilization was made possible by interim aid.... Interim aid and the prospect of the Marshall Plan made it possible to maintain stability in prices." See Price (1955).

34. Auriol (1970), p. 162. Other sources do not contradict Auriol's memoirs. See, for example, Price (1955).

35. The Marshall Plan was not left to professional politicians, potentially interested in getting along with recipient countries and building bureaucratic empires. Because Republican senators like Arthur Vandenberg had feared either the Marshall aid would be wasted or—like New Deal programs—used to solidify Democratic political bases in the United States, the Economic Cooperation Administration had "sunset" provisions built into its enabling legislation and a peculiar status as an administrative agency formally subordinate to but not reporting to or responsible to the president. Republican worries moreover set in motion a chain of events that led the Economics Cooperation Administration to be headed by a businessman: Paul Hoffman had previously been president of Studebaker.

Truman originally sought Dean Acheson as Marshall Plan administrator, but Acheson demurred. Senator Arthur Vandenberg had been the key to getting the program shell fueled with appropriations. Vandenberg had worked hard to separate Marshall Plan administration from the ongoing governmental bureaucracy. Acheson believed—correctly—that the appointment of a State Department insider like himself would be taken as a rejection of what Vandenberg had worked for. Acheson suggested that Truman, instead, ask Vandenberg for his choice—and he speculated that Vandenberg would recommend Paul Hoffman. Truman did ask, and Vandenberg did so recommend.

36. Between 1948 and 1952, trade among European countries increased more than five times as fast as European trade with other continents. The economies of Europe were once again permitted to specialize in the production of goods in which they had a comparative advantage. Productivity received another boost.

37. Statistics in this section are from Boltho (1982).

38. The hypotheses advanced in this and the succeeding paragraph are developed at more length in Eichengreen (1989b).

39. This point, made forcefully for Britain by Matthews (1967), applies to other European countries as well. See Glyn et al. (1990).

40. Broadberry (1991), table 6, computed from Matthews, Feinstein, and Odling-Smee (1982).

41. This, of course, is the famous conclusion of Kindleberger (1967), although the mechanism there linking labor markets to economic performance is somewhat different.

42. See Broadberry (1991).

43. We leave for another paper the question of what caused the postwar settlement to break down in the seventies. Two intriguing treatments of this question are

those of Marglin (1990) and Broadberry (1991), both of whom argue that the postwar settlement contained the seeds of its own destruction.

References

Acheson, Dean (1960). *Sketches from Life*. New York: Harper & Bros.

Acheson, Dean (1966). *Present at the Creation*. New York: New American Library.

Alesina, Alberto and Allen Drazen (1992). "Why are Stabilizations Delayed?" *American Economic Review* (forthcoming).

Auriol, Vincent (1970). *Mon Septennat, 1947–1954*. Paris: Armand Colin.

Arkes, Hadley (1972). *Bureaucracy, the Marshall Plan, and the National Interest*. Princeton: Princeton University Press.

Bohlen, Charles (1973). *Witness to History 1929–69*. New York: W.W. Norton.

Block, Fred (1977). *The Origins of International Economic Disorder*. Berkeley: University of California Press.

Boltho, Andrea (1982). "Growth." In Andrea Boltho, ed., *The European Economy*. Oxford: Clarendon Press.

Broadberry, S. N. (1991). "Why Was Unemployment in Postwar Britain So Low?" Unpublished manuscript, Warwick University.

Calvocoressi, Peter and Guy Wint (1972). *Total War: Causes and Courses of World War II*. New York: Pantheon Books.

Casella, Alessandra and Barry Eichengreen (1991). "Halting Inflation in Italy and France After World War II." In Michael Bordo and Forrest Capie, eds., *Monetary Regimes in Transition*, Cambridge: Cambridge University Press (forthcoming).

Collins, Susan and Dani Rodrik (1991). *Eastern Europe and the Soviet Union in the World Economy*. Washington, DC: Institute for International Economics.

Cowan, Tyler (1985). "The Marshall Plan: Myths and Realities." In Doug Bandow, ed., *U.S. Aid to the Developing World*. Washington, D.C.: Heritage Foundation.

De Cecco, Marcello (1986). "On Milward's Reconstruction of Western Europe." In *Political Economy: Studies in the Surplus Approach* 2:1, 105–14.

Díaz-Alejandro, Carlos (1970). *Essays on the Economic History of the Argentine Republic*. New Haven: Yale University Press.

Dumke, Rolf (1990). "Reassessing the *Wirtschaftswunder*: Reconstruction and Postwar Growth in West Germany in an International Context." *Oxford Bulletin of Economics and Statistics* 52:2, 451–491.

Eichengreen, Barry (1989a). "The U.S. Capital Market and Foreign Lending, 1920–1955." In Jeffrey Sachs, ed., *Developing Country Debt and Economic Performance. The International Financial System*. Chicago: University of Chicago Press, 107–158.

Eichengreen, Barry (1989b). "European Economic Growth After World War II: The Grand Schema." presented to the Conference Marking the Retirement of William N. Parker, New Haven.

Eichengreen, Barry and Richard Portes (1989). "After the Deluge: Default, Negotiation, and Readjustment during the Interwar Years." In Barry Eichengreen and Peter Lindert, *The International Debt Crisis in Historical Perspective*, Cambridge, MA: MIT Press, 12–47.

Eichengreen, Barry and Marc Uzan (1991). "The Marshall Plan: Economic Effects and Implications for Eastern Europe." *Economic Policy* (forthcoming).

Ellis, John (1990). *Brute Force*. New York: Viking.

Feis, Herbert (1950). *The Diplomacy of the Dollar, 1919–1932: First Era*. Baltimore, MD: Johns Hopkins University Press.

Gimbel, John (1968). *The American Occupation of Germany: Politics and the Military, 1945–1949*. Palo Alto: Stanford University Press.

Gimbel, John (1976). *The Origins of the Marshall Plan*. Palo Alto: Stanford University Press.

Glyn, Andrew, Alan Hughes, Alain Lipietz, and Ajit Singh (1990). "The Rise and Fall of the Golden Age." In Stephen Marglin and Juliet Schor, eds., *The Golden Age of Capitalism*. Oxford: Clarendon, 39–125.

Halle, Louis (1967). *The Cold War as History*. New York: Harper and Row.

Harris, Seymour (1948). *The European Recovery Program*. Cambridge, MA: Harvard University Press.

Hazlitt, Henry (1947). *Will Dollars Save the World?* New York: Appleton-Century.

Hogan, Michael (1987). *The Marshall Plan: America, Britain, and the Reconstruction of Western Europe, 1947–1952*. Cambridge: Cambridge University Press.

Holtfrerich, Carl-Ludwig (1986). "U.S. Capital Exports to Germany. 1919–23 Compared to 1924–29." *Explorations in Economic History* 23:1–32.

Kindleberger, Charles (1967). *Europe's Postwar Growth*. London: Oxford University Press.

Kindleberger, Charles (1987). *Marshall Plan Days*.

Kostrzewa, Wojciech, Pater Nunnenkamp, and Holger Schmeiding (1990). "A Marshall Plan for Middle and Eastern Europe?" *World Economy* 13:1 (March), 27–50.

Lukacs, John (1991). *The Duel*. New York: Ticknor & Fields.

Maier, Charles S. (1977). "The Politics of Productivity: Foundations of American International Economic Policy after World War II." *International Organization* 31:607–633.

Maier, Charles S. (1981). "The Two Postwar Eras and the Conditions for Stability in Twentieth-Century Western Europe." *American Historical Review* 86:327–352.

Maier, Charles S. (1987). *In Search of Stability*. Cambridge: Cambridge University Press.

Marglin, Stephen (1990). "Lessons of the Golden Age: An Overview." In Stephen Marglin and Juliet Schor, eds., *The Golden Age of Capitalism*. Oxford: Clarendon, 1–38.

Matthews, R. C. O. (1968). "Why has Britain had Full Employment Since the War?" *Economic Journal* 82:195–204.

Matthews, R. C. O., C. Feinstein, and J. Odling-Smee (1982). *British Economic Growth, 1856–1973*, Stanford: Stanford University Press.

Mayne, Richard (1973). *The Recovery of Europe, 1945–1973*. Garden City, NY: Anchor Books.

Mee, Charles (1984). *The Marshall Plan: The Launching of the Pax Americana*. New York: Simon and Schuster.

Milward, Alan S. (1965). *The German Economy at War*. London: Methuen.

Milward, Alan S. (1984). *The Reconstruction of Western Europe 1945–51*. London: Methuen.

Pogue, Forrest C. (1990). *George C. Marshall: Statesman 1945–49*. New York: Viking Press.

Sweezy, Paul (1942). *The Theory of Capitalist Development*. New York: Oxford University Press.

Tinbergen, Jan (1954). "The Significance of the Marshall Plan for the Netherlands Economy." In Kingdom of the Netherlands Ministry of Finance, *The Road to Recovery: The Marshall Plan, Its Importance for the Netherlands, and European Cooperation*. The Hague: Kingdom of the Netherlands Ministry of Finance.

United Nations (1948). *International Capital Movements During the Interwar Period*. Lake Success, NY: United Nations.

United Nations (various years), *Economic Survey of Europe*. Geneva: United Nations.

United States Mutual Security Agency (1953). *The Structure and Growth of the Italian Economy*. Rome: MSA.

Wallich, Henry (1955). *Mainsprings of the German Recovery*. New Haven: Yale University Press.

van der Beugel, Ernst Hans (1966). *From Marshall Aid to Atlantic Partnership: European Integration as a Concern of American Foreign Policy*. New York: Elsevier.

van der Wee, Hermann (1986). *Prosperity and Upheaval*. Berkeley: University of California Press.

Wexler, Imanuel (1983). *The Marshall Plan Revisited: The European Recovery Program in Economic Perspective*. Westport, CN: Greenwood Press.

9

Panel Discussion: Lessons for Eastern Europe Today

Olivier Blanchard
Wilhelm Nölling
Richard Portes

Olivier Blanchard

What have we learned about postwar reconstruction from this conference, and—more importantly in the current context—which of the lessons are applicable to the reconstruction of Eastern Europe today? Let me organize my thoughts around four points.

1. I am struck by the diversity of reconstruction strategies—or in some cases lack of strategies—followed by different countries on the one hand, and the commonality of medium-run outcomes on the other.

Consider the following examples, taken from the various papers and from the discussion they triggered:

Germany endorsed and followed free trade and convertibility, making a religion of it; the paper by Herbert Giersch and Holger Schmieding puts much emphasis on the importance of trade in the postwar German expansion. But, during the same period, France went through alternating periods of heavy exchange controls and decontrols, and of trade restrictions.

What free trade actually meant varied across countries, a point made by Rudi Dornbusch in his comparison of the Japanese and the German experiences. In Germany, the focus was on import competition as the key to good health and competitiveness. But in Japan, domestic markets were sheltered instead, and the emphasis was on export growth as the key to success.

France went heavily into planning, and the first few plans, from 1947 on, were far more than indicative. The allocation of credit was largely controlled by the state. In Italy, the state holding company, IRI, was able to fend off attempts to eliminate it and played a central role in the reconstruction process. Elsewhere, markets and private firms were given a larger role in the allocation of investment.

While most countries had an initial bout of inflation, some were able to keep inflation roughly under control therafter. Again, Germany after the monetary reform is the primary example. But others, such as France, suffered repeated bouts of inflation until the late fifties.

I have no doubt that a cross section regression of the growth performance of the various countries on the factors listed above—from exchange controls, inflation, stability, and the like—would yield a few significant coefficients (although, based on the results from a study by Stanley Fischer of the effects of macroeconomic policy on growth, I suspect that the results would not be as impressive as say, the claims in the paper by Patrick Minford ...). But, when one looks at postwar growth rates, the basic impression is that all countries had impressively high growth, no matter what strategy was being pursued. From 1948 to the late fifties, all major countries had a rate of growth in excess of 3 percent, most in excess of 4 percent. These are impressive rates, by historical standards, and even more so compared to where Europe had been prewar. And while investment was high, most of the growth was due to the Solow residual.

Does this mean that we should relax, that after a few years of upheaval eastern Europe will also grow, nearly no matter what? One senses that the answer is a clear no. The question is why. This takes me to the second point.

2. In thinking about reconstruction in Eastern Europe, two types of experiences come to mind. The first is indeed postwar reconstruction. The second is the reconversion of regions in decline. Of those, we have plenty of examples, from regions depending on shipbuilding to regions depending on coal, steel, or textiles. And the general picture is one of slow, painful, and costly transformation.

Why do the two types of experiences differ so much? To a first approximation, postwar reconstruction was a process of building upon what existed, a movement out along a ray. But reconversion, by its nature, implies changing, perhaps destroying the existing structure, not building upon it. This is much harder to achieve. To take a related example, remember how large the macroeconomic effects of the increases in the price of oil in the seventies turned out to be.

Which reference is more appropriate for Eastern Europe? Clearly, the initial stabilization and liquidation of the overhang evoke postwar reconstruction. But once the macro house is in some order, reconversion of regions seems the more relevant reference by far. In East Germany today, the basic remaining issue is that of how fast to close the large East German manufacturing firms. And the debate is not much different from earlier ones, in West Germany, about closing the shipyards in the North. In other countries, things are both better and worse. A country like Poland is basically like East Germany, but without the deep pockets of the Treuhandt: the costs of the transition cannot be deferred by borrowing. But Poland can choose real wages, both directly and through the exchange rate; this does not change the fact that much will have to close, but it gives more breathing time.

So what can we learn and not learn from postwar reconstruction for Eastern Europe?

3. We can clearly learn about stabilization and monetary reform. Both the Italian experience up to 1946 and the German monetary reform are particularly useful in that respect. But there the lessons seem to me to be the same as from Latin America. And those lessons have been incorporated in IMF programs or in, say, the Polish stabilization plan of 1990. We can learn also about the role of foreign aid in smoothing ripples, in preventing short-run cash flow problems from becoming fiscal crises. But I have agreed to leave a discussion of Marshall aid to the other members of the panel.

4. We cannot learn much about restructuring. I shall cover three issues that are central to Eastern Europe today and where postwar experience seems to be of no help.

The first is the issue, which I mentioned earlier, of how fast to close certain factories. Should closings take place early, leading to a large but hopefully short increase of unemployment, followed by a burst of job creation? Or will high unemployment drain fiscal resources, create a class of permanently unemployed, trigger a political crisis, and stop the process of reconversion? These questions were just not important ones after the war: there was not much to close. The reconversion of the defense industry was the only issue, and in most cases, it probably involved returning to previous lines of business that had been abandoned during the war. (A study of the reconversion of the defense industry would be an interesting one).

The second related issue is how fast to expose firms to foreign competition—to go for full convertibility and low tariffs, or to protect them for a while. Even if the lessons of the postwar are that fast exposure to foreign competition strengthens, they do not apply to Eastern Europe, at least not without some more work. The structure of production was mostly right at the end of the war, the price incentives having been distorted not very much and for not very long. The jolt from foreign competition was small and stimulating. The structure of production in Eastern Europe is mostly wrong. Exposure is more likely to kill than to strengthen.

The third issue is how to organize labor relations. Many papers stress the importance of social consensus after World War II, especially in comparison to the aftermath of World War I. Without denying that some systems of labor relations work better than others, social consensus is more likely to have been the effect rather than the cause of the good growth performance. As was emphasized by Richard Layard in his comments at the conference, expectations of real income growth after a Great Depression and a world war were low, and productivity growth happened to be high. It was easy to satisfy workers' aspirations while maintaining healthy profits. These conditions are just not present in Eastern Europe. Expectations are high, and growth of real income will take a while. The immediate aftermath of the postwar period was associated with high growth; the initial part of the transition in Eastern Europe has been associated instead with large contractions.

Bibliography

Fischer, Stanley (1993) "Growth, Macroeconomics and Development," *NBER Macroeconomics Annual*, MIT Press.

Wilhelm Nölling

I would like to concentrate on one aspect, namely, financial aid for the Eastern European countries. Financial aid is not all they need. On the contrary: I think they need conceptual help, they need fresh ideas, they need help in reorganizing. They can't do it by themselves. But I will concentrate on financial aspects because I believe that without financial aid, conceptual help—fresh ideas—can't be put into effect. That is my basic assumption.

But I would like to start with three assumptions whose relevance or validity cannot be denied. The first is that there is an urgent need for liquidity. You may call it capital, you may call it cash savings, or what have you. I call it liquidity. This need is prevalent in all of the Eastern countries. They all are suffering from lack of hard currency. They cannot import because they don't have the funds. And, of course, if they cannot import from us, for example, then we won't be able to supply. That might become an issue if the recession forces become stronger in the course of the next year. And I think regardless of that, the economic engines are over there. They won't move unless they get fuel. By fuel I mean some sort of liquidity. In view of the very heavy external burden they have to service—there's no moratorium—it is literally impossible for them to take off, to have a chance for reconstruction. So this is assumption number one.

My second assumption is that capital in the usual sense—derived either from public revenues and/or credits from capital markets, thereby tapping private savings—will not be available to these countries in any measure, in any amount required. When you look at the financial situation of all the countries around us (with the exception of Japan, of course), Germany cannot do much more; France has refused to accept responsibility. If you look at Great Britain's public finance situation—at the situation in France, Italy, and America and so on—then my conclusion is that all these countries are very hard pressed to find resources adequate to the challenge, to the task.

So if we—and that is my conclusion here—if we agree on the need for a new Marshall Plan, then we must take the trouble to ask, where do we get the money? What are the sources or the potential sources to provide liquidity?

And then my third assumption and my third point is that there are lessons to be learned from the way the Germans financed unification. Last year ... we were willing to transform worthless "East-mark" savings into deutsche marks at the very generous rate of 2:1, thereby printing the money to do this. In Germany we don't talk about this, the Bundesbank especially doesn't like being called a printer of money under the circumstances of unification. But that's what actually happened. We could have raised the money in order to have the East Germans preserve their savings, by of course raising taxes here, or capital market sources could have been used. But we did not do this. Instead, we actually provided them with this printed money. Moreover, it is high-powered money, but I don't want to go into this in detail.

The second feature of financing unification is, of course, higher taxes and money derived from capital markets. And it is very interesting—and I want to come to my main conclusion—the amounts are interesting. West Germany—for all practical purposes it is the economy of West Germany—needs to finance the eastern part to the extent of about 150 or 160 billion marks annually. West Germany now supplies 70 percent of the GNP of the eastern part, and it amounts to 5 to 6 percent of the GNP in the western part of our country.

If we stop here for a moment and think about the magnitude involved in helping the eastern part, my suggestion is that if we supplied them with half of it in hard currency, it would reduce the situation in an unimaginable way. I mean, it would really help. You look at the foreign debt situation of all the countries, the debt service burdens, and so on. For if we assume for a moment the idea that half of what Germany has to provide and has to finance—let's say only 80 billion marks or 50 billion dollars—I feel that would help. On the other hand, there is no source, as I mentioned, in the world available to supply 80 billion marks or 50 billion dollars. Therefore, my conclusion has been since May, since I have been advocating this, to turn to the International Monetary Fund and to find out whether special drawing rights could be turned into this "money printing machine" needed to supply the eastern parts—and the other parts of the world as well—with the necessary liquidity. (It shouldn't be called printing money, of course, as this would cause shock waves outside of this room.) But I was quite encouraged by what the Japanese did after the war. Of course, printing money, as Hamada said, increased inflationary pressure or brought about inflationary pressure. But by doing it in a tailor-made way and attaching conditions to a very substantial increase in special drawing rates and enabling the countries to draw and to go to their banks and have it used as a collateral, then I think we could overcome this particularly bad situation. That is my suggestion. And I would like you to comment on this. This is nothing really new, because in Washington a couple of weeks ago this proposal was put on the table; it was strongly resisted again by the Germans and the Americans and so on. But the idea that we could alleviate the situation in a very substantial way is not new; I mean, it is on the table. But we should think about it. The idea could be promoted, maybe even by a conference like this.

Let me next turn to the use—or rather the misuse—of funds and investment from abroad in order to modernize the Soviet Union's industry. And it isn't a very impressive picture when you look at the figures for what they bought and were then unable to install and so on and so on. So I have always maintained that it won't help in this respect, throwing money at the problems over there. When developing the concepts I think it is important to follow them as far as they can go. We cannot tell them that they have to adopt the German type or style of social-market oriented economy. That is impossible. And I agree with all who stress the point that domestic endeavors—and the responsibility of these states—cannot be overestimated. I would quantify it a little bit differently. When you said 99.1 percent or something like that, I would say that maybe 90 percent is their responsibility and that we maybe have to contribute 10 percent. We have to move away from placing the sole responsibility for solving their problems—or keeping some kind of a peace over there—on these societies that are undergoing restructuring.

I think it is not justified to draw conclusions from the experience of Latin America and to say, look at the experiences we derived and if they apply over there we've got to leave them alone and let them get out of their misery as the Latin Americans seem to have done, or have not done at all. It's an open question whether they have succeeded in any sense. I am guided by a pessimistic view as to the options available. I don't think we have many options when we look at it from a global point of view, not from the Central European point of view.

That is my assessment of the situation, and as I mentioned, there are some paradoxes. On the one hand, the amounts needed, it is my contention are small in comparison to what the financial figures of the Western world entail, small in comparison. At the same time, they are most difficult to raise. I think the savings and the real transfer that are needed will be achieved simultaneously. They will be created in a truly Keynesian fashion. And I agree with you that it has to do with the state of the world economy, whether the United States will derive the right benefits, or Germany, or France and so on.

So far looking at our experience here, what we can proudly say is that going into debt in favor of helping our East German brothers has benefited all our neighbors. Look at their export figures: they are very impressive. If we can avoid the collapse of the Eastern world, benefits will be derived by all the countries in the Western world, either directly or indirectly. And as I said before, the real transfer can come about mainly by keeping wheels turning that otherwise would stop. If the wheels of production and distribution stop in Eastern Europe, we will be forced to help them and to feed them, and they will not work as they could if we supplied them with the means to keep these wheels going.

If other wheels turn around faster and can produce, then we can achieve the savings and improve the real situation. That is the answer I would like to give to this question. And under certain conditions—I agree fully—this can be denounced as an inflationary stimulus. But I think we can attach conditions that can minimize this threat.

My last point is that if the Soviet Union and the Eastern world are considered to be mainly a problem for us here in Germany, I think that we will soon find out that Germany cannot cope. If we succumb to the hundreds of millions of hungry and starving people in the East—which is not too gloomy a prospect—I think it will affect all of us. So we are all in one boat. I would like to stress this very much. It is not a problem you can leave Germany alone with; this isn't possible. It is too much of a problem.

And nobody is going to benefit in Europe or elsewhere if the Germans collapse—which, of course, I hope will not happen.

Richard Portes

I start with the relation of the transformation of Central and Eastern Europe to the reconstruction of Western Europe after the war. The East European economies are very different from the postwar example. I do not agree with Rudi Dornbusch that we can just put the economic agents in a room and rely on them to do what's necessary: sex, or markets, or whatever. Even if they can manage to have sex or the economic equivalent without any further education, it has to be the right kind: they must have safe sex. They need a structured environment and institutional framework. That was much easier after the war, and "catch-up" could not have worked without the appropriate legal system, properly trained accountants and bankers, and so forth. This is not a call for morality but for the practical necessities.

My second reservation about the postwar analogy is that the system that prevailed before the collapse of communism was qualitatively different from the example of the war command economy. The physical allocation mechanism and absence of meaningful prices were much more extreme than under wartime rationing and materials allocation. It certainly was nothing like the postwar Swedish or British examples of socialism. Nor is it in other respects like Latin America. The distortions are an order of magnitude greater. They lasted much longer, and they affected the behavior of economic agents much more deeply.

A third difference is one of the key issues for economic policy in making this tremendous change. The history of decades of command planning undermines the *credibility* of whatever new policies and institutions are put in place. To establish credibility will be much more difficult than in many of the past cases.

In the postwar reconstruction in Italy, the overall orientation of policy, dirigiste or not, has been discredited by fascism and war. In the United Kingdom, according to Patrick Minford, dirigisme was glorified by bolshevism and war. But certainly in Eastern Europe today, dirigisme is totally rejected, most notably in the extreme Klausian version of laissez-faire. In Czechoslovakia, that extreme position is in practice modified by Vaclav Klaus's role as a politician. Thus, for example, despite his convictions, he did not go to a floating exchange rate. And even in this environment of extreme laissez-faire, there may still be some role for industrial policy. The magnitude of the structural and relative price changes required raises major problems of trying to coordinate on a completely different equilibrium. Those coordination problems are much more extreme in this context than elsewhere.

Macroeconomic policy in Eastern Europe must choose between currency reform and price-level adjustment in order to reduce real balances without setting off a subsequent inflationary spiral. I find no clear lessons here from the different examples of Germany and Italy. But there are two points that are often overlooked. First, stabilization cannot and probably should not achieve zero inflation. In Latin America and elsewhere, there is a well-known 20-percent barrier, and it may not be such a desperately bad thing. Mexico has been stuck there, for example, and things are going extremely well. Second, contrary to much of the discussion of "monetary overhang," stabilization policy need not worry about encouraging households to save. As unemployment grows, they will quickly get used to needing precautionary savings. And they will save, as in Poland. In aggregate, however, much of the required savings must come from retained earnings, if only because the financial markets and the capital market are not going to provide any other source of investment finance.

Herbert Giersch put very well what I would have said about choosing the level of the exchange rate. I would simply add that certainly in the case of Poland, and possibly in Czechoslovakia, we have seen that the initial undervaluation was pushed too far.

The lesson of our discussion of openness and of the way in which Erhard was rescued by the Korean War is the importance of foreign demand in underpinning a supply-side response. In this case, the key is access for the East European countries to the European Community markets. It will take courageous political decisions in the Community to overcome obstacles in the current negotiations of the association agreements and in their implementation so as to give Eastern Europe the foreign markets that sparked the *Wirtschaftswunder*.

Access is not just a short-run question of coal and steel, textiles, clothing, and agriculture. It is a longer-run question and a vexed issue in the negotiation of the association agreements as to what sorts of safeguards are included—safeguard clauses, antidumping clauses, etc. That is of great importance for foreign investors. No matter how much we open up now, we shall not get serious foreign direct investment in these countries unless there is assurance that five years down the road, when the investments come on stream, the EC markets will not shut down as soon as there is some minor threat of market injury to some little area.

Both the need for stabilization and the need to open up require a much faster move to convertibility than most of us had originally thought was desirable or even feasible. What these countries need initially is convertibility at a fixed rate and then, subsequently, some kind of exchange-rate rule, a clear policy to guide an adjustable peg. A nominal anchor is essential, not just to orient monetary policy and defend against inflation but also to provide a point of reference for the tremendous adjustment of relative prices that is necessary.

Instant convertibility would make any form of payments union otiose. Is the apparent success of the postwar European Payments Union misleading? Indeed, should Western Europe have gone to convertibility immediately? Recall that the United Kingdom tried in 1947 but could not maintain it. The initial conditions are in fact quite different. The West European countries did not need convertibility for reconstruction in the same way as the East Europeans do for transformation. A direct link of domestic to foreign prices as a basic building block of the market economy is essential in Eastern Europe now; it was not after the war for the reconstruction of a preexisting market economy with a capital stock that had suffered damage and depreciation but whose structure was not highly distorted.

Convertibility with exchange-rate stability will require foreign support and debt consolidation. Finland may have paid its debt; Germany did not. The German example is more relevant for the East European case. The recent Mexican experience shows how to construct a successful debt-reduction agreement. Provided that the major reforms are put in place, as they already have been in Hungary, a suitable debt-reduction agreement can be of immense help. At some point the Hungarians are just going to have to learn that lesson. It will prove politically impossible to keep consumption down indefinitely in order to service one of the highest debt burdens in the world.

Debt reduction and debt service reduction are the only likely source of really substantial financial aid for these countries, and then only if they themselves push very hard for it. That has already been the lesson of Poland, although the banks have unconscionably delayed in following the Paris Club—just as they did in 1981 with disastrous consequences. The bias of such aid would be toward Bulgaria, Hungary, and the Soviet Union. That may or may not be justifiable, but realistically any big money can only come from debt relief.

There are several things we have not learned from the postwar or subsequent experience. We have not learned how to implement mass privatization, nor even how to put a huge sector of large state enterprises on some kind of commercial basis, all simultaneously. We know very little about whether that privatization process should or should not precede deconcentration (demonopolization) of the economy. There is no unanimity about the nature of the financial system that should be put in place, although some system must be implanted as quickly as possible. And Anglo-Saxon financial institutions may be much less suitable than a German or Japanese-style structure.

Migration may have been good in different respects and in different ways in the German and Italian cases. Nevertheless, I do not think it would be particularly good for Eastern Europe, because of the brain drain. If migration were unconstrained, it would be open and large; it would be the migration of the wrong kind of people for Eastern Europe to lose, though good for Western Europe to receive.

A point we have ignored almost completely, except briefly in the discussion of Japan, is agriculture. That is terribly important in the East European cases. The Hungarian example, starting in 1965, showed what could happen even in the command economy if you actually gave incentives to the farmers. In Bulgaria, Romania, or the Soviet Union, there is tremendous potential that could be realized in this way. Of course, this would make the issue of market access even tougher—in the best of circumstances, it might even finally destroy the Common Agricultural Policy.

For whatever financial aid and technical assistance we do provide, conditionality is essential. But it must be perfectly clear. In Eastern Europe, there have been so many international organizations wandering about and so many missions that it is close to an occupation army, especially if we add on the merchant bankers and the management consultants (leaving out the academics). The consequence is multiple and inconsistent conditionality: they are hearing too many kinds of advice, much of it related to aid. There must be more coordination in this conditionality, if not in the aid itself.

On intraregional trade, I agree with Rudi Dornbusch. It has completely broken down. And if the same thing happens in the "Soviet Disunion" as has happened in Eastern Europe, there will be a catastrophic fall in production because of the greater interdependence among the republics than between the East European countries and the Soviet Union. If the Soviet republics go to separate, inconvertible currencies, putting the pieces back together will make the Marshall Plan and the European Payments Union look like child's play.

Index

Acheson, Dean, 218
Adenauer, Konrad, 11, 17
Agartz, Victor, 12
Agriculture, 199
Algerian War, 87
Allies
  currency reform deadlock and, 64–67
  Soviet Union and, 35
Antitrust Law of 1947, 158
Argentina
  European reconstruction and, 211–214
  populist overregulation trap, 222
  postwar growth, 192–193
Atlee, Clement, 116, 120, 121
Autonomous collective bargaining, 10

Balanced budget philosophy, in Finland,
  149
Banking Law of 1926, 69
Banking Law of 1936, 67, 69, 76
Bank of Italy, 67
Bank of Japan, 173
Bank of Japan Note Deposit Ordinance,
  172
Barter, 1
Basic Law, 24
BDI (Federation of Industries), 19
Belgium, 199
Bevan, Nye, 119
Bevin, Ernest, 119, 130, 218
BHE, 13
Bizone, 24, 35
  central planning abolishment, 3
  currency reform, 5
  industrial production, 4
  output development, 20
Black markets, 35, 38, 169

Bolsheviks, 116
Boom, postwar, 205–206
Bottlenecks, Marshall Plan and, 208–210
Bretton Woods system, 120–121, 192, 220
Britain, 132–133
  central government finances and, 129
  command economy, 115
  Conservative party, 116, 123, 130
  controls, 128–131
  full-employment policy, 50
  government spending, 122–124
  interactive complications, 135–136
  Korean War and, 119
  Labour government, 115, 116, 132
  Marshall Plan and, 119, 136
  monetary policy, 120–121
  recovery, postwar, 117–122
  regulation, 128–131
  socialism, 115
  taxation and interaction with benefits,
    124–128
  welfare state, 123–124
British Overseas Airways Corp., 130
Budget deficits, 3
Bundesverband der Deutschen Industrie
  (BDI or Federation of Industries), 19
Butler, Rab, 116, 120
"Butskellism," 116

Caisse des Dépôts, 105
Capital flows, 19–20
Capital formation, 3, 147
Capital stock, 21, 32–33
Capital taxation, 127
Central bank (Bank deutscher Länder), 3
Centre for Economic Policy Research
  (CEPR), 141–142

Christian Democratic Party, 77
Churchill, Winston, 116, 120
Clay, Lucius, 36, 217
Coal production
  in Japan, 161
  lack of, in Italy, 61
  Marshall Plan and, 209–210
  recovery, 203–205
  shortages, in Britain, 199
Codetermination law, 11
Colm, Gerhard, 174
Communist party support, in France, 103
Company statute law, 11
Competition, 24, 48
Conseil National du Crédit, 105
Conservative government, 120
Constant returns model, 95–96, 99
Consumer price index, 21
Convertibility, 24, 240
Counterpart Fund Special Account, 175
Credit squeeze, in Britain, 121
Currency convertibility on current account,
  19
Currency reform, 36–37
  deadlock, 64–67
  in West Germany, 2–3, 4–5
Czechoslovakia, 182

DCE (domestic credit expansion), 121
Decontrol of economy (Leitsätze), 3
De Gasperi, 71
De Gaulle, General Charles, 84, 87
Democracy, 24
Denmark, 199
De Stefani, Alberto, 67
Destruction, from World War II, 197–198
Deutsche mark (DM), 2, 19
Deutscher Gewerkschaftsbund (DGB or
  German Federation of Trade Unions),
  11, 19
Devaluation, 23, 86, 88
DGB (German Federation of Trade
  Unions), 11, 19
DM (deutsche mark), 2, 19
Docile union argument, 47
Dodge, Joseph, 160, 174–175
Dodge Line, 160, 162, 175–177, 179–182,
  184
Dodge Plan, nucleus of, 174
Dollar gap, 15, 75, 119
Domestic credit expansion (DCE), 121
Durable demand, 46

Eastern Europe
  extension of aid for, 190
  financial aid for, 234–238
  Finland recovery and, 150–151
  gloomy outlook in, 139–142
  Marshall Plan and, 221–223
  reconstruction in, 232–233
East Germany, 20, 232–233
Economic growth, in European nations,
  during Marshall Plan years, 194–195
Economic order, importance of, 20
Economies of scale, 117
Eden, Sir Anthony, 120, 129
Education Act of 1944, 120, 122
Educational reforms, Japanese, 160–162
Efficiency, ordo-liberal policies and, 31
Einaudi, 71, 72, 76, 77
Eisenhower, President Dwight, 179
Emergency Finance Measures, 179
Emergency Monetary Measures Ordinance,
  172
Emigration, from Finland to Sweden, 151
Employment, 7–8, 40
Enaudi, Luigi, 67
Energy shortages, Finland recovery and,
  145
EPU. See European Payments Union (EPU)
Equalization claims, 3
Erhard, Ludwig, 8, 49
  Bizonal coalition and, 24
  calls for moderation of wages, 12–13
  central planning abolishment, 3, 17
  1948 reform package, 36–40
  popularity, 43
ERP (European Recovery Program). See
  Marshall Plan
Europe
  balance-of-payments, 200
  Eastern. See Eastern Europe
  economic substitutions, 209
  economy after two wars, 197–206
  liberalization, Marshall Plan and, 15–16
  reconstruction, political economy of,
    210–214
  trading system in late 1940s, 14
  transportation infrastructure, 208
  Western. See Western Europe
European Monetary System, 77
European Payments Union (EPU), 218, 240
  currency convertibility on current
    account, 19
  dissolution of, 19

establishment of, 16—18
liberalization of foreign trade and, 37
European Recovery Program (ERP). *See*
    Marshall Plan
Exchange rates, 23—24, 43
Exogenous demand shocks, 48
Expectational errors, theory of, 12—13
Export mix, 22

Fair Trade Commission, 158
Family financial combines, dissolution of,
    158—159
Fascism, 57
Faure, Edgar, 87
Federation of Industries (BDI), 19
FILP (Fiscal Investment Loan Program), 161
Financial aid, for Eastern Europe, 234—238
Financial stability, Marshall Plan and,
    215—217
Finland, recovery in, 143—151
Fiscal Investment Loan Program (FILP), 161
Foreign exchange constraints, Marshall
    Plan and, 208—210
France, 199, 235
    American aid and stabilization, 87—93
    Communist party support, 103
    devaluations, 86
    economic reconstruction, 83—111
    economy during 1945—1959, 83—87
    endogenous growth models and, 111
    exogenous growth models and, 110—111
    financial markets, inefficiencies of,
        104—105
    growth rates, high, 108—109
    growth strategy, 50
    investment, postwar, 98—108
    Marshall Plan and, 16, 85, 87—88,
        216—217
    national accounts data, 86
    openness, lack of, 100
    production externalities, 101—102
    property rights uncertainty, 102—104
    reconstruction, growth theory and, 93—98
    stabilization, announcement effect and, 93
    strikes, postwar, 103
    war losses, 84—85
French zone, 20
Friedman, Milton, 44, 182

Gaitskell, 116
Gambino, Amedeo, 71

GARIOA (Government Account for Relief
    in Occupied Areas), 172
GATT (General Agreement on Tariffs and
    Trade), 19, 178
GDP
    British, 124—127
    in postwar Britain, 117—118
General Agreement on Tariffs and Trade
    (GATT), 19, 178
General Headquarters (GHQ). *See* Supreme
    Commander of Allied Powers (SCAP)
General House Survey (GHS), 128
George, Lloyd, 120
German Federation of Trade Unions
    (DGB), 11, 19
German unification, 235
Germany, 61
    centrally administered economy, 1
    defeat, growth and, 182
    impact of reforms, 4—14
    industrial production, 2
    medium run postreform, 38—42
    Nazi, economy of, 10
    1948 reforms, 36—37
    prereform, uncertainty in, 35—36
    prereform period 1945—1948, 32—36
    repressed inflation, 1
    short run postreform, 38
GHS (General House Survey), 128
GNP deflator, 18
Goldsmith, Raymond, 174
Government Account for Relief in
    Occupied Areas (GARIOA), 172
Gross investment ratio, 40
Growth
    autonomous effects, 45—48
    export-led, 5—10
Growth theory, French reconstruction and,
    93—98

Hoarding, of raw materials and
    semifinished products, 1
Hoover, Herbert, 195
Human capital
    economies of scale and, 117
    growth and, 46—47
    postwar growth spurt and, 22—23
Hungary, 182
Hyperinflation
    Japan and, 156
    threat, in Italy, 68—71

Ikeda, Prime Minister, 179
IMF (International Monetary Fund), 178
Immigration, 46
Import liberalization, 24
Incentives, in prereform Germany, 33–35
Income distribution, 47
Income Doubling Plan, 179
Income tax rate, top marginal, 3
Industrialized countries, inflation, 122
Industrial production. *See* Production,
     industrial
Inflation, 5–10, 231–232
  in industrialized countries, 122
  in Italy, 64–65
  stabilization in France, Marshall aid and,
     87–93
  in United Kingdom, 122
Internal migration, postwar growth spurt
     and, 23
International Monetary Fund (IMF), 178
Investment
  Eastern economies and, 140–141
  private, Marshall Plan and, 206–207
  public, Marshall Plan and, 207–208
Ishibashi Keynesian policy, 179
Israel, 20
Italy, 235, 238
  agricultural production, 71
  agriculture, 199
  Allied invasion of, 57
  bank loans and deposits, 69–70
  credit squeeze, 73–74
  defeat, growth and, 182
  deficit, 62–63
  economy after World War II, 58–63
  hyperinflation, threat of, 68–71
  Marshall Plan and, 209–210
  monetary overhang, buildup of, 62–63
  money growth, 72–73
  open inflation, first phase of, 64–67
  postwar experience, 77–78
  postwar liberalism, limits of, 76–77
  public debt, 62–63
  raw material imports, 68–69
  stabilization, 71–74
  stabilization crisis, 74–76

Japan, 61, 155
  American occupation policy, 159–160
  balance-of-payments, 171, 177
  boom in volume, 177
  chronology of postwar events, 184

defeat, growth and, 182
dissolution of zaibatsu, 158–159, 181
educational reforms, 160–162, 181
expansionary policy under Ishibashi,
     180–181
exports, 182
fixed exchange rate and, 181
government debts, 162
growth rate of GNP deflator and money,
     164–165
hyperinflation and, 156
industrial production, 163
inflation, 172
interest rates, 163
investment rate, 166–167, 178
Jimmu Boom, 177
Keynesian unemployment, 180
labor reforms, 159–160, 181
land reforms, 158, 181
macroeconomic significance of
     reconstruction, 179–181
microeconomic significance of
     reconstruction, 181
monetary overhang, 180
monetary stabilization process, 162–
     176
occupation policy, 183–184
political-economy aspect, 182–183
postwar experiences, WWI vs. WWII,
     156
prices, postwar, 163, 168–169
real factors behind reconstruction,
     157–162
reforms, postwar, 157–162
savings rate, 166–167, 178
social reforms, 160–162
subsidies, 169–171
surrender of, 155
Trade Financial Special Account,
     171–172, 174
transition to high-speed growth era,
     177–179
Japan Democratic Party, 178
Japan Liberal Party, 178
Japan Teachers' Union, 178
Jimmu Boom, 177

Keiretsu, 159
Keynes, J. M., 43–44, 173
Keynesian macroeconomic policy, 9
King-Robson growth model, French
     reconstruction and, 96–98

Korean War
  boom from, 8–9
  Britain and, 119
  end of, 177
  exogenous demand shocks and, 48
  French military expenditures, 87
  macroeconomic indicators, 176
  postreform programs and, 42
  West Germany and, 16–17, 18
Kouri spiral, reverse, 47

Labor reforms, Japanese, 159–160
Labor relations, organization of, 233–234
Labor Relations Adjustment Law of 1947, 159
Labor Standards Law of 1947, 159
Laissez-faire, 31, 238
Länderrat, 24
Land reforms, Japanese, 158
Lapland reconstruction, 143, 144
LDP (Liberal Democratic Party), 178
Liberal Democratic Party (LDP), 178
Liquidity, 234–236
Lloyd, Selwyn, 127, 131
London Debt Agreement, 20, 24
London School of Economics (LSE), 121
Long-term growth, social contract and, 218–221
LSE (London School of Economics), 121

MacArthur, General Douglas, 136, 155, 157
Macmillan, 120
Macroeconomic policy, growth and, 232
Marginal tax rates, 128
Market conforming, 31
Market economy, transition to, 2–4
Market economy consensus, economic transition and, 140
Market forces, free play of, 217–218
Marshall, George C., 189, 196
Marshall Plan, 36, 48, 109, 193
  alleviation of resource shortages and, 190
  announcement of, 73
  bottlenecks and, 208–210
  Britain and, 119
  European liberalization and, 15–16
  folk image, 191–192, 194–197
  foreign exchange constraints and, 208–210
  France and, 85, 87
  growth vs. WWI growth, 192
  implications for Eastern Europe, 221–223
  Italy and, 75
  London Debt Agreement and, 20
  political effects, 16
  private investment and, 206–207
  public investment and, 207–208
  purpose, 194
  role of, 214–221
  slow release of, 38
  stabilization of external debt in France, 88–89
  United Kingdom and, 125–126
  vs. United Nations Relief and Recovery Administration, 196–197
  Western European growth and, 190–191
Material Mobilization Plan of 1937, 161
Metal industry, Finnish investments, 144
Migration, from Eastern economies, 141
Miike coal mine strike, 178, 179
Mills, John Stuart, 43–44
Minimum wage laws, 130–131
Ministerial Committee for Credit Control, 71
Ministry of International Trade and Industry (MITI), 159
Mitsubishi Shoji, 158
Mitsui Bussan, 158
Mobility, 47
Monetary and fiscal policy, 20
Monetary circuit, 63
Monetary overhang, 239
Monetary reform, 233
Monetary stabilization process, in Japan, 162–176
Monnet Plan, 107
Morgenthau proposal, 35
Mussolini, B., 57
Mutual Security Assistance, 15–16

National Assistance boards, 127
National Health Service, 122–123
National Health System, 120
Nationalist political party, 13
Nationalization, 103–104, 130, 217
National Railway Union, 178

Occupation fees, 89
OECE (Organization for Economic Cooperation in Europe), 87
OEEC (Organization for European Economic Cooperation), 16, 18, 19

Ordo-liberal policies, 37
  description of, 29, 30—31
  efficiency and, 31
  failure of, 41
  incentives, 46
  initial success of, 42
  role in postwar recovery, 48—49
  support for, 42
Organization for Economic Cooperation in
  Europe (OECE), 87
Organization for European Economic
  Cooperation (OEEC), 16, 18, 19
Overvaluation, of Western European
  currencies, 23

Pacifism, 183—184
Perón, Juan, 211—213
Pessimism of recovery, 29
Poland, 182, 233
Police labor, 47
Policy role, in postwar recovery, 48—49
Political consensus, economic transition
  and, 140
Postwar growth spurt, explanation, 20—25
Powell, Enoch, 120, 123—124
Price decontrol, 37
Price level stabilization, 39
Price liberalization, 37
Priority Production System, 161—162
Private investment, Marshall Plan and,
  206—207
Production, industrial
  European, in 1938, 58
  Italian, 58—62
  liberal reforms of 1948 and, 6
  postwar, 45
  after WWII, 198—199
Public debt, financing by money creation, 3
Public Finance Law of 1947, 175
Public investment, Marshall Plan and,
  207—208
Purchasing power theory of wages, 12

Radcliffe Committee, 121
Ramsey growth model, 94—95, 99, 107
Raw materials, lack of, 173
Reconstruction Finance Bank, 161, 175, 179
Reconstruction process, 7
Redistribution of wealth, 4
Reichsmark (RM), 2
Rent Decontrol Act of 1957, 131

Repubblica Sociale Italiana, 57
Restructuring, 233

San Francisco Peace Treaty, 158—159, 177
Savings, composition, 40
Sayers, R. S., 121
SCAP (Supreme Commander of Allied
  Powers), 155, 157
Schäffer, Fritz, 17
Schumpeterian entrepreneur, 37, 50
Sectoral growth, 41
Social consensus, economic transition and,
  140
Social contract, long-term growth and,
  218—221
Social Democrats, 24, 36
Social reforms, Japanese, 160—162
Social responsibility, of unions, 13—14
Solow residual, 232
Soviet Union, 182
  Finnish war reparations and, 144
  output decline, 139—140
  Western Allies and, 35
Stabilization, 5—10, 233
Stalin, Joseph, 115
Stock market, 106
Subsidies, Japanese, 169—171
Supergrowth, 205—206
Supreme Commander of Allied Powers
  (SCAP), 155, 157
Sweden
  Finland's recovery and, 144, 149—150
  removal of rewards and, 117

Taft, Robert, 195
Tanzi-Oliveira effect, 89—90
Tax system, 3
Textile industry, Italian, 60
Thatcher, Margaret, 116
Thorneycroft, Peter, 120
Tokyo, Japan, 179
Tories, 120, 136
Trade, external terms, 21—22
Trade Financial Special Account, in Japan,
  171—172, 174
Trade Union Law of 1945, 159
Trade unions, Japanese, 177—178
Transportation infrastructure, European,
  208
Truman, President Harry S., 189, 195, 196
Truman Doctrine, 196

Uncertainty, in prereform Germany, 35–36
UNECE (United Nations Economic
    Commission for Europe), 41
Unemployment, distribution, 40–41
Unions, 21
  in Britain, 130–131
  expectational errors and, 12–13
  inflation and, 7
  organizational weakness of, 10–11
  political distraction of, 11–12
  social responsibility, 13–14
  West German, 10–14
United Kingdom
  economic performance, relative, 133–135
  food exports to Germany, 3
  inflation, 122
  Marshall Plan and, 16, 125–126, 136
United Nations, humanitarian aid, 195
United Nations Economic Commission for
    Europe (UNECE), 41, 140
United Nations Relief and Recovery
    Administration (UNRRA), 196–197
United States
  food exports to Germany, 3
  Marshall Plan assistance to European
    countries, 15
  withdrawal from Western Europe, 195
UNRRA (United Nations Relief and
    Recovery Administration), 196–197
U.S.-British Bizone, 2, 3
U.S.-Japan Security Treaty, 178–179

Vandenberg, Arthur, 196, 223

Wage control, 37
Wage Council Acts of 1945 and 1948, 130
Wage policy, West German, 12–13
Weimar Republic, 10, 11
Western Allies. See Allies
Western Europe
  agriculture, 199
  democracies, stability of, 189
  differences in countries, 142
  on eve of Marshall Plan, 194
  growth, Marshall Plan and, 190–191
  reconstruction, 238
  after war, 142–143
West German Bundestag, 24
West German tariff schedule (1949–1950),
    19
West Germany, 20
  agriculture, 199

balance-of-payments crisis, 16–18
central bank, 18
currency reform, 4–5
economic integration, 24
European liberalization and, 18–20
favorable trade balance, 14
foreign trade expansion, 21
growth, 45–48
  vs. British growth, 133–135
inflation rate in, 18
internal economy, 14–15
labor force, 20
labor unions and, 10–14
monetary reform, 233
1948 reforms, shortcomings of, 23
from 1945–1951, 31–42
postwar growth spurt, 20–25
postwar performance, 50
postwar recovery, 29
recovery, 43–45
recovery stages, 49–50
restitution with Israel, 20
speedy return to normality, 20
transition to market economy, 2–4
unexpected postwar growth performance,
    42–49
Work ethic, 22, 46
World War I
  international capital markets after, 200
  speed of recovery, 201–205
World War II
  destruction from, 197–198
  speed of recovery, 201–205

Yoshida, Prime Minister, 182–183
Young, Ralph, 173

Zaibatsu, dissolution of, 158–159, 181
Zysman, John, 161